INVESTIGATING
SUBJECTIVITY

OTHER RECENT VOLUMES IN THE
SAGE FOCUS EDITIONS

INVESTIGATING SUBJECTIVITY

Research on Lived Experience

Carolyn Ellis
Michael G. Flaherty
editors

SAGE PUBLICATIONS
International Educational and Professional Publisher
Newbury Park   London   New Delhi

For Art and Gretchen

For information address:

SAGE Publications, Inc.
2455 Teller Road
Newbury Park, California 91320

SAGE Publications Ltd.
6 Bonhill Street
London EC2A 4PU
United Kingdom

SAGE Publications India Pvt. Ltd.
M-32 Market
Greater Kailash I
New Delhi 110 048 India

Printed in the United States of America

Library of Congress Cataloging-in-Publication Data

Investigating subjectivity: research on lived experience / Carolyn Ellis, Michael G. Flaherty.
     p. cm. — (Sage focus editions ; 139)
    Includes bibliographical references and index.
    ISBN 0–8039–4496–9 (cloth). — ISBN 0–8039–4497–7 (pbk.)
    1. Social psychology—Methodology. 2. Subjectivity.   I. Ellis,
Carolyn.   II. Flaherty, Michael G.
HM251.S8369   1992
301'.072—dc20
                                  91–45333
                                     CIP

92 93 94 95 10 9 8 7 6 5 4 3 2 1

Sage Production Editor: Tara S. Mead

Contents

Acknowledgments

Many people and organizations helped us with the 1990 Stone Symposium, "Sociology of Subjectivity," which provided the starting point for this project. We wish to acknowledge the support of the Society for the Study of Symbolic Interaction Gregory Stone Memorial Fund, the American Sociological Association Problems of the Discipline Small Grants Program, the American Sociological Association Section on Emotions, Eckerd College, the College of Arts and Sciences and the Department of Sociology at the University of South Florida, and the Eugene Weinstein Memorial Fund. We are also thankful for the assistance of Art Bochner, Lloyd Chapin, Julia Davis, Gretchen Flaherty, Shelia Kalet, Kim Miller, Michele Murteza, James MacDougall, Linda O'Bryant, Debra Ross, Carleen Shapiro, Jim Sperry, Amy Wang, Tom Warren, Leslie Wasson, Annette Weiser, and Birgit Wilhelm.

An Agenda for the
Interpretation of Lived Experience

CAROLYN ELLIS
MICHAEL G. FLAHERTY

This book focuses on *subjectivity,* meaning human lived experience and the physical, political, and historical context of that experience. It is our intention to return to the goals formulated by pioneers such as Weber, who saw sociology as centrally concerned with understanding human subjectivity. Sociology, Weber (1947, p. 88) said, "is a science which attempts the interpretive understanding of social action. . . . In 'action' is included all human behaviour when and in so far as the acting individual attaches a subjective meaning to it." Despite Weber's characterization of our discipline, subjectivity per se has been neglected as a topic of sociological inquiry.

Why has so little attention been given to subjectivity? Katz (1988) contends that many sociologists feel repelled or threatened by the unruly content of subjective experiences. They shy away from the investigation of subjectivity in much the same fashion that individuals avoid unpleasant or dangerous activities. Subjectivity can be both unpleasant and dangerous: unpleasant because emotional, cognitive, and physical experiences frequently concern events that, in spite of their importance, are deemed inappropriate topics for polite society (including that of sociologists); dangerous because the workings of subjectivity seem to contradict so much of the rational-actor worldview on which mainstream sociology is premised.

This volume grew out of the 1990 Stone Symposium, the "Sociology of Subjectivity," sponsored by the Society for the Study of Symbolic

Interaction. The scholars who assembled at that symposium shared a commitment to the premise that "human beings act toward things on the basis of the meanings that the things have for them" (Blumer 1969, p. 2). The works published in this volume elaborate that premise through research on subjective experience and attempt to broaden the current concentration on the sociology of emotions to include cognitive, discursive, physical, political, and historical dimensions of subjectivity.

Issues in the Study of Subjectivity

Sociologists now generally recognize that emotional processes are crucial components of social experience. Although this turn toward including emotions within the domain of sociology has been a useful corrective to the dominance of rational-actor models of human nature, most of the work on emotions has been restricted to issues of conceptualization or debate over theoretical frameworks (Harré 1986; Kemper 1981, 1987; Scheff 1985; Shott 1979; Thoits 1989). During the 1980s, the sociological study of emotions held the promise of something akin to an intellectual revolution (Kuhn 1970). As the sociology of emotion enters the 1990s, however, it has begun to take on the appearance of a "stalled revolution," to use Hochschild's (1989, p. 12) apt phrase. What started as a revolution is in danger of being co-opted by the dominant paradigm of mainstream sociology, which transforms emotional experience into models of rational action. This volume addresses four issues in the sociology of emotions that have stood as obstacles to the development of a more comprehensive understanding of subjectivity and offers a view of emotion that diverges from rational-action models.

First, most methods of sociological research employed in the sociology of emotions establish distance between experiencing subjects and their lived experience. These methods are based on the assumption of rational order and give access only to the surface public self (Goffman 1959), not the inner feeling self or its relationship to emotional experience in the world. Examples of these methods include surveys, questionnaires, computer simulation, videotaping, and discourse analysis as well as the use of advice books, marriage manuals, child-rearing manuals, and popular magazines. These orthodox methods have constrained the range of questions researchers ask about emotions and, consequently, the answers likely to be found. Traditional methodological tools tend to limit work on emotion to behavioral expressions, resulting in an unbalanced emphasis on outer displays of emotions; when subjective reports are collected, they are conventionally reported in terms of preconceived categories of the researchers that privilege individual and discrete emotions.

Second, emotional processes are treated as separate from other kinds of subjectivity, such as thinking and somatic experiences. With few exceptions (Glassner 1988; Jacobus, Keller, & Shuttleworth 1990; Kemper 1990; Sanders 1989), sociological writing has ignored the body. Moreover, many who do consider the body tend to sever it from subjective experience (Denzin 1985). Sociologists have paid more attention to cognitive processes, but this represents vestiges of the rational-actor model. The cognitive bias in sociology has put those who study emotion in a defensive position, in which many act as if they must choose between emotion and cognition. As a result, emotional and cognitive orientations are viewed as competing perspectives, instead of "blur[red] together in the person's stream of experience" (Denzin 1989, p. 121; James [1890] 1950, pp. 185-87). While some scholars depict emotions as elements of rational behavior (Hochschild 1979, 1983), and others describe cognition as an ingredient of emotional processes (Schachter and Singer 1962), little has been done to unravel the complex manner in which emotion, cognition, and the lived body intertwine.

Third, emotions are isolated from their social context. Sociologists have concentrated their efforts on micro-processes and individual emotions during a particular historical period. This perspective is misleading because it implies that subjectivity reflects only a personal response to a unique situation. Analysis of political and cultural forces that condition emotional experience across time and space is neglected. Consequently, we have little knowledge of the social distribution of subjectivity with respect to inequality and the ways that systems of subjectivity change over time. When historically oriented researchers (Cancian and Gordon 1988; Stearns and Stearns 1986) do consider changing attitudes toward emotions such as anger and love, they concentrate on rules instead of connecting social conventions to feelings and discussing what these changes mean for people's lived experience.

Fourth, the study of emotional lived experience is treated as outside the sociological domain because emotions cannot be studied "scientifically." This reflects the tension among social scientists concerning their relationship to the natural sciences on one side and the humanities on the other. A call for investigations of lived experience raises the specter that sociology may be tilting toward the humanities. Likewise, coming into contact with our subjects' lived experiences can make us feel uncomfortable and embarrassed (Ebaugh 1988; Ellis 1991a). Researchers who write about their own emotions risk being seen by colleagues as emotional exhibitionists. One reason for this is that researchers, and the colleagues who read their work, typically have been males from upper-middle-class, Anglo-American, professional back-grounds where emotions are suppressed or, at most, viewed as private experiences (Rosaldo 1987).

This volume addresses these four issues in an attempt to invigorate the investigation of subjective experience. Emphasizing thick ethnographic de-scriptions of emotions grounded in lived experience, these authors do not represent consensus on method. Instead, they rejuvenate various traditional interpretive procedures and advance new methodological techniques for examining emotional processes. In some cases, authors analyze texts pro-duced by laypeople for reasons other than research. In other cases, authors construct texts by eliciting their subjects' responses or by becoming the phenomenon and reflecting on their own streams of consciousness. Included among their methods and materials are interviews, participant observation, systematic introspection, performance, the analysis of archival records, and documents from mass media such as films, newspaper accounts, autobiog-raphies, and novels. While realizing that writing about experience always is removed from actual "raw" experience (Denzin 1991), the overriding con-cern of these writers is shrinking the distance between the experiencing subjects and their accounts of lived experience.

A number of the authors in this volume have broadened the scope of their inquiries to explore the interconnections among emotional, cognitive, and physical experiences. The current diversity within sociology makes this an especially auspicious time to integrate research on subjective processes and transcend old divisions. It is as unrealistic to treat aspects of subjectivity separately as it would be to view education, occupation, and income as unrelated determinants of social class.

In this volume, authors focusing on how emotions feel also recognize that emotions have rational components and resonate in the physical body. Similarly, authors who emphasize cognitive processes acknowledge that there is an emotional horizon for cognition because, in large measure, people think about the same things they care about. Hence this collection attempts to bridge the divisions among researchers with different but complementary perspectives on the investigation of subjectivity.

Subjectivity is situated such that the voices in our heads and the feelings in our bodies are linked to political, cultural, and historical contexts. Emo-tional and cognitive responses to our bodies, for example, are conditioned by prevailing definitions of health, beauty, and stigma. The languages of various cultures and subcultures differ in the capacity to articulate subtleties of subjective processes. Likewise, dramatic events and barely noticed trends of history alter the ways in which people think and feel about themselves. All of these themes are evident in this volume, where feminist story lines weave in and out of historically located plots and men are allowed new voices filled with passion and compassion.

These authors are not embarrassed by their own subjectivity. Their personal stories remind us that emotions are not the exclusive properties of subjects (Ellis 1991b). In their attempt to understand the dynamics of subjectivity, these writers experiment with creative genres of presentation, often viewed under the purview of the humanities, to convey the lived experience of thoughts and feelings. In addition to using field notes and personal narratives, they experiment with fiction, poetry, and drama. They attempt to "shape their work in terms of its necessities rather than perceived ideas as to what they ought or ought not to be doing" (Geertz 1980, pp. 166-67).

Humanistic and Scientific Modes of Interpretation

The authors of this book see lived experience as an interpretive rather than a causal story. An interpretive story "lives willingly with plurality, embracing the power of language to make new and different things possible; . . . focuses on how we talk about the world and tries to deal with it; . . . recounts improvisations, changes, contradictions, ambiguities, and vulnerabilities" (Bochner 1990, pp. 5-6). Our goal of interpreting the meaning of our own and other people's lives may require that we continue blurring the distinctions between humanistic and scientific modes of inquiry (Geertz 1980). The study of subjectivity requires sociology to take its place as quasi-science, quasi-humanities (Zald 1988). As such, the goal is to arrive at an understanding of lived experience that is both rigorous—based on systematic observation—and imaginative—based on expressive insight (Bateson 1972).

Instead of viewing experience as a series of solvable problems (Marcel 1949; Neumann 1989), authors in this volume attempt to capture and evoke the complex, paradoxical, and mysterious qualities of subjectivity. Instead of subordinating lived experience to the "tyranny of reason" or the "consolation of order" (Jackson 1989, p. 16), they follow Keats (1958, p. 193) in their attempt to cultivate the apprehension of "being in uncertainties,/Mysteries, doubts, without any irritable reaching after fact and reason." They return from their explorations with descriptions and interpretations intended "to keep a conversation going" (Rorty 1979). Ultimately, it is a conversation through which we can come to know ourselves and others and the positions from which we speak; a conversation that unites the humanities and the sciences.

We see the process of subjectivity as having an existence sui generis—an existence that cannot be reduced to "more basic" forces in the mechanics of physiology or the dynamics of interpersonal relations (Jackson 1989). Grounding our interpretations in lived experience connects the internal with the social and is in accord with the goal of formulating an understanding of subjectivity from within (Denzin 1989), that is, on its own terms, and not merely as epiphenomenal to other levels of analysis.

These works attempt to deal with the "ethnographically particular" without eschewing that which is "existentially common to all human beings" (Jackson 1989). The writers describe the moment yet realize that "every human situation is novel, emergent, and filled with multiple, often conflicting, meanings and interpretations" (Denzin 1989, p. 25). They feel for their subjects and their research, yet they are able to tack back and forth between an "insider's passionate perspective and an outsider's dispassionate one" (Van Maanen 1988, p. 77). Their research methods mirror life as the authors move between fluctuating levels of absorption and detachment, managing multiple selves and roles, even when their own experience is the object of investigation.

In exploring new territory, these authors have been forced to confront certain questions concerning the production and analysis of textual materials. What is the relationship of fiction to ethnography (Krieger 1984)? What is the relationship of narratives to lived experience? What is the role of ethnographers' interactions with those they study? As Jackson (1989, p. 3) puts it: How do we clarify "the ways in which our knowledge is grounded in our practical, personal, and participatory experience in the field as much as our detached observations?" How does one decide what to tell others about the analysis of narrative materials, and what considerations govern the selection of texts for the sake of presentation and substantiation? Addressing these issues illuminates the interplay between knower and known, between the humanities and the sciences.

Windows on Lived Experience: The Texts

The interpretive approach to the study of emotion, cognition, and the lived body opens curtains for viewing the workings of subjectivity. In this light, four vistas emerge as an organizing structure for this volume: the interpretation of existing texts; the writing of new texts; the experiencing of time, place, and activity; and transformations of the subjective self. Through the use of innovative materials and procedures, the authors offer portals to the world of subjective experience.

The authors in Part I are concerned with the interpretation of existing texts. They offer readings of films, diaries, biographies, letters, calendars, and children's fiction as representations of lived experience. Their investigations exemplify the use of cultural artifacts as documents of human subjectivity.

In "The Many Faces of Emotionality: Reading *Persona*," Norman Denzin suggests that "nearly everything that is present in Bergman's movie is absent from our contemporary theories." The aims of the film, Denzin says, should also be goals for students of emotionality. Bergman takes an interpretive perspective that directly confronts the problem of representing subjectivity. He shows that emotionality is a gendered, interactional production. Using close-ups and long shots, split-screens, mirrors and reflections, doubling of characters, and characters speaking for each other, Bergman shows that it is impossible to separate the observer (filmmaker) from the observed (emotionality). Denzin reminds us that, like the film, life is not lived linearly: "It is lived through the subject's eye, and that eye, like a camera's, is always reflexive, nonlinear, subjective, filled with flashbacks, after-images, dream sequences, faces merging into one another, masks dropping, and new masks being put on." The film's conclusion is open-ended and illusive, as is the real world of lived experience, a world characterized by multiple meanings and ambiguities.

Laurel Graham offers four textual representations of one year in a woman's life, Lillian Moller Gilbreth (1878-1972), a highly influential pioneer of scientific management. As her texts in "Archival Research in Intertextual Analysis: Four Representations of the Life of Dr. Lillian Moller Gilbreth," Graham uses the book and film versions of *Belles on Their Toes,* a biographical account of the Gilbreths, and archival records consisting of Gilbreth's own letters and calendars. Graham points out intertextual inconsistencies that show variations in the construction of Gilbreth's lived experience, dependent on authority, medium, genre, and anticipated audience. Archival texts, Graham suggests, can provide alternative kinds of information to the texts of popular culture. When taken as "incomplete and partial" narratives and incorporated into intertextual analyses, archival texts can assist our understanding of the connection between mythologies and cultural representations. In this case, archival records give us a subversive feminist reading of a year in the life of Lillian Gilbreth.

Bronwyn Davies also reflects on the nature of women's subjectivity and its relation to lived and told stories. In "Women's Subjectivity and Feminist Stories," she blends rational argument, emotion, and lived bodily experience to detail the contradictory imperatives that inform the potential of those who are positioned as women. The embodied being, she claims, "is not the unitary rational being invented in the enlightenment . . . but a multiple being, finding ways to incorporate both sides of any of these dualisms previously divided along sex lines." The main story line for women is the romantic one, like Sleeping Beauty, in which woman is nothing until the prince kisses her. New feminist stories, she suggests, must take binary pairs, such as male/female, reason/emotion, mind/body, and rework them as necessary elements of subjectivity. The task becomes looking for and generating new story lines and new forms, especially those made available to children. Davies demonstrates that fiction and personal stories present avenues to the multiple wholeness of lived experience.

In Part II, authors experiment with the new ways of writing texts that Davies proposes, and they show the multifaceted, ambiguous, and multiple meanings of lived experience portrayed in Bergman's film, in the works on Gilbreth, and in women's stories. Believing that the time has come to produce our own postmodern narratives, and not just talk about the need to do so, authors in this part write personal stories, dramatic accounts, and poetry that express the complexities, contradictions, and revelations of lived experience. These narratives constitute a nascent literature written with the canons of ethnography in mind.

Carolyn Ellis and Arthur Bochner create a multivoiced narrative that describes the processual and emotional details of an abortion. The result is a text meant to be performed as a "staged reading" so that nuances of feeling, expression, and interpretation can be communicated more clearly, and emotional response and identification can be evoked. In "Telling and Performing Personal Stories: The Constraints of Choice in Abortion," the researchers treat their experiences as primary data and reflect on the subtle shadings and ambiguities of emotionality for both genders. Especially significant is the juxtaposing of the masculine and feminine voices with regard to an experience in which the male participant's voice normally is silenced. That men can feel deeply about such an event offers us insights into men's subjectivity and suggests a new story line for them as well as for women who must cope with the politics of conflicting abortion ideologies and divergent responses from others.

Carol Rambo Ronai tells another personal story in "The Reflexive Self Through Narrative: A Night in the Life of an Erotic Dancer/Researcher." She becomes the phenomenon, a dancer in a strip bar setting, by using multiple reflections to explore her own conduct and emotions as she moves back and forth between the roles of researcher and dancer. Dancing and writing about dancing, she shifts forward, then backward, then sideways through time, demonstrating that her researcher self is intimately connected to her dancer self and that becoming the phenomenon is a complicated process. Then she discusses the problems inherent in self-ethnographic research. Eschewing the separation of audience and text, she invites readers to make her experience intelligible by examining their own experiences in reaction to hers.

Laurel Richardson continues the experimentation with form by exploring the role of poetry in linking lived, interactional experience to the research and writing enterprises of sociologists. In "The Consequences of Poetic Representation: Writing the Other, Rewriting the Self," she concentrates on the personal consequences she experienced as a result of presenting an interview in the form of poetry. Although, in this case, the researcher and subject are two different people, Richardson has intentions related to the introspective studies above. While Ellis and Bochner, and Rambo Ronai, try to disentangle the voices of participants from those of researchers, Richardson discusses how the subject has entered her life, how her sociological and poetic voices have been integrated, and how her relationship with the subject—her other—changed her and allowed her to see herself and her world in different ways.

A subjective sense of ourselves is one of the principal elements in lived experience. In Part III, authors explore ways in which one's sense of self is conditioned by the peculiarities of time, place, and activity. Their studies reveal how cognition and emotion are intertwined as individuals define themselves and interpret the meaning of their experience.

One example of how cognition and emotion work together is variation in perception of time. Ordinarily, our inner sense of time is roughly synchronized with the passage of standard temporal units, as measured by clocks and calendars. Under certain conditions, however, we feel that time is passing quickly or slowly. In "The Erotics and Hermeneutics of Temporality," Michael Flaherty investigates the experience of lived duration. His findings are based on a collection of personal narratives in which individuals describe situations that provoked the sensation of time passing very slowly. He argues that the perception of time is shaped by emotional and cognitive processes that reflect the individual's subjective involvement with the situation. From analysis of the narratives, he formulates a theoretical interpretation that embraces the full range of variation in the perception of time.

A sense of self depends on place as well as time. In the chapter, "Wild Life: Authenticity and the Human Experience of 'Natural' Places," Gary Alan Fine claims that interpretation of place provides a frame for generating meaning. Fine explores subjective elements of "being in the wild" and contends that the idea of nature provides a lens for experiencing a different understanding of self and reality. People believe that culture and nature are separate realms of experience, and their beliefs have cognitive as well as emotional components. Fine's research among people who collect mushrooms shows that beliefs about the difference between culture and nature act as self-fulfilling prophecies with important implications for conduct and identities. Thus subjective processes are intrinsic to the social construction of reality.

Mark Neumann also studies the experience of self in nature. His research takes us into the world of tourists at the Grand Canyon. In "The Trail Through Experience: Finding Self in the Recollection of Travel," Neumann examines narratives of tourists to understand their struggle to make travel experiences meaningful and to "author" a self in the process. These narratives provide insight into the broader meaning of travel. "As people assign meaning and significance to their travel experiences, they reveal how culture and identity become incorporated through travel, the kinds of selves people find and lose while away from home, how identities are made as people confront others, and the peculiar and paradoxical ways that everyday life reappears as people seek to escape in their journeys."

Part IV deals with the transformations of our identities, or selves, in response to personal and physical changes, historical events, and transitions. Authors of these chapters remind us that subjective processes are experienced in the lived body and influenced by cultural and geographic environments.

Virginia Olesen's chapter, "Extraordinary Events and Mundane Ailments: The Contextual Dialectics of the Embodied Self," emphasizes the experience of the lived body and its integral role in the evolution of self-image. Olesen examines both extraordinary and mundane circumstances that lead to transformations in the experience of self. Her discussion of the extraordinary is grounded in published and reported accounts of individuals' subjective experiences (including her own) during and after the 1989 San Francisco earthquake. From a series of interviews, Olesen explores individuals' accounts of mundane ailments and how they cope with them. Olesen's research exemplifies the need to integrate knowledge of cognition, emotion, and the lived body.

In "The Self, Its Voices, and Their Discord," John Gagnon discusses sources and transformations of the self since the early stages of the nineteenth century. The self, he says, is the name that has been given to that voice in us that speaks last or seems truest to our most authentic feelings or thoughts at the moment of speech. He shows that "the definition of the self, its internal organization, its origins in the individual life history, its transformations throughout the life cycle, and its relation to cultural production have been influenced by changes in the material conditions of everyday life and changes in intellectual styles of explanation." Gagnon connects intrapersonal aspects of subjectivity to the dynamics of social and historical forces. His work demonstrates that if we want to understand lived experience, then we must examine our narrative materials against the backdrop of historical and cultural contexts.

This volume addresses subjectivity as lived experience in its physical, political, and historical contexts. We believe it should be judged according to its objective of provoking feelings in our readers that "they have experienced, or could experience, the events being described" (Denzin 1989, pp. 83-84). Assessment of how well we have achieved this goal can be formulated as answers to the following questions: Have we made subjectivity more intelligible? Do readers experience something akin to the emotions, thoughts, and bodily sensations we attempt to convey? Does the prose evoke cognitive, emotional, or physical response or identification? Were readers reminded of similar situations or different situations but with similar conditions? Have readers redefined a personal problem as a public issue as a result of reading our texts? Do readers have some increased understanding of the connection between subjectivity and sociocultural dynamics? Do readers recognize themselves—their feelings, thoughts, and everyday experiences— in the texts? If this volume provokes these responses, our goals will have been achieved and we will be pleased about the "way this has turned out."

References

Bateson, G. 1972. *Steps to an Ecology of Mind.* New York: Ballantine.
Blumer, H. 1969. *Symbolic Interactionism.* Englewood Cliffs, NJ: Prentice-Hall.
Bochner, A. 1990. "Embracing Contingencies of Lived Experience in the Study of Close Relationships." Keynote Lecture to the International Conference on Personal Relationships, Oxford University.
Cancian, F. and S. Gordon. 1988. "Changing Emotion Norms in Marriage: Love and Anger in U.S. Women's Magazines Since 1900." *Gender and Society* 2:308-42.
Denzin, N. K. 1985. "Emotion as Lived Experience." *Symbolic Interaction* 8:223-40.
———1989. *Interpretive Interactionism.* Newbury Park, CA: Sage.
———1991. "Representing Lived Experiences in Ethnographic Texts." In *Studies in Symbolic Interaction.* Vol. 12, edited by N. K. Denzin. Greenwich, CT: JAI.

Ebaugh, H. R. 1988. *Becoming an Ex: The Process of Role Exit*. Chicago: University of Chicago Press.

Ellis, C. 1991a. "Sociological Introspection and Emotional Experience." *Symbolic Interaction* 14:23-50.

———1991b. "Emotional Sociology." In *Studies in Symbolic Interaction*. Vol. 12, edited by N. K. Denzin. Greenwich, CT: JAI.

Geertz, C. 1980. "Blurred Genres: The Refiguration of Social Thought." *The American Scholar* 29:165-82.

Glassner, B. 1988. *Bodies*. New York: Putnam.

Goffman, E. 1959. *The Presentation of Self in Everyday Life*. Garden City, NY: Doubleday.

Harré, R. 1986. "An Outline of the Social Constructionist Viewpoint." Pp. 2-14 in *The Social Construction of Emotions*, edited by R. Harré. Oxford: Basil Blackwell.

Hochschild, A. 1979. "Emotion Work, Feeling Rules, and Social Structure." *American Journal of Sociology* 85:551-75.

———1983. *The Managed Heart*. Berkeley: University of California Press.

———1989. *The Second Shift*. New York: Viking.

Jackson, M. 1989. *Paths Toward a Clearing: Radical Empiricism and Ethnographic Inquiry*. Bloomington: Indiana University Press.

Jacobus, M., E. F. Keller, and S. Shuttleworth. 1990. *Body/Politics: Women and the Discourses of Science*. New York: Routledge.

James, W. [1890] 1950. *The Principles of Psychology*. Vol. 1. New York: Dover.

Katz, J. 1988. *Seductions of Crime*. New York: Basic Books.

Keats, J. 1958. *The Letters of John Keats 1814-1821*, edited by H. E. Rollins. Cambridge: Cambridge University Press.

Kemper, T. D. 1981. "Social Constructionist and Positivist Approaches to the Sociology of Emotions." *American Journal of Sociology* 87:336-62.

———1987. "How Many Emotions Are There? Wedding the Social and the Autonomic Components." *American Journal of Sociology* 93:263-89.

———1990. *Social Structure and Testosterone*. New Brunswick, NJ: Rutgers University Press.

Krieger, S. 1984. "Fiction and Social Science." Pp. 269-87 in *Studies in Symbolic Interaction*. Vol. 5, edited by N. K. Denzin. Greenwich, CT: JAI.

Kuhn, T. S. 1970. *The Structure of Scientific Revolutions*. 2nd ed. Chicago: University of Chicago Press.

Marcel, G. 1949. *The Philosophy of Existence*. New York: Philosophical Library.

Neumann, M. 1989. "The 'Problems' of Evidence in Cultural Studies." Paper presented at the International Communication Association, San Francisco.

Rorty, R. 1979. *Philosophy and the Mirror of Nature*. Princeton, NJ: Princeton University Press.

Rosaldo, R. 1987. *Culture and Truth: The Remaking of Social Analysis*. Boston: Beacon.

Sanders, C. R. 1989. *Customizing the Body*. Philadelphia: Temple University Press.

Schachter, S. and J. E. Singer. 1962. "Cognitive, Social and Physiological Determinants of Emotional State." *Psychological Review* 69:379-99.

Scheff, T. 1985. "Universal Expressive Needs: A Critique and a Theory." *Symbolic Interaction* 8:241-62.

Shott, S. 1979. "Emotion and Social Life: A Symbolic Interactionist Analysis." *American Journal of Sociology* 84:1317-34.

Stearns, C. and P. Stearns. 1986. *Anger: The Struggle for Emotional Control in America's History*. Chicago: University of Chicago Press.

Thoits, P. 1989. "The Sociology of Emotions." *Annual Review of Sociology* 15:317-42.

Van Maanen, J. 1988. *Tales of the Field: On Writing Ethnography.* Chicago: University of Chicago Press.

Weber, M. 1947. *The Theory of Social and Economic Organization,* edited by T. Parsons. New York: Free Press.

Zald, M. 1988. "Sociology as a Discipline: Quasi-Science and Quasi-Humanities." Paper presented at the American Sociological Association, Atlanta.

PART I

Interpreting Texts

1

The Many Faces of Emotionality

Reading Persona

NORMAN K. DENZIN

Unarguably one of the most difficult and enigmatic of contemporary films (Johnson 1985, p. 2418),[1] Ingmar Bergman's *Persona* (1966)[2] contains within itself the essential ingredients for a postmodern, interpretive sociology of emotionality, subjectivity, and everyday life. It is simultaneously historical, autobiographical, interactional, sexual, and gender specific, framed around epiphanic movements, and most centrally preoccupied with language, speaking, the masks that hide the self, and the ability of the person to strip away masks and become an essential, feeling, flesh-and-blood human being, with no disguises.

In his double play on *persona,* the mask and the person behind the mask, Bergman with this film sets an agenda for our field.[3] I wish to sketch out the implications of this text for contemporary discourse on the above topics but, first, a synopsis of the movie.

It is a man's story about two women. During a performance of *Electra,* Elisabeth Vogler (Liv Ulmann), a noted actress, stops speaking and remains absolutely mute for one moment before continuing with the play. The next day, she lapses into mental and physical inertia, refusing to speak or move. Her doctor, finding nothing physically or mentally wrong with Elisabeth, places her in the care of a young, well-adjusted nurse, Alma, who bears an uncanny physical and facial resemblance to Elisabeth. The two women are sent to a seacoast island, where Alma is to treat Elisabeth. Before they leave, three significant events occur. Elisabeth receives a loving letter from her husband, in which he tells her "we must look at each other as if we were children, full of kindness and good things. You taught me this." The letter contains a photograph of their son. She tears the photo in half. Shortly after this, Elisabeth watches in horror a television news broadcast about the Vietnam war in which a Buddhist monk burns himself to death. Screaming, she withdraws in fear into the corner of her room. The next day, her physician diagnoses her muteness as a form of playacting and tells her to remain that way "until you find it uninteresting, finished, and can leave it as you have left, by and by, your other roles." The doctor continues his analysis, telling Elisabeth that this muteness is the result of the

> hopeless dream about being, not doing, but being. Aware and watchful every second . . . the abyss between what you feel for others and what you are for yourself . . . the burning need to be unmasked. At last to be seen through, reduced, perhaps extinguished. Every tone of voice a lie. . . . Every gesture false. The role of wife, the role of friend, the roles of mother and mistress, which is worst? Which has tortured you the most? . . . Where did it break? . . . Your role as *Electra* . . . gave you a rest . . . but [now] you have nothing left to hide behind. And so you were left with your demand for truth. . . . Kill yourself? No—too nasty. . . . But you could be immobile. You can keep quiet. Then at least you're not lying. Then you don't have to play a part. . . . But reality plays tricks on you. Your hiding place isn't watertight. Life starts leaking in everywhere. And you're forced to react. No one asks whether it's genuine or not. . . . It's only in the theatre that's an important question. (Script extract from Bradfield 1972, pp. 41-42)

Upon arriving on the island, Alma discards her nurse's uniform. While on the island, Alma does all the talking. Drunk one night, she relates a sexual orgy she experienced in her late teens. Elisabeth reports this story in a letter to her doctor. Alma reads the letter and confronts Elisabeth with this betrayal. Alma becomes violent and accuses Elisabeth of using her ("You've used me. You've told me nothing!"). Elisabeth's husband visits and talks to Alma as if she were his wife. He speaks of their son. Alma becomes more hysterical. Words fail her as she relives Elisabeth's experiences as an actress and a mother. She enters a near schizophrenic state, speaking in short phrases without meaning. The next day, she confronts Elisabeth, who is covering up a torn picture of her son, and tells her she had been challenged to play the role of mother, had hated it, hated her son, and was now attempting to escape from everything by remaining voiceless. (The night before, Elisabeth is shown gazing at the most famous photograph from the Holocaust, the scene with the child about to be shot by the Nazis.) At the end of her speech,

Elisabeth is discovered to have put the pieces of her son's torn photograph back together. (This scene is then repeated with Elisabeth telling it to Alma.) Thus Alma's challenge has worked. The next day, at Alma's urging, Elisabeth speaks the word *nothing*. The following day, the women pack and leave the island. Alma has returned to wearing her nurse's uniform. The film ends with shots of Bergman and a cinematographer on a dolly, a shot of Elisabeth back on stage, and a picture of a young boy touching a photography that turns into two faces, Alma's and Elisabeth's.

Filled with reflexive signifiers from beginning to end, all of which inform viewers that they are viewing a film made by Bergman,[4] the text then comes full circle on itself.[5] Alma discovers what the physician already knew, that Elisabeth was playing another role. What the physician didn't know, however, was that the role she was escaping from was that of mother. By forcing Elisabeth to relive her experiences as a mother, Alma brings her out of her muteness. This involves a confrontation with the word *nothing*. Alma knows and Elisabeth now understands that being must involve a transcendence of nothingness. As reality leaks into the everyday, action of any sort is meaningful. There is no escaping being.

Elisabeth's illusion, that reality can be escaped from, is thus destroyed. But the destruction occurs under the arm of patriarchy. For example, the father/husband on two occasions carries the message of the son; and it is Alma's reenactment of Elisabeth's motherliness that brings her out of her mute state. Bergman thus brings two messages. The first is philosophical and is about being and meaning. The second is sexist, and patriarchal, and about women's place in the social order and the proposition that full being only comes from the full embracement of the maternal function.[6] The two messages cannot be separated in Bergman's text, and the presence of the second jeopardizes the force of the first.

Our Project

Arguing, then, that nothingness is a mask, that silence is a form of talk, that *persona muta* is also a part one can play, this film challenges students of emotionality, communication, and everyday life to expose the masks, or personas, that our respective fields hide behind. Elsewhere (Denzin 1989, 1991), I have suggested that the various sociologies of emotion and everyday life pass under a single heading, which I called "scientist," even though they are currently divided into two camps, the positivistic and the constructionist (see Kemper 1990, especially the chapters by Collins, Hammond, Thoits,

Kemper, Smith-Lovin, and Heise; and for more clearly interpretive-constructionist views, the contributions in Franks and McCarthy 1989). Positivistic sociologies seek external sociological and psychological explanations of this phenomenon called "emotionality," and they carry labels like the ritual chain theory, the power-status theory, and the feeling-rules-management theory. Each of these perspectives attempts to inscribe an objective, scientific account of human experience, containing it within a deterministic, quantitative, predictive, often biological framework.

Alongside these formulations now emerges another cluster of approaches that are more interpretive, subjective, feminist, biographical, and narratively inspired (see, for example, the readings in Franks and McCarthy 1989). Subjective in orientation, these new orientations reflect a commitment to grasp experience from the subject's point of view. But, like their empiricist counterparts, they seek "scientific" accounts of emotionality and contemporary life, which privilege the researcher over the subject, method over subject matter, and maintain commitments to outmoded conceptions of validity, truth, and generalizability. They refuse to address how the subject's experiences are transformed into textual representations that are only stand-ins for the actual experience being described and analyzed. That is, lived experience can only be represented indirectly, through quotations from field notes, observations, or interviews. These strategies of representing lived experience create the impression that the subject exists outside discourse, in a world of self-mediated and self-defined experiences (Denzin 1990, p. 201). In fact, the sociologist creates the subject through the strategic use of textual materials that are intended to bring the subject alive in the writer's text. Such representations suppress the actual processes that lead to the subject's construction in the text (Clough 1989, p. 163; Denzin 1989, p. 199).

As they edge their way backward into the "postmodern" space, these new approaches seek to still give the researcher the mask of scientist to hide behind. We maintain a belief in a form of "realism" that we think allows us to accurately map the world of the empirical. Not artists but scientists, sociologists want to capture the real. In this move, they sustain an allegiance to a movement that started in the nineteenth century with the realist, naturalistic, melodramatic novel, a movement that rose to prominence in the twentieth century with social realism in film, modernism in art, and positivism in the social sciences.

Social realists eschew a strict correspondence theory of truth, but they are not willing to go all the way over to a conventionalist (feminist) theory, which holds that the relation between *internal and external referents of discourse is largely arbitrary and changeable.* Realist epistemology holds that the world out there exists independent of our perceptions of it.

As social realists, the new subjectivists take their place in a long tradition that has been simultaneously positivist and postpositivist, or interpretive. From Weber to Durkheim, Mead to Watson, Blumer to Lazarsfeld, Marx to Althusser, this tradition has maintained a commitment to a science that renders the invisible world visible. It has maintained a commitment, as just noted, to the production of a series of realist, melodramatic, social problem texts that have created an identification with the powerless in society. These works of realism reproduced and mirrored the social structures that needed to be changed. They valorized the subjectivity of the downtrodden individual (for excellent instances of this approach, see Ellis and Bochner, and Rambo Ronai, in this volume). They made a hero or heroine of the sociologist who could write moving texts about the powerless. They created a body of textual work that kept the private/public divisions alive and well in American sociology.

Social realism in sociology continued, then, the narrative, realist traditions of Romantic and Victorian fiction. In the twentieth century, the narrative tradition quickly grafted itself into mainstream scientific-positivist realism. This realism was short-lived, however, to be replaced by the new governing aesthetics and philosophies of science peculiar to modernism and post-modernism (see Jameson 1990, p. 155). Thus the new texts move uneasily between old-fashioned correspondence theory positivism and the new poststructuralisms and subjective methods that come with the postmodern period.

Today, social realism is under attack. It is now seen as but one narrative strategy for telling stories about the social world out there. In its place comes poststructuralism and grammatology, new writing and reading styles grafted into the cinematic society, where a thing exists if it can be captured in a visual or printed text. Poststructuralism undermines the realist agenda, contending that things do not exist independent of their representations in social texts. Accordingly, if we want to change how things are, we must change how they are seen, written about, and heard (see Richardson in this volume). How they are seen is itself determined by the older realist and modernist agendas that presumed worlds out there that could be mapped by a realist, scientific method.

It is this hegemonic vision that must be challenged, and too many constructionists refuse to take up the challenge. They still want a world out there that proves their theory right or wrong. But how do they find that world and bring it into existence? How do they record what it does when they push against it? Unfortunately, they seldom answer these questions. Social realism will not produce the science of subjective experience that so many seek. Paradoxically, it is realism that got us into this situation where the subjective is now valued.

Suppose that we drop the mask of social realism. What would happen? Imagine for a moment that you collectively assumed the persona of Elisabeth. Cast me in Alma's identity. You remain silent for a moment; let me do the talking. Strip away your theories and let me ask you some questions and make some observations. A variety of theories now litter our field as it opens itself to other influences: semiotics, phenomenology, postmodernism, critical theory, poststructuralism, feminism, Marxism, narrative theory, deconstructionism, and cultural studies. These theories are windows with shutters, ways of seeing that close doors, yet they all point in the direction of two conclusions and one question: Our standard theories are no longer working, and we must look for new approaches. The new will reveal itself in the texts we write about our subject matter, but where and how do we look? A different approach is sought.

A Cultural Studies That Makes a Difference

The interdisciplinary movement known as "feminist cultural studies" speaks to the above needs, drawing as it does on all the human disciplines and the theoretical formations that now gather under the interpretive, critical umbrella. A feminist cultural studies examines three interrelated problems: the production of gendered, ethnic, political cultural meanings; the textual analysis of these meanings; and the study of lived cultures and lived experiences and their connections to these worlds of representation. Culture—the taken-for-granted and problematic webs of significance and meaning that human beings produce and act on when they do things together—is shaped by the larger meaning-making-institutions-of-society-at-large. The representations of human experience as given in the mass media, film, social science, novels, art, politics, and religion constitute a critical layer of materials to be interpreted. Such texts inevitably confuse "nature and history" in a way that suggests "ideological abuse" (Barthes [1957] 1972, p. 11), the hidden privileges of patriarchy, and the myth of autonomous interacting individuals producing unique structures of personal experience.

Two models of interpretation currently operate in the human disciplines (Derrida 1972, p. 264). The first seeks to decipher, unravel, and discover the truth, the origins, the centers, the essences, the inner structures, and the obdurate meanings that operate within and shape particular forms of experience, interactional sites, social texts, and social institutions. This view has dreamed, throughout sociology's history, of representing and capturing human beings in society and doing so scientifically. This is the classical and neoclassical version of sociology as a science of society. It holds a firm grip on most sociologists today. Its influences are present in both the positivist and the constructionist approaches to the study of subjectivity and everyday life.

The second approach to interpretation (Derrida 1972, pp. 264-65) is not directed to the study of origins, centers, structures, laws, or empirical regularities. It holds that human beings are never fully present, to themselves, or others, except through a process of deferral and delay. It argues that language is also only a process and hence never fixed in its representations or meanings. It contends that society, as conceptualized by experience, can never be fully captured because language will not allow this to occur. Hence experience can only be given in texts (interviews, field notes, life stories, films, and the like) that are themselves indirect representations of what they purport to represent. It seeks instead to examine how current textual practices (including theory and research) reify structures, subjects, and social experience. It proposes to deconstruct these practices so as to reveal how they keep in place a politically repressive picture of the social that is out of touch with the world as it is lived and experienced.

A cultural studies that makes a difference builds on this second model of interpretation. It treats the personal as political. It works to connect personal troubles to public issues within a radical and plural democracy that regards personal troubles as the site of struggle. It seeks to give a voice to the voiceless, as it deconstructs those popular culture texts that reproduce stereotypes about the powerless. Understanding that texts repress, while they create and support tyrannical political structures, this deconstructive attitude resists the reactive, commercialized versions of the postmodern. It advocates pluralism and cultural diversities but cautiously repudiates a laissez-faire attitude toward diversity, seeking instead a radical, nonviolent pluralism that represses no one and liberates all.

Back to Persona

Can we point to a moment in our collective history when we, like Elisabeth, fell silent during a performance? Can we pinpoint a moment when the hopeless dream of building a full-fledged theory of emotionality, subjectivity, communication, and everyday experience suddenly awakened us? When did we realize that our theories are and were playing tricks on us, that our every gesture was false, that our past identities no longer worked, that we now had noting left to hide behind? Perhaps we haven't yet awakened from our dream and are still performing our parts in *Electra* or *Oedipus Rex*. But maybe we have awakened and perhaps the 1990 Stone Symposium (and the publication of this volume) is that awakening. Let's assume it is and move forward from that assumption.

Back to the film. Nearly everything that is present in Bergman's movie is absent from our contemporary theories, even those that are gender specific. His text contains all that we need. Reconsider the images in *Persona*: death, Vietnam, the Holocaust, sexuality, pregnancy and abortion, childhood, the theater, anger, fear, horror, dread, death, terror, an oppressive patriarchy, and the proposition (however implicit) that there are gender-specific emotional experiences. Consider his two subjects: flesh-and-blood human beings, presented in the here and now. No grand theories of interpretation here. Just two women, one silent, the other vocal. What does Bergman give us? His film is a historically specific (the Holocaust and Vietnam), self-reflexive account that crosses the bridges between Jungian psychoanalysis and Sartrean existentialism in a way that connects the profound moments of meaning in everyday life with epiphanic experiences. His text directly confronts the problem of representing subjective, feminine experience and shows that emotionality is a gendered, interactional production. His methods of shooting and editing use close-ups and long shots (emphasizing intimacy and detachment), split-screens, after-images, mirrors and reflections, indirect lighting, the doubling of characters, reversals in dialogue, subjects speaking for each other, simultaneous voices, long silences, and a constant self-referentiality that proclaims the impossibility of separating the observer (filmmaker) from the subject. Understanding that strict realistic cinema will not capture what he is after, Bergman goes for an interpretive-subjective approach that obliterates the usual distinctions between time, space, linearity, and meaning. Even his conclusion is open-ended and illusive, for in this world only multiple meanings and ambiguities operate.

Language as speech is Bergman's problem. How does silence speak? Is there a language of silence that speaks being's meaning? How does being represent itself in and through language? Bergman's answer is direct. Being's meaning is given in perception (see Merleau-Ponty 1964, p. 58), in the visual field that anchors self to other. Understanding that this field cannot be written about, only represented, Bergman creates a visual feast of faces and images that merge into one another. His challenge to us, then, is to learn how to write visually, in a way that reflects how what is seen is felt, knowing then that seeking is feeling.

Writing Emotionally

To write visually is to produce a new form of the social text, a form that is itself part visual, part montage, and part cinematic. Such a text writes itself across its own subject matter, for example, mixing the printed text, which may be multicolumned, in multiple scripts, with photographs, lyrics from sings, lines from films, and so on.[7] This new form finds one of its expressions in a new form of historiography called the "mystory" (Ulmer 1989, Pt. 3). Nostalgia, mourning, and melancholia are the pervasive postmodern theoretical emotions, although they are not present in this volume. From Jameson to Lyotard and Baudrillard, the lament is the same; things are not as they used to be. A certain sadness lingers over their texts.

Ulmer (1989) challenges this argument, offering in its place a playful pedagogy for the age of video and television. Ulmer's project builds on the three modes of discourse—orality, the written text, and the video text—which together constitute the stuff of contemporary discourse. The technology of postmodern culture has shifted from print to video. Orality in the video age incorporates three levels of sense making—common sense, the popular, and the scientific. These three discursive structures, which involve science, popular culture, everyday life, and private experience, circulate through all levels of culture, from "high" to "low" and back again (Ulmer 1989, p. vii).

Teletheory introduces a new genre of discourse, "mystory," into the postmodern stream. A mystory is "always specific to its composer . . . . [it] brings into relation your experience with three levels of discourse—personal (autobiography), popular (community stories, oral history or popular culture), expert (disciplines of knowledge)" (Ulmer 1989, pp. vii, 209). A "mystory" begins with a personal experience, the sting of memory. It locates personal, popular culture, and scholarly items significant to the writer. Once located, these items are researched in terms of their representations in the popular, and scientific, archives of the culture. Fragments of this information most relevant to the oral life story are then assembled in an order that displays a humorous, playful, aggressive witlike relationship to the text and the events that are recorded. In Ulmer's words (1989, p. 211), as the writer of a "mystory," "I am the target of the aggressive wit that replaces the monumental melancholy associated with the pedagogy of specialized high culture." (Ulmer's "Derrida at the Little Bighorn: A Fragment" [1989, pp. 212-43] is an example of such writing.)

A "mystory" personalizes the postmodern. It connects the contradictory currents of this contemporary culture to the writer's personal biography. As a pedagogical device, it allows the writer as teacher to lead the student into the production of a cultural text that blends orality, print, and video into a personal document that universalizes the singularity of the student's experiences. Ulmer's aggressive wit replaces the nostalgic, mournful longing for that day when the postmodern disappears.

In the mystory, the feeling eye, and ear, embrace and produce their own emotionality. My experience is always sensuous, and embodied; I feel what I hear and see. Emotionality lies in the plane of the perceptual field that is felt and experienced from within as one face conveys to another how she feels about what she sees and hears in the other's face and voice. I tell these experiences in mystory. The mystory tells my emotional stories.

Even if the ineffable cannot be expressed in words, it can be expressed in the face, in the eyes, in the gestures, in the silences that join. These visual and heard representations express my emotionality. What is seen and then felt is itself anchored in historically specific fields of experience that move outward from the person into collective and personal time. Backward to the Holocaust, forward to the dead monk in Vietnam, and the rock music playing outside Noriega's castle in Panama City, my reactions to Elisabeth's torn photograph are also historically framed. As she gazes at the Jewish boy about to be killed, and the monk who burns himself to death, I hear rock and country music in my head, and stories of others about to die or who have fled from a loved one or who have retreated into silence behind state-imposed walls so as to escape guilt from past misdeeds. My seeing her see herself tear up an image of her child reminds me of the fragility of my relationship to myself, my children, and my historical moment as well.

The Storyteller's Plot

Bergman is a storyteller, and the teller's most powerful effects come

> when he [or she] convinces us that what is particular, integrated and different in a cultural practice [like filmmaking or doing the sociology of emotion and subjectivity] is part of a cultural plot that makes coherent sense of all cultural practices as a totality: not a totality that is there, waiting for us to acknowledge its presence, but a totality fashioned when the storyteller convinces us to see it his [or her] way. (Lentricchia 1990, p. 335)

Our most powerful effects as storytellers come when we too expose the cultural plot and the cultural practices that guide our writing hands and lead us to see coherence where there is none or to create meaning without an understanding of the broader structures that tell us to tell things in a particular way.[8] Our commitment to a realistic, melodramatic view of meaning and social life must be seen, as argued above, as a form of plotted discourse that does neither us or those we write about any good; that is, lives may not have beginnings, middles, and happy endings; nor can they necessarily be told in straightforward, linear time, through representational, realistic texts.

Erasing the boundaries between self, other, and history, Bergman invites me to embark on a project that has the following characteristics. I now focus only on flesh-and-blood subjects and their representations in my texts (mystories) and the texts of others. I abandon a preoccupation with a subject of my construction, calling this the analytic subject. I now dispense with distinctions between the analytic and the empirical subject, the one who answers interviews. Looking always for representations of lived experience, I understand that lived experience can only be given indirectly, through textual representations. While I seek the "wild being" who exists outside textual representations, and comes into containment only under duress, I understand that no one exists outside a text and that texts produce subjects (see Denzin 1990, p. 213).

These texts, however, ought not be constructed under the hegemonic system of naturalistic realism; for life is not lived realistically, in a linear manner. It is lived through the subject's eye, and that eye, like a camera's, is always reflexive, nonlinear, subjective, filled with flashbacks, after-images, dream sequences, faces merging into one another, masks dropping, and new masks being put on. In this world called reality, where we are forced to react, and life leaks in everywhere, we have nothing to hold on to but our own being.

This being the case, our project, as students of emotionality and subjectivity, becomes clear. Ever alert to any new angle that will shed light on our phenomenon, we look constantly to how each of us constructs the other out of the bits and pieces of history and meaning our culture makes available to, or forces upon us, including gender, race, and class and the structures of patriarchy. Stepping up one level, our work enters the terrain of cultural studies (Carey 1989, pp. 89-110) and becomes simultaneously critical, feminist, phenomenological, and interpretive. Seeing emotionality in the fields of perception that envelop us, we undertake an interpretive project that studies how others, with sensitivities greater than our own, have themselves wrestled with the meaning of emotionality for the human being. At the same time, we undertake projects that experiment with new forms of writing and representation (see Richardson in this volume), including first-person accounts of our own emotionality (for example, Ellis and Bochner, and Rambo Ronai, in this volume). Learning from Elisabeth's muteness that a smug withdrawal from the world is impossible, we also learn from Alma that you can't make this being called emotionality reveal herself to you until she's ready. But once she's properly approached, she will speak. This is what we learn from Bergman's *Persona*. Now, how do we listen?

Notes

1. *Persona* was also chosen by a poll of international critics as one of the ten best films ever made (Johnson 1985, p. 2418).

2. The film *Persona* (1966; released in the United States, 1967). Origin: Sweden. Produced, scripted, and directed by Ingmar Bergman; AB Svensk Filmindustri; Bibi Andersson (Alma), Liv Ulmann (Elisabeth Vogler), Margaretha Krook (Doctor), Gunnar Bjornstrand (Herr Vogler), Jorgen Lindstrom (Boy).

3. An interviewer, in discussing the word *persona* with Bergman, remarked, "Originally *persona* means the masks used by actors in classical drama. It also means the various personages in a play. But Jung has a definition which I think suits your film admirably— I'd like to hear what you think of it. The consciously artificial or masked personality complex which is adopted by an individual in contrast to his inner character, with intent to serve as a projection, a defence, a deception, or an attempt to adapt to the world around him." Bergman (1969, p. 202) replied, "It . . . fits well in this case. There's something extremely fascinating to me about these people exchanging masks and suddenly sharing between them." Asked to describe the film, Bergman said, "It's about one person who talks and one who doesn't, and they compare hands and get all mingled up in one another" (Bergman 1969, p. 196). I'm indebted to Robert Carringer for introducing me to this film and for showing me how to start reading it.

4. As the film begins, a black screen is shown, then blazes of light as a film projector's carbon-arc lamps begin to burn, then film begins running through a projector, followed by various images: a bit of silent comedy, a spider, a nail being driven through the palm of a hand, bodies in a morgue, a young boy who reaches out toward an indistinct shape that becomes a women's face and then changes from one woman's face to another. The faces are those of Elisabeth and Alma. In the middle, the picture disintegrates, as if something is wrong with the projector. At the end, Bergman and his cinematographer, as noted above, are shown shooting film as a reflection of Elisabeth appearing in a film is revealed.

5. Throughout, there are scenes that appear as dreams or fantasies. Shortly after their arrival, Alma is sleeping. Elisabeth passes through a curtain into Alma's bedroom, and the two figures merge into one. In other key moments, the images and faces of the two women merge, giving the impression of a doubling of character that is unified into a single figure.

6. Penley ([1973] 1976) offers an extended analysis of Bergman's negative treatment of women, who range in his films (e.g., *Persona, Cries and Whispers, Secrets of Women, The Silence, Fanny and Alexander*) from being highly neurotic, and self-destructive, to purely erotic, or earth or harsh mother figures.

7. McGuire (1991) provides an exemplary text. A mystory analysis of the discourses on anorexia nervosa, her handwritten and typed text is written across a text that is made up of the Xeroxed photographs of the bodies of beautiful women as presented in fashion magazines.

8. My plot, of course, is deconstructive, weaving an unstable line between a critique of social realism and a call for mystories that report, from the subject's point of view, epiphanic emotional experiences.

References

Barthes, Roland. [1957] 1972. *Mythologies*. New York: Hill & Wang.

Bergman, Ingmar. 1969. "Bergman on *Persona*." *Rasunda*, February 10, pp. 195-214.

Bradfield, Keith. 1972. *Ingmar Bergman,* Persona *and* Shame: *The Screenplays of Ingmar Bergman*. New York: Grossman.

Carey, James W. 1989. "Overcoming Resistance to Cultural Studies." Pp. 89-110 in *Communication as Culture*, by James W. Carey. Boston: Unwin Hyman.

Clough, Patricia Ticineto. 1989. "Letters from Pamela: Howard S. Becker's Writing(s) for Social Scientists." *Symbolic Interaction* 12:159-70.

Denzin, Norman K. 1989. "Interpreting the Social Constructionist Position in the Sociology of Emotions." Paper presented to the annual meetings of the American Sociological Association, Roundtable Session, "The Social Constructionist-Positivist Debate," August 9.

———1990. "Harold and Agnes: A Feminist Narrative Undoing." *Sociological Theory* 8:198-216.

———1991. *Images of Postmodernism: Social Theory and Contemporary Cinema*. London: Sage.

Derrida, Jacques. 1972. "Structure, Sign, and Play in the Discourse of the Human Sciences." Pp. 247-65 in *The Structuralist Controversy: The Languages of Criticism and the Sciences of Man*, edited by Richard Macksey and Eugene Donato. Baltimore: Johns Hopkins University Press.

Filmfacts. 1967. "*Persona*." 10(April 15):59-61.

Franks, David D. and E. Doyle McCarthy, eds. 1989. *The Sociology of Emotions: Original Essays and Papers*. Greenwich, CT: JAI.

Jameson, Fredric. 1990. *Signatures of the Visible*. London: Routledge.

Johnson, Timothy W. 1985. "*Persona*." Pp. 2418-21, in *Magill's Survey of Cinema*. Vol. 5, *Foreign Language Films*, edited by Frank N. Magill. Englewood Cliffs, NJ: Salem.

Kemper, Theodore D., ed. 1990. *Research Agendas in the Sociology of Emotions*. Albany: State University of New York Press.

Lentricchia, Frank. 1990. "In Place of an Afterword: Someone Reading." Pp. 321-38 in *Critical Terms for Literary Study*, edited by Frank Lentricchia and Thomas McLaughlin. Chicago: University of Chicago Press.

McGuire, Gail. 1991. "Writing the Anorexic Body." Unpublished manuscript, Department of Sociology, University of Illinois at Urbana-Champaign.

Merleau-Ponty, Maurice. 1964. "Film and the New Psychology." Pp. 48-59 in *Sense and Non-Sense*, by Maurice Merleau-Ponty; translated by Hubert L. and Patricia Allen Dreyfus. Evanston, IL: Northwestern University Press.

Penley, Constance. [1973] 1976. "Cries and Whispers." Pp. 204-08 in *Movies and Methods.* Vol. 1, edited by Bill Nichols. Berkeley: University of California Press. (Originally published in *Women & Film*, 1973)

Ulmer, Gregory. 1989. *Teletheory*. New York: Routledge.

2

Archival Research in Intertextual Analysis

Four Representations of the Life of Dr. Lillian Moller Gilbreth

LAUREL GRAHAM

There is a growing interest in the relationships between cultural texts and dominant ideologies.[1] Investigators of popular culture, for example, have demonstrated how popular texts naturalize politically conservative and patriarchal ideologies. Borrowing from Barthes's *Mythologies* (1957), they examine how movies, books, music, and other cultural artifacts employ thematic and stylistic devices to convey mythologies (e.g., Denzin, 1991; Doane 1987; Gledhill 1985, 1987; Hall 1980; Ray 1985). These mythologies are implicit cause-and-effect chains, often guiding textual characters along the path of mainstream, conservative ideologies. Although mythologies are ideological, popular texts sell them as "the truth." With careful observation, mythologies can be deconstructed; that is, their hidden presence in the text can be made explicit and their capitalist and patriarchal underpinnings can be critiqued.

AUTHOR'S NOTE: I wish to thank Norman Denzin, Andrew Pickering, David Breeden, and "the bonded cohort" (Linda Detman, Virginia Husting, and Dale McConkey) for helpful comments. A special thanks to Helen Schroyer, chief librarian of the Gilbreth Collection, Purdue University, and to Ernestine Gilbreth Carey, for her help and encouragement.

One approach for deconstructing mythologies is intertextual analysis. This involves comparing several texts that hold some feature in common, perhaps a set of representational techniques, a plot line, or a substantive topic (e.g., Schatz [1981] compares genre films; Denzin [1991] compares films about alcoholics). Intertextual analysis can be used to compare several texts depicting the same period in one person's life. With multiple readings of each text, the analyst can identify contradictions among the accounts that then help locate the mythologies operating in each text. In cases when historical characters have left behind their own unpublished records of their lives, such as letters and diaries, these documents provide valuable additional texts. Because they typically are not written to be sold in a capitalist popular culture market, archival documents are likely to suggest new angles for deconstructing more popular versions of a story. This chapter illustrates how intertextual analysis can be strengthened by including archival documents among the texts to be compared.

To explore this technique, I treat a set of archival records as a multifaceted cultural text, incomplete and partial like any other. I include this text in a comparison of four versions of one woman's story. All four of my texts recount the struggle of Lillian Moller Gilbreth (1878-1972) to stabilize her efficiency engineering career after her husband's death. In reverse chronological order, they are a Hollywood movie (*Belles on Their Toes* [1952]), the book that inspired the movie (*Belles on Their Toes* by Frank Gilbreth, Jr., and Ernestine Gilbreth Carey [1950]), a biography of Gilbreth and her husband (*Partners for Life* by Edna Yost [1949]), and Lillian Gilbreth's own calendar, which she called her "diary" along with her personal letters (Gilbreth Collection [1924-25]). Each of these accounts draws upon a set of dominant ideologies about women's duties in marriage, motherhood, and science to tell its story. At the same time, each text reinforces a traditional mythological relationship between these cultural conceptions. Briefly stated, this mythological system urges women to find happiness in the domestic sphere and to pursue a scientific career only if it is financially necessary. Each text offers its own twist on this general mythology.

By coincidence, when lined up chronologically, these four texts are also ordered by anticipated popularity. The older the text, the less commercially popular its author(s) expected it to become. This is most evident when looking at the extremes: the Hollywood movie and the archives. For economic and historical reasons, Hollywood movies tie themselves most noticeably to traditional ideologies. As Robert Ray (1985, p. 27) writes, "The determinedly commercial nature of the U.S. film industry compelled a kind of filmmaking peculiarly responsive to the dominant ideologies of American life." Put bluntly, capitalist and patriarchal mythologies help sell cultural texts, especially movies.

At the other extreme, archival documents are often written as pragmatic devices for organizing one's daily life. Certainly, ideologically constituted subjects write these accounts, drawing upon cultural myths to represent their experiences. Because archival documents are not written to be sold to the public, however, their expressions of dominant ideology are not mandated for the sake of marketability. The noncommercial character of archival records makes the story they tell fragmented and unstable, an account that can help locate mythological systems at work in commercially popular versions of the same story.

Between these two extremes, I include two additional kinds of texts, a book and a biography, which were intended by their authors to be more popular than the archive but less commercially successful than the film. Moving backward through these four texts (from film to book, biography, and then archive) will allow an incremental deconstruction of the mythologies conveyed in each text.

Stories of Lillian Gilbreth

Historians and engineers have called Dr. Lillian Moller Gilbreth "the world's foremost female industrial engineer," and they have credited her with bringing psychological theories and practices into management research (Trescott 1983). She and her husband, Frank Bunker Gilbreth (1868-1924), were industrial engineers and pioneers of scientific management. They worked as partners from around 1904 to 1924 to develop their own methods and ideals of scientific management, which complemented and challenged those of Frederick Taylor. Frank spent much of his time in consultation with manufacturers to find ways of improving industrial efficiency.[2] Lillian acquired a special interest in the human side of industrial management and earned a Ph.D. in psychology in 1915. She also served as writer, editor, and research assistant in the motion study laboratory they set up in their Montclair, New Jersey, home. During those years, she gave birth to their 12 children (11 of whom survived to adulthood) and divided her energy between motion study research and caring for this large family.

Together the Gilbreths published many books and articles and, by the 1920s, they thought that their research was finally beginning to get the recognition it deserved. In June 1924, they were scheduled to travel to Europe, where Frank was to give a series of lectures and serve as an organizer for the first international management conference. Shortly before his departure, he died of a heart attack. Lillian went to Europe to deliver the lectures in his place, thereby initiating her career as an autonomous efficiency expert. Over the next 40 years, her interests diversified into such fields as department store management, household management, and engineering for the handicapped. Her eventual success, however, did not come without some initial struggle: According to most accounts of her life, she overcame monumental barriers to women in engineering in the first 12 months after Frank's death, from the summer of 1924 to the summer of 1925 (e.g., Gilbreth and Carey 1950; Yost 1949).

The availability of four texts addressing this particular period in Lillian Gilbreth's life permits intertextual deconstruction of the myths concerning the American woman as wife, mother, and scientist. Each text plays on Lillian's negotiation of the duties she felt toward men, her children, and her career to tell a story of how she succeeded in stabilizing her career. Locating the points of contradiction or discontinuity among these four stories will illuminate the multidimensionality of dominant patriarchal and capitalist myths in American society. This will also show how different types of texts draw on different aspects of American culture and then throw these myths back at it.

The four accounts differ markedly on several dimensions. Most notably, three of these texts—the film, book, and biography—are publicly accessible, while the archive is not. It is equally obvious that the authors' purposes in writing these texts were different. Lillian's calendar and letters were written primarily for pragmatic reasons. The calendar notes were organizational aids for getting her through the workweek. Many of her letters during this period were written to businessmen telling them how motion study could help their specific enterprise. In contrast, biographer Edna Yost wrote for a general readership as a way of saluting two admirable individuals.[3] Frank Gilbreth, Jr., and Ernestine Gilbreth Carey wrote the book *Belles on Their Toes* (1950) for adults and children: It was intended as a tribute to their mother and as a collection of humorous tales about their family to follow *Cheaper by the Dozen* (1948).[4] The motion picture *Belles on Their Toes* (1952) was based on the book but was reworked for the screen by Phoebe and Henry Ephron. In this movie, Lillian struggles to get her career going after Frank died while her oldest daughter Anne struggles to find a husband. With this sequel, producers hoped to achieve the huge box office sales earned by its predecessor, the 1950 film *Cheaper by the Dozen*.[5]

Reading Cultural Texts

Borrowing from film studies, I assume that each cultural text contains enough information to yield a wide range of political readings but that each text structurally encourages a *realist reading* (or *hegemonic reading* or *dominant reading*—I interchange these terms; Denzin 1989b, 1991; Gledhill 1985; Hall 1980). This realist reading accepts the text as a truthful depiction. Realist readings emerge from the reader's emotional identification or empathy with textual characters, and this emotional involvement keeps readers interested in the plot.

Texts facilitate a realist reading by using stylistic techniques and thematic paradigms to draw the reader into the story (Ray 1985). Films use techniques such as lighting, color, camera angle, and music to generate an emotional involvement. They are saturated with quick shifts between scenes, preventing careful reflection by the viewers, who instead can consume the meanings implied with little effort (Benjamin [1935] 1968). Well-tested thematic paradigms also help foster a realist reading. Dream scenes, a story (or movie) within a movie, and reunions are some examples of Hollywood's recurrent thematic conventions.[6]

Hollywood films almost always employ the thematic tactic of presenting a great crisis in the opening scenes and then resolving this crisis throughout the rest of the movie. Viewers have come to expect this tension and resolution from any American movie. It is particularly pervasive in films from the era of *Belles on Their Toes,* however, which commonly built a slightly new story around a formulaic plot. Between World War II and the early 1950s, Hollywood relied upon rigid stylistic and thematic conventions to produce movies of several genres (e.g., the western, the family melodrama, the horror film, the combat film; see Schatz 1981, and Ray 1985). Audiences' expectations permit a certain economy of presentation in such films by filling in the unspoken but previously projected gaps in the story. In genre films, a prevalent cultural tension is often transplanted into the personal biographies of individual characters, and their resolution of the crisis brings a mythical effacement of the cultural tension (Ray 1985). American films and especially genre films are optimistic that the protagonist will solve his or her problems within the bounds of dominant ideologies.

Taken together, these presentational techniques discourage critical reflection by viewers. Instead of being critical, viewers often suspend their disbelief, which lends a certain kind of authority to the text (Kuhn 1982, pp. 131-32). Indeed, genre films sell the best when audiences allow themselves to be taken in by the plot. What a film sells is not merely an entertaining story: Films sell the mythological connections between cultural crises and the particular solutions to these crises that they legitimate on screen. They tie dominant ideologies to the resolution of personal problems with which the audience can identify. In naturalizing ideologically approved solutions, films teach audiences how to live within the interpretive confines of dominant ideologies and within the physical confines of the social structures that these ideologies protect.

Despite the mythologizing power of popular culture, the possibility always remains that some readers will construct subversive readings (Denzin 1991; Gledhill 1985; Hall 1980). A subversive reading is one that challenges dominant myths of capitalism and patriarchy by interpreting the subject as struggling against these ideologies and social forces. Subversive readings are critical of the cause-and-effect chains naturalized in a text; they identify its mythologizing techniques, both stylistic and thematic, and thereby undermine its power. From within the film itself, one can derive an alternative, subversive interpretation of the causes and effects presented that posits the blame for personal problems on capitalist and patriarchal structures. Subversive readings locate the solutions to these problems in the rejection of dominant ideologies.

Subversive readings require a very active reader, one who views narrative as ideological and seeks to deconstruct its dominant mythologies. Subversive readings are themselves ideological, partial, imperfect. When developed to counter particularly crippling mythologies, however, such as the myth that women should not want to be scientists, they can be politically useful. This pragmatic, political legitimation for doing subversive readings is the most powerful reason for approaching texts in this manner.

Unfortunately, subversive readings are difficult to construct. The odds are not stacked in their favor: It simply takes more interpretive energy to criticize the plethora of cause-effect chains and ideologies presented than to accept them. A wide variety of subversive readings are possible for any text, but none of them is very probable.

Recently, the tactic of deconstructing texts via multiple readings has been extended to two of the other textual forms that concern this chapter. For example, children's books have been deconstructed in a similar manner by researchers interested in early childhood sex and gender socialization (e.g., Davies 1990). Recently, the mythologizing mechanics of biographical writing have come under scrutiny as well (Denzin 1989c). Archival documents are not written to create a cohesive, marketable story, so their mythologies are more fragmentary. Nevertheless, they too rely upon ideology and can be deconstructed in the same way that books and films have been.

With any of these types of cultural text, subversive readings are difficult to produce. Investigators begin by carrying out multiple readings of a text. Then they delineate its prevalent themes, construct a realist reading of the text, interpret that reading for its dominant ideological meanings, construct a subversive reading and contrast it with the realist reading, and, if possible, secure additional readers' interpretations of the text (see Denzin 1989b, p. 40). An American text's dominant ideological meanings are difficult for Americans to discern because we live our lives with these myths flooding our popular media. They do not shock us in the way that an African tribe's myths might shock a Western anthropologist.

One way to illuminate myths, and thereby to facilitate a subversive reading of a text, is to look outside the text to alternative accounts of its story. As I argued at the outset, intertextual analysis provides a practical technique for locating a text's myths as well as clues for deconstructing them. The novelty in my intertextual analysis is that it includes archival documents as ideological text to facilitate the deconstruction of more popular narratives.

Each of my four texts explains how Lillian Gilbreth was able to get the family consulting business back on its feet after Frank's death, without breaking up the family. Taking each text separately, first I construct a realist reading. For space considerations, I give only brief attention to the stylistic and thematic methods each text uses to encourage a realist reading. I search for the mythologies in each text by trying to identify implicit cause-and-effect chains and questioning how the text naturalizes these links. To help identify the mythologies in these texts, I compare each text to all of the others but, in particular, to the one that directly preceded it chronologically. Shifting backward from very popular to less popular accounts, I give special attention to what information was left in, what was taken out, and what was modified in each version of the story. The points of contradiction among these accounts illuminate implicit mythologies operating in each text. I read these myths for their ideological content, examining how these mythologies connect to capitalist and patriarchal ideologies. This clears a path for a subversive reading.

The Texts and Their Mythologies

The Film

The movie *Belles on Their Toes* (1952) is a nostalgic portrayal of the Gilbreth family in the 1920s. It begins where *Cheaper by the Dozen* (1950) left off: in 1924, just after father Frank Gilbreth has died. This sequel concentrates on the first months as Lillian struggles to establish her own career and as the children do their part to help make ends meet, and then it leaps ahead 20 years to show that they succeeded.

The movie opens at a commencement ceremony in the 1940s but quickly slips back in time 20 years to a scene of the Gilbreth family at home busy with cleaning chores and singing a song. The crisis facing the Gilbreth family is announced almost from the opening scene: Lillian's husband Frank has died and she must provide economically for her 11 children without him. In the short term, this means she must leave the children with the family handyman for five weeks to carry out Frank's speaking engagements in Europe. In the long term, she will need to become a full-fledged career woman, balancing family and work, to keep the family together and fed. How will she manage two jobs at once? If she puts too much time into the business, she risks losing the closeness and happiness in her family; and if she dwells too much on meeting the emotional needs of the family, she risks losing the family business. If this happens, the money will run out and she will have to turn the younger children over to her wealthy relatives. Her twofold project, to meet the economic and emotional needs of her family, sets up the plot for the entire film. The way she solves her problem provides a behavior lesson for viewers.

Shortly after the film begins, Lillian sets sail for Europe. When she returns, she tells her oldest daughter Anne that her talks in Europe did not go well and that most clients have abandoned her, refusing to take instruction from a female management consultant. She expresses her difficulty clearly: How will she be able to convince the business world that she can consult with clients and teach motion study as well as Frank could?

The film's answer to this question is multidimensional. She succeeds because of persistence, because she makes some concessions to become more of a teacher than a motion study consultant, and because she has faith in two men. On screen, Lillian thanks these two men for her business success: (1) Frank Gilbreth, the husband who, despite his own absence, drives the plot with the values and practices he instilled in his wife and children, and (2) a client named Sam Harper, who takes it as his mission to find Lillian more clients and to help her succeed in business while trying to kindle a romance with her. As for keeping the family together and providing each child with a college education, she thanks only her dead husband Frank; it was because of a promise to him that she was determined to finance a college education for each child, and this promise prodded her through the trials of career building.

The film ends as it opened, with Lillian sitting at her youngest child's college graduation. This provides a final signifier of her success. She drifts into a memory of Frank taking the family for a Sunday drive. When Anne asks if she was sleeping, she replies that, no, she was just thanking someone who loved them all very much. It is her love for Frank and her determination to carry out his goals for the family that solve her dilemma in the movie.

A deconstruction of this film might begin by recognizing that Hollywood movies, like *Belles on Their Toes*, were traditionally made to be consumed once in neighborhood cinemas (Doane 1987).[7] Cause-and-effect chains are demonstrated quickly, making themselves seem compelling. This film is part of the family (or maternal) melodramatic genre. Produced at the height of the genre era, it takes a well-tested narrative formula, gives it new names and faces and some unique minor features, and then presents it as something new to the consuming public (Schatz 1981). Robert Ray (1985, pp. 131-32) notes that, not only did Hollywood mass produce genre films during this era, it "turned more and more to the pre-sold picture, a movie based on an already successful novel." To the extent that viewers knew the book *Belles on Their Toes,* the film *Cheaper by the Dozen,* and the genre of family melodrama, this film was assured a certain popularity.

By creating a great dilemma in the opening scenes, this film captures viewers' attention, and the threat of breaking the mother-child bond commands personal identification with the characters on screen. Shot almost entirely in domestic settings, this film marks itself as a family melodrama. Following two plots, Lillian's attempt to make her career work, and the courtships of the older daughters, especially Anne, this film fits what Schatz (1981, p. 233) calls the "widow/lover variation" of the family melodrama. In particular, this film speaks to women and mothers. It fits well into Mary Ann Doane's (1987) conception of maternal melodrama because much of the film is pictured through the eyes of Lillian (although often also through a "male gaze") and because it treats problems defined as female: "domestic life, the family, children, self-sacrifice, the relationship between women and production versus that between women and reproduction" (Doane 1987, p. 3). Like most maternal melodramas, it relies on pathos to construct its meanings: Lillian's risk of losing her career or her happy family gets us sympathetically involved in the film, and this suspense generated at the outset is not finally resolved until the last child graduates in the closing scene. The film uses 20 years of elapsed time to demonstrate that she has solved her dilemma.

Belles on Their Toes shows its female protagonist overcoming socially induced hardships but does not condemn society for creating her hardships.

In fact, a realist reading finds it actually strengthening several dominant myths of 1950's America through its story line. These myths concern women's need for men and children and their incompetence in careers, especially scientific careers. So, while this film about an ambitious "career woman" might be expected to challenge such myths, a casual reading finds it glorifying traditional values.

For example, at first it seems that Lillian is career oriented, forgoing her duties as mother to pursue a career; however, once she returns from Europe, we learn that she will work as often as possible within the confines of the family home to maximize her time with the children. Later we learn that, when she is away on business, she worries about each and every one of them and that she only feels comfortable traveling because the older daughters are home to give their siblings first-rate care.

One might suppose that Lillian's widowed, working woman character would challenge the mythical necessity of marriage for female happiness. Instead, this film overplays Lillian's dedication to Frank, nearly making her own life seem like a service to him. She is not the independent career woman of more recent films such as *Aliens* (1986) but the wife of an invisible husband. In effect, the absence of the husband is what makes it tolerable for Lillian to work in this film. If he were present, and she simply chose to work because she liked working, the film would threaten patriarchal ideologies. In accepting the help of Sam Harper to get her career going, Lillian acts out a myth that women cannot succeed in a career on their own merits; they need the help of men. When her career finally stabilizes, Lillian teaches in her own home and does not travel as frequently as Frank did until much later. In her actions and symbolically, she is precluded from the world of "real" science, for that is a man's world; instead, she teaches about efficiency in her parlor, enclosed in a domestic scene. On all four counts—marriage, children, career, and science—this film poses no threat to dominant American ideologies of the 1950s.

Several features of the film help to tame the radical behavior of its protagonist and thereby bolster conservative myths; for example, it is a nostalgic "fringe musical."[8] The film uses music to evoke images of an era when families were big and hardworking. With no television to pacify them, they choose to interact more often, to play games, to sing together, and to participate in the housework. The music also serves to discourage potential radical readings of the text. For instance, when the children become cranky about eating only cheap beans for most of their summer, they do not fight and make Lillian's plan fail; instead, they sing a song about how tired they are of eating beans. Songs pacify them at potential sites of rebellion.

This film also prevents Lillian from looking radical by giving her some of its most reactionary lines. For example, near the closing scene, when she realizes Anne has been postponing marriage in order to fill in as pseudomother for the younger Gilbreth children, Lillian exclaims that she does not want spinster daughters around the house and encourages Anne to marry her beau. Indeed, the title of the film, "Belles on Their Toes," is a description of how the Gilbreth daughters will have to *be* if they expect to find good husbands. Husbands are more important than careers throughout this film.

Lillian's career is made to seem acceptable only because it is economically necessary. She regrets leaving the children home with only the inept handyman Tom to supervise them, but she must or the family will have to break up. Regarding women and work, the message of this film is unmistakable: Women can pursue careers, but only if they must for economic reasons.

The Book

The book *Belles on Their Toes* was written by two of the Gilbreth children as adults. It chronicles the adventures of the Gilbreth children as they minimized their own hardships with a healthy attitude, sacrifice, and plenty of hard work after their father's death. Like the film, the book takes the daughters' struggles to find husbands as one of its primary themes. But, unlike the film, the book gives little systematic attention to Lillian's career. The last line of the Foreword reads: "This is a book about the Gilbreth family after Dad died. It is primarily the story of Mother." The book, however, presents an edited version of Lillian's life as mainly a mother, not as a career woman or engineer.

Most stories in the book seem to be told more for their humor and to demonstrate the love and affection in the family than to constitute a plot or a unified theme. Furthermore, although the book is written in the third person, there are frequent stylistic reminders that this is a loosely autobiographical account; the authors were these children at one point in time. Their recollections get added credibility, and their messages get added power.

The book also constructs a dilemma in its opening pages, but its dilemma is less threatening and it has a different slant than the film's. In the opening chapter, "Something for Dad," the risk is framed this way (Gilbreth and Carey 1948, p. 3): "Mother was going to try to operate the business herself—that was one reason the trip to Europe was necessary. If she failed, the family might have to be divided or to move in on Mother's relatives on the West Coast." When Lillian was invited to go to Europe to give Frank's speeches, "at first it seemed out of the question. And then it seemed to be the one opportunity of keeping the family together" (Gilbreth and Carey 1948, p. 6). Thus, in both film and book, the risk is family dissolution. The difference is that the film exaggerates the book's representation of this risk; for instance, the film depicts cousin Leora, who will take some of the children if Lillian cannot manage them, as evil, whereas the book is not judgmental of "Mother's relatives" and is not so certain whether the children would have to live in separate homes. The film speeds up and caricatures the dilemma presented in the book.

The book also gives a more positive impression of Lillian's European trip. By this account, the children, who are staying at the Gilbreth's summer home on Nantucket, receive a call from Lillian before her arrival telling them that "the talks at London and Prague had gone well—very well, she thought. And she had plans for opening a motion-study school at our house in Montclair" (Gilbreth and Carey 1948, p. 57).

This text is less concerned with explaining what Lillian did to succeed than with explaining how the children helped. In a sense, it pushes forth a capitalist behavior lesson for children: scrimp, save, and work hard when your family needs you and you will achieve your goals and make your parents proud. Older daughters helped their mother with domestic chores and put their spare energy not into careers but into the manhunt. This book affirms the merits of capitalism and 1950's patriarchy for young readers.

Even though the book ignores much of Lillian's career, we can piece together reasons for her success from the text. How does this book explain her success in keeping her family and business intact? First, it does not dwell on what Lillian risks if she fails to balance her occupations correctly. The threat of family dissolution is only hinted at as one possible consequence of Lillian's failure, not as inevitable. Instead of the evil cousin Leora, the Gilbreth family would live with their Grandmother Moller on the West Coast. Leora enters late in the book as merely a nosy relative, not someone who is trying to break up the family. Thus the book does not latch onto Leora as a symbol of family dissolution the way the film does.

One of the most glaring discrepancies between the film and book is the film's invention of Mr. Sam Harper. This character must have been imagined by the screenwriters, because the book, biography, and diary contain no similar character. The absence of Sam Harper precludes a widow/lover-type plot in the book and makes Lillian seem more self-reliant. She can be given a trifle more credit for her own successes in the book than in the film.

Mainly this book tells how the children contribute to help Lillian bypass the risk of family disruption. They saved hundreds of dollars from their budget during that summer on Nantucket by calculating more efficient methods of meeting their own needs (as inculcated in them by their father while he was alive). Consider this dialogue (Gilbreth and Carey 1948, p. 62):

"We spent $296.00," said Martha, who always knew the bank balance to the last penny.

"I don't know how you did it," Mother told us, shaking her head. "Why if we can keep going at that rate, I know everything will be all right."

"And we've been eating like kings," Ernestine put in.

"I'd like you to help me run the house, just as you've been doing," Mother said. "And I'd like Martha to keep the budget—goodness knows I never could manage money that well."

"You'll have to make out a requisition form in triplicate when you want even two cents for a stamp," Anne warned.

The children save the day (and the year) in this book and they do so in a humorous, believable way.

The Biography

The third text, *Partners for Life: Frank and Lillian Gilbreth's Transformation of Scientific Management, 1885-1940* (Yost 1949), is a linear, humanist, realist biography.[9] It takes as its subjects both Frank and Lillian Gilbreth and follows their lives from childhood through Lillian's career well after Frank's death. I focus on the last four chapters, which address Lillian's capacity to run the business and the household without Frank. This book is written in a nostalgic, romantic style, never questioning the inherent goodness of Frank and Lillian and the ingenuity of their work. The biography therefore takes on a heroic feel, as if it were these two people against the world. Often, it is the battle for public recognition of Frank's contributions, driven by Lillian's unwavering love and fidelity, that propels Lillian's career.

The biography is not so dependent on a problem-solution scheme for delivering its meanings. Thus the risk is not framed in such a dangerous light. Lillian's choice was not to send the kids to her relatives without her, nor to assign the kids to separate homes; the choice was whether to take all of her children and move closer to her relatives in California—where she could continue writing but not consulting—or to try making the firm succeed—

which would necessitate staying in Montclair but would allow the family to continue on undisrupted. There is no suggestion that the family would be divided. Thus the book and film's tear-jerking fear of the mother-child bond breaking 11 times is absent from the biography. Further, the biography states that the Gilbreth children were never left alone without an older Gilbreth relative staying with them (Yost 1949, p. 309). This suggests that the handy-man and older daughters were not their only guardians while Lillie was away carrying out her career responsibilities. Her career was not so threatening to the children's security as the other texts suggest.

To show how the biography is linear, humanist, and realist, I shall consider each of these characteristics independently. The lives of Lillian and Frank are explained in a linear fashion by instinct, early childhood experience, developmental learning, diligence toward seeking truth, respect for workers, and, above all, their ultimate love for life and for each other. Lillian is motivated primarily by her natural caring instinct, which she developed further under Frank's influence. As a child, she was extremely shy and was taught at home by her mother. Her affluent childhood left her unprepared for managing a large family on a tight budget, but her inner strength and skills, absorbed from Frank, saw her through difficult times. Her love for him motivated her to continue achieving his goals after his death. His desire to find "the one best way" became her desire by osmosis.[10] Indeed, it is the union of values, ideals, virtually of spirit that gives this biography a romantic feel, and the telos of absolute, unperishable love makes the plot linear—all goes toward love.

The biography is humanist because the unity of each character is uncon-tested. The Gilbreths each possess natural and learned character traits that follow them through life and explain successes in various endeavors. One "self" is presumed for each person, such that, when Lillian must cope with the loss of a husband and with having no authority to tell her what to do, some buried feature of her static "self" surfaces to guide her. She does not change her own nature but rediscovers hidden aspects of herself that she had learned by watching Frank.

This biography is realist through and through.[11] Prevalent themes center on the attempt to get the recognition for Frank that is rightfully his. Words and phrases like "recognize the importance," "finally paid tribute," "credit for," "pioneer," "recognition still withheld" all assume a natural direction that scientific management was to take. This implies that there is some underlying correct method of management research and that Frank had discovered it. Taylor and his disciples had conspired to cover up the true merit of Frank's work and so it would become Lillian's mission to restore respect for her dead husband.

The biography includes a certain type of information excluded from the film and book and thereby permits a more subversive, casual reading than do the more popular texts. Lillian's academic achievements, her master's degree in literature and her Ph.D. in psychology, are glossed over in the film and book. Yost's account, however, discusses these achievements at length, juxtaposing them with Frank's high school education. Another revelation that the more popular texts fail to divulge is that Lillian actually likes her work.[12] The biography claims that Lillian and Frank had begun planning a motion study course in their home long before his death. Lillian's decision in 1924 to open a course in her home was not then, by this account, a compromise of her career plans for the sake of her single-parent family but the realization of a long-term plan. These pieces of information suggest that Lillian valued her career highly and did not merely work for the sake of the family but because she found engineering rewarding.

Like the book, however, the biography generally portrays Lillian's solo career as propelled by the wishes of her late husband, who is a powerful presence even in his absence. And, like many biographies of women scientists, Yost's contribution depicts Lillian as brilliant and highly unusual in her capacity for hard work and sacrifice.[13] Yet Lillian's sacrifices are minute in comparison with the rewards she accrues from the deep sense of love she feels from Frank both before and after his death: Fulfillment in her life comes more from Frank than it does from science. Once again, we have a text that attributes the lion's share of credit for Lillian's successes to this man.

The Diary and Letters

Lillian called her appointment calendars her "diaries." Like most diaries, hers was no doubt mentally edited before it was written. But, unlike most people, the Gilbreths also *rewrote* their appointment calendars, making corrections, deletions, and so on. Lillian rewrote the Gilbreths' 1924-25 calendar in 1941, long after Frank's death, and next to each entry she inscribed a set of initials indicating whether the original entry was in Frank's or her own handwriting.[14]

This diary is above all a pragmatic text, with many issues left open. Prefabricated structures of meaning are not so numerous as in the other texts. Yet these papers still offer only a mediated perspective on her lived experience. Lillian's calendar merely sketches which pieces of information were useful and necessary for her as she went about her daily work during this period. For example, it lists appointments, birthdays, lunch dates, and deadlines. She refined many of her letters with particular readers in mind sometimes to make herself seem less aggressive.[15]

What did she do as Frank's partner in Gilbreth, Inc.? Usually, Lillian tends to belittle her own contributions to the firm. In a letter dated May 13, 1926, Lillian accepted a speaking engagement before a joint meeting of the ASME (American Society of Mechanical Engineers) and the SIE (Society of Industrial Engineers), on these terms (Gilbreth Collection, Container 135 [NHZ 0830-42]): "Please be sure to announce me as Mrs. Frank B. Gilbreth, for I want Frank's friends to feel that it is his message that I bring." But, in her application for admission into the ASME in April of 1926, Lillian describes her own work between 1914-24 as central (Gilbreth Collection, container 131 [NHZ 0830-1]):

> In 1914 our Company began to specialize in management work. I was placed in charge of the correlation of engineering and management psychology, and became an active member of the staff making visits to the plants systematized in order to lay out the method of attack on the problems, being responsible for getting the necessary material for the installation into shape, working up the data as they accumulated, and drafting the interim and final reports. I was also in charge of research and teaching, and of working up such mechanisms, forms and methods as were needed for our type of installation of Scientific Management, Motion Study, Fatigue Study, and Skill Study. . . . During Mr. Gilbreth's frequent and prolonged absences both in this country and abroad, I was in responsible charge of all branches of the work.

This account finds a much more active Lillian prior to Frank's death than do any of the other accounts. Frank's name went on many of their published papers, but the archives, and historical accounts based on the archives, make it appear that she was doing much of the work. Price (1987, p. 359) claims that Lillian wrote two books from 1915 to 1917, which were published under Frank's name. Much of the technical writing during these years and some of the professional correspondence is signed by Lillian. All of this suggests Lillian was devoted to her career even prior to Frank's death.

According to Lillian's diary, how did she get the business back on its feet? The first issue to consider here is how far the business had deteriorated. The diary gives little indication that the business was put in grave danger by Frank's death. The Gilbreths were proceeding as normal in the spring of 1924, stretching their connections into Europe. Appointments with various clients and associates were numerous that autumn of 1924, as were Lillian's speaking engagements. After Frank died, Lillian sent out invitations to a number of businesses describing the motion study course she was planning.

Much of the correspondence during this period was with Miss Eugenia Lies of Macy's department store or with the new clients Miss Lies had introduced to Lillian. Up until his death, Frank had been sending requests to Macy's Vice President Straus to arrange a meeting to show him how motion study would save money for Macy's. In April of 1923, Frank received a flat refusal from Straus. Finally, Frank went to Macy's and presented his case, but still no contract was signed. In May of 1924, Miss Lies, an executive at Macy's, sent Frank an organizational chart of Macy's and, in early June, Frank responded by sending her process charts and leaflets advertising "The Gilbreth One Best Way." Then Frank died. The next correspondence to Miss Lies is from Lillian in December of 1924 when Lillian agreed to meet Miss Lies to discuss micro-motion study. Shortly thereafter, Lillian began working on the floor at Macy's to get a feel for how motion study could be fruitfully applied there. In January, she wrote back to Miss Lies saying that she wanted to arrange an interview with Mr. Straus because, after working on the floor, she was convinced of the value of starting motion study work at Macy's. Soon, Straus agreed to send Miss Lies herself, as the Macy's representative, to be trained by Lillian Gilbreth in the first motion study course. This initiated a close relationship between Gilbreth, Inc. and Macy's that Frank had been denied.

The first Montclair motion study course had three students and a camera-man. A close working relationship seems to have developed between Miss Lies and Lillian that winter.[16] By the end of the course, Lies was enthusiastic about the Gilbreth methods and had recommended the course to many different people in America and abroad. Lies agreed to speak to other potential Gilbreth clients (including Sears, Roebuck and Company) to show them how well scientific management worked for Macy's and to convince them that it would also work in their own businesses. Once the first course proved successful, new courses were planned, and an alumni club formed in which these businesspersons and management instructors met to improve their understanding of motion study and to make business connections. Lillian continued to offer motion study courses until 1930.

The diary and letters from this period show Lillian building upon previous business contacts to establish a new facet of her career, motion study instruction in her home, that would be more tolerable for a woman in the eyes of business colleagues. Working in her home was not an unusual plan invented because of her new single-parent status; rather, she and Frank had always done much of their work in their home and had taught summer schools for professors at their former home in Providence, Rhode Island. The idea for an in-house motion study course could be read as a logical extension of these summer school courses.

Lillian navigated around social obstacles to her career plans, constantly aware that she would never be viewed as an equal by many of her colleagues.[17] The archives illuminate these social barriers to her career in an unapologetic way, without the constant attempt to make Lillian's actions seem traditional. Because these documents were not written to be sold to the public, there are no checks to ensure that readers will interpret her as a traditional wife and mother. Although particular letters might trivialize her career goals, the tendency to assimilate her story into dominant ideologies is not as evident in the archives as it is in the other texts.

A Dustier Path to Subversion

Working backward through these texts, from the slick Hollywood movie to the dusty archives, I have deconstructed the image of Lillian Gilbreth as a woman who worked only out of economic necessity. I have begun piecing together a subversive, feminist understanding of this year in her life. My subversive reading looks beyond popular texts into relatively unknown, archival documents to find alternative kinds of information about her life. For example, these records introduce the character of Miss Lies, a very important female ally for Lillian during the year in question. The archives are equally informative in the events and characters they leave out. A "Sam Harper" character is absent from Lillian's calendar and memos, suggesting, contrary to the film, that she did not rely on a male client to stabilize her career.

This kind of deconstruction receives added credibility because archival documents were actually written by the character under study. These documents provide a look at Lillian Gilbreth's own explanations of her career struggle. Her words can serve as a weapon to counteract the mythologizing power of popular accounts. Although I want to use the authority of her words for this political end, I also want to destabilize the authority of any text, including Lillian's own. This kind of contradictory ambition is becoming a goal in diverse theoretical contexts (e.g., Clifford and Marcus 1986; Haraway 1989).

Instead of forcing us to elicit a feminist statement from within conservative texts, intertextual analysis points us toward subversion along an alternative path. Juxtaposed with popular texts, archival information can snap us out of a passive daze and force us to be more critical of implicit ideologies.

Including archival information in an intertextual analysis avoids the political dilemma sometimes posed by arguing that every text is subversive. For instance, do we want to spend our time searching for feminist messages in pornography? Probably not, but neither do we want to categorically deny the possibility for such messages to be conveyed. Although every narrative may be read subversively, intertextual comparison simplifies this goal. The words of individuals whose lives have been represented in popular culture offer a new perspective on their lives, one that is not burdened with the obligation to sell itself in a capitalist marketplace.

Intertextual analysis need not resort to "correspondence realism" or any claim regarding the truth or falsity of cultural representations. Philosophical transformations of the postmodern era make such realism difficult to uphold (Baudrillard 1981; Lyotard 1979). Yet, in presenting this chapter, I have neglected to comment on the ideological character of my own selective reading of the archival documents in the Gilbreth collection. From these documents, I might have pieced together an account equally conservative as the film *Belles on Their Toes*. Instead, I built a subversive reading in conjunction with my own feminist perspective. The fragmented nature of archives permits active, interpretive involvement while popular books and films discourage personal and idiosyncratic interpretations. The benefits of including archival research in intertextual analysis stem from this openness to contrasting ideological interpretations.

Notes

1. I will use *text* or *cultural text* to refer to recorded narratives regardless of whether they are inscribed on paper or film.

2. First names may seem unconventional here, but, because I will refer to several members of the Gilbreth family, this is the least cumbersome method.

3. This admiration is evident throughout the biography. For example, Yost's (1949, p. 3) opening chapter begins: "When shall we see their like again? The everyday facts of their partnership seem to preclude a repetition of the phenomenon of the Gilbreths, for it was a partnership rooted in the most amazing fulfillments of love and marriage as well as in work of an unusual character for a woman." Additionally, book reviews in both *The New York Times* (June 26, 1949, p. 23) and the *Christian Science Monitor* (July 6, 1949, p. 14) claim that Yost's affection often obscures ultimate truths about the Gilbreths.

4. The acknowledgment in *Belles on Their Toes* reads: "TO MOTHER/who deserves better treatment." Like its predecessor, this book was chosen as a "Book of the Month" (Ernestine Gilbreth Carey, personal communication, 1991).

5. Although the film *Belles on Their Toes* is a sequel to *Cheaper by the Dozen*, the screenplays were not written, produced, and directed by the same individuals. *Cheaper by the Dozen* was rewritten for the screen and produced by Lamar Trotti and directed by

Walter Lang. The screenplay for *Belles on Their Toes* was written by Phoebe and Henry Ephron, directed by Henry Levin, and produced by Samuel Engel. Both are Twentieth Century Fox productions. According to *Filmfacts* (Steinberg 1980, p. 21), *Cheaper by the Dozen* was the fourth top-money-making film of 1950. *Belles on Their Toes* must have disappointed its producers by not faring as well economically.

6. Katovich (1989) discusses how movies use reunions to deliver their themes.

7. There is a lot more to say in deconstructing this film than I have space for here, especially in its construction of the "supermom" figure. I address this issue specifically in a paper titled "Reading *Belles on Their Toes*: How to Be a Mother and a Scientist at the Same Time," presented at the Midwest Sociological Society meeting (Graham 1990).

8. Clive Hirschhorn (1981, pp. 416, 423) in *The Hollywood Musical* defines it as a "fringe musical," because it is "not sufficiently musical to merit a main entry."

9. For more on these three characteristics of biographical writing, see Denzin (1989c, chaps. 2 and 3).

10. Frank Gilbreth's goal in any consultation with industry was to find what he called "the one best way to do work." This motto appeared on his letterhead and became his trademark.

11. This quotation (Yost 1949, p. 302) gives a sense of the romanticism and realism of the text: "So now these two, developed more greatly possibly because of their need to overcome opposition, were of a recognized stature to reap the rewards it has long been the custom of professional groups to bestow in a man's lifetime. Each recognition was doubly dear because of its delay. Probably few of his peers knew how deeply their lack of recognition of the originality and importance of his work had hurt Frank Gilbreth, for he could compensate successfully with enthusiasms that covered his real feelings."

12. Yost (1949, p. 348) writes: "One of her daughters relates the surprise with which she realized, long after she was a grown woman, that 'mother really loved work' and was not doing it solely to support her family."

13. See LaFollette (1988) for more on this tendency in biographical writing about women in science.

14. Her original handwritten copy is also available in the archives (Gilbreth Collection, container 109 [NHZ 0850-2]).

15. For example, in her communications with Colonel Sheehan of the SIE in June of 1924, her only career goal is to carry on with Frank's work and to "live out all of his plans" (Gilbreth Collection, container 135 [NHZ 0830-42]).

16. It seems Miss Lies became a family friend as well. In January of 1925, Lillian's daughter Ernestine Gilbreth, who was interested in a career in sales, began corresponding with Miss Lies (Gilbreth Collection, container 134 [NHZ 0830-20]).

17. An excellent example of this struggle for acceptance in the engineering community is documented in her requests for letters of reference for admission to the American Society of Mechanical Engineers in 1925 and 1926 (Gilbreth Collection, container 131 [NHZ 0830-1]).

References

Barthes, Roland. 1957. *Mythologies*. New York: Hill & Wang.
Baudrillard, Jean. 1981. *For a Critique of the Political Economy of the Sign*. St. Louis: Telos.

————1983. *Simulations.* New York: Semiotexte, Foreign Agents Press.

Benjamin, Walter. [1935] 1968. "The Work of Art in the Age of Mechanical Reproduction."
Pp. 219-53 in *Illuminations,* edited by Hannah Arendt. New York: Harcourt Brace & World.

Carey, Ernestine Gilbreth. Personal correspondence with the author. April 30, 1991.

Christian Science Monitor. 1949. Book review of *Partners for Life.* July 6, p. 14.

Clifford, James and George Marcus, eds. 1986. *Writing Culture.* Berkeley: University of
California Press.

Davies, Bronwyn. 1990. "The Formation of Gendered Subjectivities in Relation to Lived and
Told Narratives in Early Childhood." Paper presented at the Stone Symposium, St. Petersburg
Beach, FL.

Denzin, Norman. 1989a. *Interpretive Interactionism.* Newbury Park, CA: Sage.

————1989b. "Reading *Tender Mercies*: Two Interpretations." *The Sociological Quarterly*
30(1):37-57.

————1989c. *Interpretive Biography.* Newbury Park, CA: Sage.

————1991. *Hollywood Shot by Shot: Alcoholism in American Cinema.* New York: Aldine de
Gruyter.

Doane, Mary Ann. 1987. *The Desire to Desire: The Woman's Film of the 1940s.* Bloomington:
Indiana University Press.

Gilbreth, Frank Bunker and Lillian Moller Gilbreth. 1924. N-File: Container 109, Gilbreth
Collection, Purdue University.

————1925. N-File: Container 134, Gilbreth Collection, Purdue University.

————1926. N-File: Container 135, Gilbreth Collection, Purdue University.

————1946. N-File: Container 131, Gilbreth Collection, Purdue University.

Gilbreth, Frank B., Jr., and Ernestine Gilbreth Carey. 1948. *Cheaper by the Dozen.* New York:
Thomas Y. Crowell.

————1950. *Belles on Their Toes.* New York: Thomas Y. Crowell.

Gledhill, Christine. 1985. "Recent Developments in Feminist Criticism." Pp. 817-45 in *Film
Theory and Criticism.* 3rd ed., edited by Gerald Mast and Marshall Cohen. New York: Oxford
University Press.

————1987. "The Melodramatic Field: An Investigation." Pp. 5-42 in *Home Is Where the Heart
Is: Studies in Melodrama and the Woman's Film,* edited by Christine Gledhill. London:
British Film Institute.

Graham, Laurel. 1990. "Reading *Belles on Their Toes*: How to Be a Mother and a Scientist at
the Same Time." Paper presented at the Midwest Sociological Society meetings in Chicago,
April.

Hall, Stuart. 1980. "Encoding/Decoding." Pp. 128-38 in *Culture, Media, Language,* edited by
S. Hall, D. Hobson, A. Lowe, and P. Willis. London: Hutchinson.

Haraway, Donna. 1989. *Primate Visions.* New York: Routledge.

Hirschhorn, Clive. 1981. *The Hollywood Musical.* New York: Crown.

Katovich, Michael A. 1989. "Portraying the Reunion on Film: A Case Study of a Social Form."
Pp. 213-35 in *Studies in Symbolic Interaction.* Vol. 10 (part A), edited by Norman Denzin.
Greenwich, CT: JAI.

Kuhn, Annette. 1982. *Women's Pictures: Feminism and Cinema.* London: Routledge & Kegan
Paul.

LaFollette, Marcel C. 1988. "Eyes on the Stars: Images of Women Scientists in Popular
Magazines." *Science, Technology, & Human Values* 13(1):262-75.

Lyotard, Jean-François. 1979. *The Postmodern Condition: A Report on Knowledge.* Minneap-
olis: University of Minnesota Press.

The New York Times. 1949. Book review of *Partners for Life.* June 26, p. 23.

Price, Brian. 1987. "One Best Way: Frank and Lillian Gilbreth's Transformation of Scientific Management, 1885-1940." Ph.D. dissertation, Purdue University.

Ray, Robert B. 1985. *A Certain Tendency of the Hollywood Cinema, 1930-1980.* Princeton, NJ: Princeton University Press.

Schatz, Thomas. 1981. *Hollywood Genres: Formulas, Filmmaking, and the Studio System.* Philadelphia: Temple University Press.

Steinberg, Cobbett S. 1980. "Film Facts." p. 21. New York: Facts on File Inc.

Trescott, Martha Moore. 1983. "Lillian Moller Gilbreth and the Founding of Modern Industrial Engineering." Pp. 23-37 in *Machina Ex Dea: Feminist Perspectives on Technology,* edited by Joan Rothschild. New York: Pergamon.

————1984. "Women Engineers in History: Profiles in Holism and Persistence." Pp. 181-204 in *Women in Scientific and Engineering Professions,* edited by Violet B. Haas and Carolyn C. Perrucci. Ann Arbor: University of Michigan Press.

Yost, Edna. 1949. *Partners for Life: Frank and Lillian Gilbreth's Transformation of Scientific Management, 1885-1940.* New Brunswick, NJ: Rutgers University Press.

3

Women's Subjectivity and
Feminist Stories

BRONWYN DAVIES

In this chapter, I draw together reflections on the nature of women's subjectivity and the relation of that subjectivity to lived and told stories, and to feminist stories in particular. This is not a linear story about women's subjectivity that has as its central organizing feature a rationally planned and executed argument. Rather, this story is a mixture of rational argument, of emotion, and of lived bodily experience, intertwining what we think of as fantasy and reality, and embracing contradictory positions. Although each fragment is illuminating in and of itself, together they represent the complex interplay of women's subjectivity and feminist stories.

I draw on episodes from my own life and on feminist stories and images to illustrate the ways in which poststructuralist theory can inform our thinking about the experience of being female, feminine, and feminist. Feminist poststructuralist writers such as Cixous (1981, 1986) have argued for a multiple wholeness for women that incorporates both sides of the current oppositional and hierarchical dualisms through which femininity and masculinity are currently constructed. In this chapter, I explore the formation of female/feminist subjectivity and in particular the place of story in that formation. This exploration is aimed at locating the ways in which feminist subjectivity is impeded or enhanced through the taking up of particular story lines as one's own and examing the changes taking place in lived and told feminist narratives as we find ways to constitute ourselves outside the male/female dualism.

Women

In what sense do I speak here of "women" and their subjectivity? I am not speaking in an essentialist sense about all people who happen to have female genitals but about the discursive category female/woman and the experience of being discursively constituted as one who belongs in that category. Often feminist discussions fall apart on the terms *woman* and *man,* because it is assumed that the speaker is saying "all women" or "all men," and anyone can instantly think of exceptions to the apparently universalistic statement that is being made. When I talk about the experience of being "a woman," I refer to the experience of being assigned to the category female, of being discursively, interactively, and structurally *positioned* as such, and of taking up as one's own those discourses through which one is constituted as female.

The concept of positioning is central to an understanding of the way in which people are constituted through and in the terms of existing discourses (Davies and Harré 1990). Even where the process of positioning has been understood and where the interactants do not wish to position each other in terms of their sex, that they do so is almost inevitable. We are far from working out all the ways in which our speaking and acting-as-usual result from and give rise to the male/female dualism. Recently, for example, my attempt to write jointly with a male colleague became an extremely difficult process. My references to femaleness and feminism irritated him intensely, detracting, he said, from the value of what I had to say because they drew attention to the position from which I spoke. The myth of the positionless speaker as the one who speaks the most valuable truths was one he was not able to give up. "Masculinity" and "science" gain much of their status through their claim to positionless "truth"; that is, a truth that, no matter who one is or where one stands, would still be the same.

Men (and especially male scientists) have believed that they speak as *man,* a category inclusive of men and women. But their position has been a privileged one and often was totally incorrect when it presumed to speak for or of anyone other than white middle-class males. Women, in contrast, have always had their position as female speaker *marked.* Although liberal feminists thought they could escape such marking by making the same claims as men to positionless speech, they could not be heard, even by themselves, as doing so because their own subjectivity got in the way. Having taken up as one's own the relevant emotions and the pattern of desires implicated in constituting oneself as woman, asking to be heard as if one were a man becomes extremely problematic (Riviere 1986; Walkerdine 1989).

But, when I attempted to point out to my colleague the positioned nature of his speech (and the sexism that such unacknowledged positioning implies), he was deeply offended. His understanding of the nature of positioning within one discourse did not undo his belief in the myth of the positionless position within another, more powerful discourse about science. I was questioning something that he thought all scientists should aspire to and refusing to acknowledge it as legitimate. The very fact that I was drawing attention to issues of gender, thus openly marking my position as female/ feminist speaker, meant for him that I was incapable of the same detached, scientific thought that he heard me accusing him of not having. We have all, both inadvertently and purposefully, marked women speakers as women and then accused them of speaking inferior words from that position. In this case, the difference was that I, a woman, was marking the position of male speaker, making that problematic because it was unacknowledged, refusing to prioritize scientific discourse and refusing to accept the negative marking usually attending female speech. His annoyance was understandable. The academic and the social worlds have been organized to support his illusion of positionless speech but not mine.

The discourses through which the subject position "woman" is constituted are multiple and contradictory. In striving to successfully constitute herself within her allocated gender category, each woman takes on the desires made relevant within those contradictory discourses. She is, however, never able to achieve unequivocal success at being a women. Cixous (1981, p. 250) writes of the "superegoized structure" in which women have

> always occupied the place reserved for the guilty (guilty of everything, guilty of every turn: for having desires, for not having any; for being frigid, for being "too hot"; for not being both at once; for being too motherly and not enough; for having children and for not having any; for nursing and for not nursing . . .).

The contradictory knowing that inevitably results can debilitate women in a world in which humanist discourses are hegemonic, dictating that contradictory knowing is flawed knowing (Davies and Harré forthcoming). Their contradictory subjectivity is called irrational, lacking in direction; their knowledge is intuitive, incomprehensible, or wrong. Alternatively, women who discover poststructuralist discourse can find in each moment of contradiction a clearer comprehension of their own fractured and fragmented female subjectivity (Haug 1987). They do so through recognizing the constitutive force of discourse and the means by which it inscribes in the body and emotions of the constituted subject. Once they refuse to peel off or ignore that which does not fit a linear, noncontradictory story line, and see how they are positioned within the various discourses through which they are constituted, they can begin to refuse some of those positionings and along with them the particular discourse in which those positionings are embedded. The issue ceases to be the vulnerability of the essential female self attempting to do that which history says she cannot do. It becomes instead the analysis of discursive practices and the finding of ways to collectively resist the constitution of woman inside the male/female dualism (Davies 1990). This chapter is, in part, an exploration of that possibility.

Although masculinity also is forged out of contradictory discourses, men have tended to cope differently. Among the many discursive strategies they use to deal with their lived contradictions is the distinction between self (the "I," which is unitary and private) and roles (the various "me's," which are multiple and public). Using this model, it is possible to act in contradictory ways without the coherence of oneself or one's rationality being called into question.

Although women/feminists have used the conceptual apparatus of *role*, they have often been uncomfortable with it as a means for interpreting behavior and have sought alternatives (Connell 1987; Edwards 1983; Henriques et al. 1984; Stanley and Wise 1983; Walkerdine 1981). One source of that dis-ease is that, as long as "I" and "me" are separated out, then the personal and private "I" can legitimate any social world in which the various public "me's" play out the different and contradictory roles that "society" demands. By making a strong boundary between the real "I" and the role-playing "me," it is not only possible to maintain an illusion of an essential, unitary, noncontradictory self, but the "me's" in this model need not be taken on as part of that essential self and therefore do not necessarily come within the gambit of personal and moral responsibility.

In rejecting the division between the public and the private as a legitimate and meaningful division, feminists have owned their various "me's" and not reserved these or distinguished them from some other, independent, illusory "real" self. Perhaps for this very reason, feminists have found contradictory moral imperatives much more personally troubling as they try to integrate the unintegratable into one unified, rational, whole "me/I," struggling at the same time with the overriding imperative that links being a woman with being good.

The distinction between positioning and "role" is an important one in the feminist poststructuralist framework. Role is something that is simply taken on and cast off with a "backstage" person taking up and casting off a variety of roles. One also moves through multiple positionings in any one day or even in any one conversation. Positions are discursively and interactively constituted and so are open to shifts and changes as the discourse shifts or as one's positioning within, or in relation to, that discourse shifts. Who I am potentially shifts with each speaking, each moment of being positioned within this or that discourse in this or that way. Trinh (1989, p. 35) suggests we go so far as abandon the concept of "me" in our analysis of any writing and regard "I" as no more than a requirement of the language:

> Why view these aspects of an individual which we imply in the term "writer" or "author" as projections of an isolated self and not of our common way of handling texts? For writing, like a game that defies its own rules, is an ongoing practice that may be said to be concerned, not with inserting a "me" into language, but of creating an opening where the "me" disappears while "I" endlessly come and go, as the nature of language requires. To confer an Author on the text closes the writing.

But personal histories of being positioned in particular ways and of interpreting events through and in terms of familiar story lines, concepts, and images that one takes up as one's own effectively constitute the me-ness of me separate from others. To the extent that *one takes oneself up* in terms of these familiar positionings and story lines, to the extent that one's moral commitments, patterns of desire, and ways of knowing and being are constituted through these positionings and story lines, then *they have become part of the subjectivity of that person*. This involves not just a psychosocial becoming but a physical reality in terms of the way one learns to walk and to sit and to move generally, even down to the detail of how one breathes (Haug 1987; Wex 1979).

Poststructuralist theory thus opens up the possibility of seeing the self as continually constituted through multiple and contradictory discourses that one takes up as one's own in becoming a *speaking subject*. One can develop strategies for maintaining an illusion of a coherent unitary self through such strategies as talking of roles or through denial of contradiction, or one can examine the very processes and discourses through which the constitution of self takes place. Through locating the source of a contradiction in the available discourses, it is possible to examine the contradictory elements of one's subjectivity without guilt or anxiety. Dealing with contradiction within this model can enable one to make a simple decision to act within the terms of one discourse rather than another at any one point in time, depending on its relevance, the values of its products, and so on. Or it can facilitate a decision to refuse a discourse, or to refuse the positioning made available within that discourse. It can also facilitate an understanding of the collective and discursive nature of such refusals and of the ways in which one might begin to generate alternative practices (Davies 1990).

Probably the most deep-seated taking up of oneself relates to sexuality and, in particular, choices as to hetero- versus homosexuality. These are so deeply felt that they are invariably experienced as and assumed to be "natural." Yet, as we come to understand the extensive constitutive work that goes into creating and sustaining "correctly" gendered selves, it is becoming clear that there is little about it that is unequivocally natural (Butler 1990; Connell 1987). The questioning continues as feminist biologists begin the massive task of deconstructing that which the biological fraternity assumed in their research to be the "natural order" of human/animal life (Davies 1989a, 1989c, 1990; Rogers 1988; Sayers 1986). Butler (1990, pp. 22-23) points out that the "institution of a compulsory and naturalized heterosexuality requires and regulates gender as a binary relation." The differentiation of the masculine term from the feminine term, she says, is accomplished through the "practices of heterosexual desire." The more successfully we constitute ourselves as male and female, especially in terms of heterosexual desire, the more we believe that the product of that constitutive work is natural (Butler 1990, p. 139):

> Gender is, thus, a construction that regularly conceals its genesis; the tacit collective agreement to perform, produce, and sustain discrete and polar genders as cultural fictions is obscured by the credibility of those productions and the punishments that attend not agreeing to believe in them; the construction "compels" our belief in its necessity and naturalness.

Through taking up as her own the discourses through which femaleness is constituted, each woman thus becomes at the same time a speaking subject and one who is subjected or determined by those discourses. That subjection is generally invisible because it appears not only to be natural, as Butler points out, but also to be what women *want*, a result of free choice (Walkerdine and Lucey 1989). But women's desires are the result of bodily inscription and of metaphors and story lines that catch them up in ways of being/desiring from which they have no escape unless they can reinscribe, discover new story lines, invert, invent, and break the bounds of the old structures and old discourses.

Poststructuralism offers those who have never been recognized as having the subject status that men have had a way of recognizing the means by which they have been subjected, made object, deprived of agency, and inscribed with patterns of desire that hold that oppressive cultural pattern in place. Poststructuralist discourse offers a critique of the celebration of masculinity and its equation with rationality and confirms for women their sense of self as embodied and their emotions, desires, feelings as a legitimate part of reason. For women, poststructuralism does not offer the death of the subject but the means of claiming the right to subject status—a subject who realizes, recognizes, speaks, writes her (collective) subjected condition and searches out the ways in which the patterns that hold that subjection in place can be subverted and turned to other ends.

That writing/speaking subject is not the unitary rational being invented in the Enlightenment, elaborated in various humanist discourses, and made available to (some) men ever since but a multiple being, finding ways to incorporate both sides of any of those dualisms previously divided along sex lines and through which sex difference was made to make sense (Davies 1990; Wilshire 1989). Such an incorporation aims both at disentangling those dualisms from the male/female dualism and at dismantling the dualisms themselves by reconstituting them such that they no longer take their meaning in opposition to each other but as one of a range of possibilities that incorporate rather than negate each other. Trinh (1989, p. 35) comments that "what is needed is perhaps not a clean erasure but rather a constant displacement of the two-by-two system of division to which analytical thinking is often subjected."

Cixous (1986) claims that the ideal of such multiple wholeness, an ideal and a possibility for all people, is more possible for women at this point in time than it is for men. This claim becomes vividly apparent when reading Seidler's (1989) stark analysis of male subjectivity and its equation of the masculine with the rational, the not-female, and with the absence of emotion. Unlike men, women, at least since the days of access to public education, have considered that that which is male is accessible to them, if not in fact, at least as a discursively constituted possibility. Ironically, the insistence that they maintain their femininity while gaining access to public education and the public world of work, complex as that achievement has been (de Beauvoir 1972; Riviere 1986; Walkerdine 1989), has nonetheless given them the knowledge that these opposites can be encompassed in one being. Such an encompassing of multiplicity is only problematic if one is required to be unitary and rational in the liberal, humanist, masculinist sense. Poststructuralism opens up the possibility of encompassing the apparently contradictory with ease—even, on occasion, with pleasure. In what follows, I tell some fragments of my own experience, fragments that bear little relation to the person I currently experience myself to be. The person I was in these fragments is no longer alien and strange, nor even foolish, because I can now see how I was being discursively constituted. I was simply working within the constraints of available discourses to constitute myself as comprehensible, knowable, worthwhile.

Some of My Own Contradictions

I was born in the mid-1940s in a country town in Australia. In the early 1950s in Australia, there was much talk of war, of the possibility of future wars, and of the necessity of bravely defending our shores. Being a person of value and of note seemed to be solely understood in terms of the heroism of military action expressed in terms of willingness to die for principles of freedom through taking active measures to defend our country against the "yellow peril" in the north and the dreaded threat of "communism." There was also talk of the pain that the women who waited at home experienced. There was nothing they could do to help and no way they could know what was "really happening" out there in those foreign places. Their position, the antithesis of heroism, was one of unknowing, patience, privation, hardship, and namelessness. There was a disquiet about the position of women and also a strong emphasis on the value of "womanly" qualities and the importance of the woman in the home (Freidan 1963).

Taylor talks of women in Australia in the 1940s who contested this construction. She says that,

> in their attempts to assume the burden of citizenship, they challenged the discourse of politics and war which from the time of the Greeks through to more recent times allocated to the male the task of *armed civic virtue* and the role of the warrior; and to the female, the archetypal roles of sacrificial mother and/or ministering angel as well as the task of weeping, mourning and, at times, goading to action. (Taylor 1990, p. 1)

But such contestations are not any part of my conscious remembering of my childhood. I understood as fact that women could not be soldiers, but I rejected the position of the women who hopelessly waited. I understood my rejection of that position as something original that I had thought of for myself, not recognizing that it was part of an emerging discourse being made available to me in the talk that was going on around me. My search for what else I might be, other than someone who waited, I understood and remembered as a private, individual reflection on the nature of existence. I remember thinking that the closest I could come to doing something of worth was to be a nurse and care for the heroes who actively fought for that which was of value.

But, as I listened to my parents talk, this "solution" began to seem untenable. In the eyes of my father, nurses were sexually available and therefore not, according to my mother, in the category of woman who could be respected or accorded any value other than sexual. Sexually available women could not be wives. Although my father prized sexually active women, and spent his life bemoaning the fact that my mother was not one of these, the way he talked about them made them seem laughable, sleazy, evil, and disposable.

Somehow one had to juggle these contradictory imperatives to be a good woman, to be sexually active without negating one's goodness, and to find some form of heroism not incompatible with either of these. I read voraciously, and I repeatedly came across the pattern of female heroism that combined a fear of not being worthy or loved with an extraordinary capacity to sacrifice oneself for others and to care for them, particularly if they were damaged or imperfect in some way. These characteristics I took up as my own along with the relevant patterns of desire.

At the age of 20, I met a man who had been temporarily released from jail to attend university. Following a record of violence and living outside the law, he was struggling to make something of his life "within the law." He was exceptionally talented and very much harmed by his time in jail. Who better than I to help him? I married him and the prison released him into my care. At the age of 20, carrying his child, I took on the hopeless task of making good the lack of care that he had suffered throughout his life, of loving him well enough to heal his damaged being, of sacrificing myself to the task of supporting his genius. Needless to say, I failed. The story lines through which I made sense of my life were a nonsense in the face of the damage done by the prison system, and no amount of feminine care and self-sacrifice could restore the damage. For five years, the three children and I were battered prisoners in the "domestic haven" that I had learned to want (Davies 1989b).

The romantic story lines through which I interpreted my life are one of the lived realities of the male/female dualism and they work to hold that dualism in place. Within the terms of these romantic story lines, the desire to correctly constitute oneself as woman entails taking up as one's own oppressive subject positions that none would ever rationally choose. The "choice" arises from one's history in the world as female/woman/feminine. The recognition of the story line as problematic and the possibility of refusing it and of generating alternatives come from the poststructuralist analysis of it.

Women's Subjectivity

> Is "humanity", as a reality and as an idea, a point of departure—or a point of arrival?
> (Gramsci 1957, p. 79)

Within poststructuralist thought, the person (and the idea of what it means to be a person) is collectively and discursively constituted. The collectivity of women with their shared experiences and emotions—their female subjectivity—is made possible because as "women" they are spoken into existence through the same collective set of images, metaphors, and story lines as other women. Individuals are made distinguishable from the total collective through assignment to gender category and then through naming. The assignment of gender places the child in relation to others in particular ways. The naming, done in relation to the gender assignment, both marks and heightens the assignment, making the child's gender always available in any speaking to or of the child.

Each child faces the task of performatively and conceptually distinguishing the "me" from the "not-me". The me (or I) is understood and performed as having an inner quality as well as surface appearances and historical/geographic locations. The inner quality, what we have come to know as *desire*, is not just a physical inner quality but a psychic quality. The desires of the individual are what characterize "this person" to her- or himself. This is how I "know" myself. The "real me" is the psychic me, the desiring being. Although those desires are demonstrably discursively produced and thus collective in nature, they are "taken on" by each individual as their inner core (Davies 1990).

According to Althusser (1971), subject status is guaranteed even prior to birth and is guaranteed through the familial ideological pattern of each person's origin. In the majority of cultures, this is done through the name of the father.

> Everyone knows how much and in what way an unborn child is expected. Which amounts to saying, very prosaically, if we agree to drop the "sentiment," i.e., the forms of family ideology (paternal/maternal/conjugal/fraternal) in which the unborn child is expected: it is certain in advance that it will bear its Father's Name, and will therefore have an identity and be irreplaceable. (Althusser 1971, p. 176)

Cunningham (1989) uses this quote from Althusser as a point of departure for his analysis of the autobiography of the black male slave, Douglass, who, in contrast to what Althusser takes as normative, did not know his father's name. Douglass describes himself thus:

> I was born in Tuckahoe, near Hillsborough, and about twelve miles from Easton in Talbot County, Maryland. I have no accurate knowledge of my age, never having seen any accurate record containing it.
>
> My father was a white man. He was admitted to be such by all I ever heard speak of my parentage. The opinion was also whispered that my master was my father; but of the correctness of this opinion, I know nothing; the means of knowing was withheld from me. (Cunningham 1989, pp. 47-48)

Cunningham makes a great deal of the nonsubject status of Douglass as slave, which he relates to the lack of the father's name. He relates the concept of *being a subject* to having an "ego" and ties this to the Oedipal drama acted out in relation to the master. That Douglass's mother gave him a name is considered by Cunningham not to reduce the impact of no name from the father, despite Althusser's careful disclaimers and his final statement that it is into particular kinds of families that one is born: "Before its birth, the child is always-already a subject in and by the specific familial ideological configurations in which it is 'expected' once it has been conceived." To an extent, however, Douglass also shares Cunningham's and Althusser's prioritizing of the name of the father insofar as he defines himself in terms of the absence of the father and of not knowing his father's name (and therefore presumably his own, even though his mother had given him a name). This should not be read as depriving him of subject status but, instead, as Douglass constituting himself within the terms of that same patriarchal discourse that dictates that the father, whether by his presence or his absence, is a crucial defining feature of who one is.

Cunningham compares the slaves' plight with that of women and talks of the alternative to subject status being that of object. In doing so, he is fundamentally misunderstanding what it means to *be subject*, at least in poststructuralist terms. He takes his idea of subject, at least in part (though probably unintentionally), from the liberal, humanist, masculinist (and middle-class) tradition in which humanity is assumed to be intricately connected to agency, which means the power to choose and to make decisions in relation to one's own life (Davies forthcoming). In this mode, the opposite of subject is object, that is, someone who is deprived of agency and who is subjected to the agenetic acts of others. But the meaning of subject in poststructuralist writing takes its meaning in opposition to the liberal humanist idea of the subject. The various discourses in which one participates, or in terms of which one gains a voice or becomes a speaking subject, also are the means by which one is spoken into existence (even prior to one's birth) *as subject*. These discourses subject each person to the limitations, the ideologies, the subject positions made available within them. We become not what we have learned to call our true essential selves but that which the various discourses in which we participate define as or make thinkable as a self, or a true self. The mistake that we make, according to Althusser (1971), is to see ourselves as authors of those selves rather than to recognize that discourses are the means by which individuals are taken over by various "state apparatuses." Our selves and our human nature are not the causes of what we do but the products of the discourses through which we speak and are spoken into existence:

> The fundamental innovation of Marxism into the science of politics and history is the proof that there does not exist an abstract, fixed and immutable "human nature." (Gramsci 1957, p. 140)

> What we had thought of as human nature is, rather, a regulatory fiction through which people can be ordered and located in hierarchies. (Butler 1990, p. 24)

There is another way in which Douglass and his statement about who he is are worthy of attention, which Cunningham has not noticed. His description of himself begins with the place of his birth. The absence of the father comes after that location of himself in place. As Cohen and Somerville (1990) have shown in their work on Australian Aboriginal identity, place can be a fundamental defining feature of persons. Cunningham misses the significance of this, primarily because he is caught up in the Freudian story line as *the* story line through which individuals' stories must be told. As I have argued elsewhere, this is merely one story line among many, although it is one that has been given inordinate weight in Western culture and recently within poststructuralist writing. It is possible to use the Freudian story line to make sense of and live out one's life, but it is a story line that has severe limitations and in which the male/female dualism is made fundamental to existence. It is thus a story line to be recognized as such and replaced with another (Davies 1990). In Douglass's case, he struggles to assert himself as *male*, because it is maleness in his world that guarantees agency. Part of the offense of the slave position is that there is no difference between the status of men and women and thus the male slaves perceive themselves as being deprived of the maleness/agency that is necessary for identity.

In the experience of most women, the name of the father is granted unproblematically (though only temporarily, as something to be replaced by another man's name). The name of the father is no guarantee of subject (i.e., nonobject) status in Cunningham's terms, because recognition of herself as one with a right to be heard as a speaking subject is never guaranteed. The father's name is more like a sign of temporary ownership, not a sign that this is someone with a life of her own. It is in fact her sex that names her, that subjects her to the story lines in which not only is she object but her desire and others' desire for her is organized in terms of that object status. The naming and the story lines, through which that naming is made to make sense, are not an external clothing that can be cast aside but become the very subjectivity through which each woman knows herself:

> "Sex," the category, compels "sex," the social configuration of bodies, through what Wittig calls a coerced contract. Hence the category of "sex" is a name that enslaves. Language "casts sheaves of reality on the social body" but these sheaves are not easily discarded. She continues: "stamping it and violently shaping it." (Butler 1990, p. 115)

Cixous (1986) has been of central importance in the task of reworking old discourses and generating new ones. In much of her writing, she explicitly challenges elements of existing discourses. One of her strategies is to tell the old stories again but in such a way that the unacceptable features of them become painfully clear:

> *Once upon a time . . . once . . . and once again*

> Beauties slept in their woods waiting for princes to come and wake them up. In their beds, in their glass coffins, in their childhood forests like dead women. Beautiful but passive; hence desirable: all mystery emanates from them. It is men who like to play dolls. As we have known since Pygmalion. . . . She sleeps, she is intact, eternal, absolutely powerless. He has no doubt that she has been waiting for him forever.

> The secret of her beauty kept for him: she has the perfection of something finished. Or not begun. However she is breathing. Just enough life—and not too much. Then he will kiss her. So that when she opens her eyes she will see only him; *him*; him in place of everything, all him. (Cixous 1986, p. 66)

Although this telling of Cixous's is in part through the eyes of male desire, it is also telling that reveals the absence of woman to herself inside the romantic story line. It shows the way in which woman's subjectivity, her desire, her sense of herself is inscribed in body and mind in terms of this story line and probably will be until such time as she can both understand it and its fascination for her, and write a better one. As long as this is her only or predominant story line, she will struggle to achieve the correct degree of submissiveness to be sufficiently desirable to be positioned within that story. To be in no story is inconceivable. The achievement of oneself as woman within the romantic story line is not being a subject (not-object) but being subjected. It is also positively, if destructively, taking herself up as female subject within the terms of the discourses through which she is spoken and speaks herself into existence.

Feminist writers such as Wittig have begun the task of creating new story lines with new images and metaphors that position women quite differently:

> The gypsy women have a mummified corpse which they bring out when it is not raining, because of the smell of the body which is not quite dry. They expose it to the sun in its box. The dead woman is clothed in a long tunic of green velvet, covered with white embroidery and gilded ornaments. They have hung little bells on her neck, on her sleeves. They have put medallions in her hair. When they take hold of the box to bring it out the dead woman begins to tinkle everywhere. Every now and then someone goes out on to the three steps that lead up to the caravan to look at the clouds. When the sky is obscured two of them set about shutting the lid of the box and carrying it inside. (Wittig 1969, p. 16)

In this image of Wittig's, the corpse has more beauty, even more life with its tinkling bells, than Cixous's woman, who is the object of male desire. It is the women in this story who care for this faintly absurd object and decorate it beautifully, not so that one would long to be positioned as it is, but, with tenderness and amusement, they care for its eternal being. The woman in the coffin prompts a more active reading of the absurdity of being the "love-object," suggesting not simply angry rejection for its deathlike positioning but an amused recognition and thus a possibility of movement beyond.

Women's Subjectivity and Feminist Stories

The task of generating feminist story lines that have the power to disrupt and displace the old is extraordinarily complex. This is so for a number of reasons. First, new stories are always at risk of being interpreted in terms of the old (Davies 1989c). Second, our patterns of desire are not easily disrupted, in particular to the extent that they are defined as signifying one's essential self. Third, the function of story in holding the existing order in place has not yet been fully understood. Poststructuralist and postmodern stories function in a number of ways to break up old patterns (Hite 1989). Farmer (1990, p. 4) cites Zweig on the topic of the attitudes to story that are beginning to emerge with postmodern consciousness:

> Recently, however, we have begun to expect another pleasure from the stories we read. The spectacle of life's hidden form emerging from the vagaries of experience no longer warms our hearts. On the contrary, it chills us just a little, as if the form were a prison, and the novel's end-informed story the evidence for a failure of spirit. What [we want] are disruptive moments, flashes of illuminating intensity. It is not the end which is important, but the episode; not the form, of which the end is the final clarity, as when a sculptor unveils a statue, but the illumination itself, unruly and momentary, not casting a new light over what has been lived, but compressing life itself into its absoluteness, and bursting.

Much feminist writing has precisely that quality of "bursting open" the absoluteness of experience. This is not just an angry fracturing and breaking of unwanted images and positionings—though it is also that—but the bursting forth of the bud from the death of the female winter:

> then the day came
> when the risk to remain
> tight in a bud
> was more painful
> than the risk it took
> to blossom

(a quote from Anais Nin on my physiotherapist's wall)

The binary pairs male/female, mind/body, reason/emotion, light/darkness, fact/fantasy take their meaning not only in relation but in hierarchical opposition to each other. Our new stories must rework the elements of these dualisms, such that both sides are equally valued, their meaning is no longer part of any oppositional binary form of thought, and both become necessary elements of each person's subjectivity. In the meantime, though, personal identities have been (are being) constituted in terms of those very dualities we are in process of challenging (Davies 1989c). Being a "woman" or a "man" has profound significance for *who* people take themselves to be and for the story lines through which they make sense of their own actions, emotions, bodily experience, and their positioning in relation to others (Hollway 1984). Feminists in particular are caught up in curiously contradictory ways of being as they affirm/assert the feminine, its value, and its non-otherness to masculinity and begin to envisage, to speak and write of a multiple and whole identity that does not take its meaning from the male/female dualism (Davies 1990; Davies and Harré forthcoming).

Because fantasy is understood as somehow integral to childhood, children are not immediately introduced to the fact/fantasy dualism. Adults go to some lengths to acquaint children with the world of fantasy via stories and collude in persuading children to believe that which they themselves do not believe to be true. In deep contradiction with this particular practice, however, we require of children's tellings of their own experience a sharp dividing line to be drawn between "real" and "pretend" that they then take up as an important way of categorizing their tellings. Real is legitimate and has force while pretend is dismissable and positively evil if it is not clearly marked "pretend."

Learning to separate the two clearly is a signal that one has become an adult and is a legitimate and worthy person within the terms of modern thought. But the task of separation is never complete because it is a discursively produced difference that needs constant work to achieve it as an observable difference. The fabrication of difference is manifest in those practices where what a person "really" thinks and feels becomes a matter that counselors and friends help them "discover." Such attitudes and processes are fundamental to the construction of gendered unitary, noncontradictory humanist persons who constitute themselves as having a real, discoverable essence in clear distinction to the social and discursive forces that surround and produce them.

In this humanist/modernist model, stories serve a number of functions. They can be an escape from the real world, didactic, teaching morals to the reader, or inspiration to the reader to better things. But they can also be dangerous and misleading, filling the "hearts and minds" of readers with *mistaken* versions of reality that they then confuse with real life. One such dangerous story for women is the romantic one. The danger is understood as resulting from the failure of the individual woman to separate fact from fantasy and does not recognize the way in which her understanding of what it means to be feminine is necessarily constructed out of the culture's stories and the available positionings for women within them. The specific danger of the romantic story line within a modernist understanding of story is women's tendency to construe the most ordinary and flawed of men as "their prince." Such construal can lead to inappropriate commitment, passion, and inevitable disillusion when the cracks in the supposed reality start to reveal themselves.

"Am I *really* in love?" was the anguished question we often asked each other in those days of clear separation between fact and fantasy, and we assumed that, if the answer was yes, the story line would unfold correctly with its inevitable happy ending of fulfillment and domestic bliss. If the prince was an ogre, no matter, her real love would turn him into a prince. In this model, it was my capacity to "really" love that was at fault, or else a flawed choice on my part, having not recognized an ogre that could not be changed into a prince. Either way, I was guilty.

From a poststructuralist perspective, there is no longer any "real" lived story. Stories we observe, hear, and read, both lived and imaginary, form a stock of imaginary story lines through which life choices can be made. The choices I make in any current moment will depend on the story line I take myself to be living out. If I think I am in the romantic narrative, which requires "the prince," the people with whom I choose to play out this story will be more or less able to live out the prince as I understand it, depending on whether they take themselves to be inside the romantic story line, what their particular version of the romantic story line is, and their ability and/or willingness to live out that which is necessary in my story line for them to continue to be read as prince.

In poststructuralist terms, to get out of the romantic narrative, to escape its confines, I don't need to catch myself mistakenly reading someone as prince when he is not. Instead, I need to understand the story itself, how it draws me in and how others position me within its terms. I need as well to imagine new story lines in which the problems inherent in the existing narrative are eliminated and in which the positionings available to me are not destructive in the way that the romantic narrative is. In such an interpretation, it is not the individual woman who is at fault in mistakenly living out a fantasy instead of a reality or for living it incorrectly. It is the culture that has destructive narratives through which identity and desire are organized. The task becomes one of looking for and generating new story lines. It is also one of discovering what the "hooks" are in the images and metaphors of the old story lines that can draw individual women in against their better judgment. In this postmodern version of the relation between lived and imaginary narratives, imagined stories are a valuable resource because they may hold a key to disrupting and decentering old discourses and narratives— to unstitching and fraying the patterns of desire that are held within them.

Readings of a Feminist Story

The following story was written for me by my youngest son, Daniel. I had been moaning to him about the impossibility of ever writing a feminist story because there is always the possibility of a conservative reading in which the story is understood as confirming the status quo (Davies 1989c). Daniel said he didn't think it was as difficult as all that and that he thought he could write a feminist story.

The following is Daniel's story. He was 20 at the time of writing it. It is interesting that he starts with a character who, like him, is the third child and who, like him, had a cruel father whom she never knew. I include this story as one possible answer out of the multiple answers that are needed to the questions raised in this chapter. The analysis that follows provides an example of the nonconservative reading, or reading against the grain, that we and children need to learn to do with the stories that are going on around us.

Vuthsanya

Now it so happened that a third child was born to King Rian, and was not a male. This angered the King greatly, for it had been foretold that his third child was to be gifted with great powers of knowledge and skill, especially in battle.

The King himself was a mighty ruler and man of renown. He was so angered by the birth of his third daughter that he refused to speak to her or even to see her. Her name was Vuthsanya and she only ever looked upon her father's face once. She had eyes of the blackest of black and secrets the darkest of dark.

On her twelfth birthday she left the castle and the Kingdom carrying only the clothes on her back. The King soon learned of her departure, yet he sent no search party and shed no tear. Many others did, for Vuthsanya was well liked by the people although none could claim to know her well.

The next ten years were the coldest and hardest years the Kingdom had ever known. Crops failed, sickness plagued the land, the sun seldom shone, and the King was growing old. It was then that a terrible creature came to the land. He was Teg-Mushrak, one of the ancient tormentors, who took delight in death and destruction. In looks he was something like a giant ogre, yet much more repulsive. Mushrak terrorized the Kingdom for months without rest. Rian had sent many brave knights out to finish him, but none came back.

In frustration and dismay, the King sent forth a demand for Mushrak to meet him on the field of battle. This challenge was accepted gleefully by the blood hungry Tormentor. So it was set. In one week, on Mid-Winter's Eve, the two shall meet in battle on the Felion Plains below the cliffs of Aspirion.

The day quickly came and the King went to meet his doom. The people were frightened and would not come out of their houses. Children wept and the men felt shamed for there was nothing they could do but hope.

Rian reached the plains and there was Mushrak, picking his teeth with the splintered thigh bone of a victim. He laughed and spat at Rian, who was clad in bright armor, riding a white steed, and carrying a long shining lance. "Prepare to meet your end!" yelled King Rian, as he charged toward the foul creature with blood in his eyes. But Rian was not the young warrior he once had been and Mushrak leapt aside with surprising speed and knocked Rian from his horse with a tremendous blow. The King fell to the ground and was dazed. He unsheathed his sword but Mushrak leaped in the air and dealt his head a mighty kick that rendered him unconscious, and at the ogre's mercy, of which there was none.

Mushrak was preparing to sink his teeth into his prize when he heard the beating of huge wings above him. He wheeled around and was dealt a sickening blow across the side of the head. Mushrak stumbled with blood pouring out of his face, saliva dribbling down his chin, and gave a thunderous bellow of anger. He turned to face his foe, and his anger, as great as it was, gave way to a chuckle, and then a laugh. "A woman dares to attack Mushrak, the most powerful and wonderful creature in the land," he snorted. "I will teach you the folly of your ways!"

Vuthsanya was sitting astride a black Pegasus with her long sword drawn, and no light shone from her eyes. She leapt from her mount with agility and stood to face Mushrak. She said nothing.

The giant ogre lunged toward Vuthsanya, but she nimbly ducked aside and slashed his side so that blood poured out like water.

This angered Mushrak beyond belief and he spun around, madly trying to claw at this arrogant pest. But he was no match for Vuthsanya. With two more blows, Mushrak was begging for mercy. The next blow split Mushrak's skull in two. He was dead and Vuthsanya stood tall and proud over her fallen foe.

Now King Rian awoke from his slumber and saw what had taken place and looked for the mighty warrior who had done this amazing deed, for he would most certainly be the King's new champion. But all he could see was a mighty black Pegasus flying off into the distance with a woman's figure astride. It seemed to Rian that he knew who this was, though he could not say, or perhaps would not.

Rian rode home and the people rejoiced to see their King return. To this day, people still tell the story of Rian's battle with Teg-Mushrak and how he split the monster's head in two and so saved the land. Only two people know what really happened that day, and so do you.

*   *   *

We can read this story conservatively, *with* the grain of patriarchy. In such a reading, there are many features that appear to confirm the status quo:

Fathers do not welcome or value daughters, particularly when their heart is set on a son capable of heroism;

good daughters cope with such rejection with silence and with absence, because there is nothing they can say to undo such rejection;

mothers are also silent and do nothing to question or reverse the plight of their daughters;

even where the daughter is the exception to the rule and is capable of heroism, the father will not acknowledge such heroism, nor will the daughter ask him to do so.

But there is also much about the story that makes a different reading possible, a reading that runs against the grain of discourses that constitute women inside the male/female dualism. That alternative reading provides a critique of patriarchy and gives the reader an alternative story line.

First, the father's belief in the inferiority of women is shown to be wrong. Girls *can* have powerful knowledge and be great warriors. ("It had been foretold that his third child was to be gifted with great powers of knowledge and skill, especially in battle.") Her knowledge and her strength are not only greater than his but, perhaps more important, cannot be attributed to him. As well, the powerful and all-rejecting father is shown to be dishonest, claiming her accomplishments as his own. His law rests on a shaky foundation that not only invites criticism but is recognizable as falsely depending on the unacknowledged support of women.

Second, the daughter reveals that his judgment is of no consequence to her. She can walk away from it and set up an alternative life in which she is clearly extraordinarily powerful. It is within her gift to save her father and his kingdom, which she does, but his recognition of this fact is of no consequence to her. This can be read as a profound negation of the word/ the law/the power of the father. She thus has far greater moral stature than he because she does not hold grudges or seek revenge even where this would seem to be an entirely reasonable response.

There are some additional features of the story that involve the reader in reading against the conservative grain of the story. One of these is the ending, where the author invites the reader to position her- or himself as one who knows the truth and thus as one who shares Vuthsanya's knowledge. The reader then stands with Vuthsanya against the power of the father. The story is told from the moral position of Vuthsanya but in an interestingly "unfeminine" way. The kinds of details that are normally revealed in the telling of women's lives are left completely untold. She is a genuine protagonist mixing some features of the male heroic position with some features of the heroine. As heroine, she is, at the beginning, vulnerable in the way that heroines usually are. She is at risk of being rejected by a central male figure; in this case, the father. She has no safe domestic scene and is cast adrift, presumably with the task of finding a new one. But she turns this around. Her story becomes one that is more typical of the male hero. She is powerful, competent, and strong. The home base that she creates is not described and, perhaps more important, neither is she (except for the blackness of her eyes whose most prominent quality is what they hide). She is not the object of another's gaze, nor does she need anyone else to make her safe.

Because the story begins with the familiar scene of rejection, it has the power to "hook" a female reader who can connect with the subjectivity of Vuthsanya and know her vulnerability. It maintains this connection in a number of ways. Vuthsanya remains caring in that she saves her father when he needs it and she does not confront or demand in an "unfeminine" way. Her warriorlike skills are the most significant point of departure in her character from current accepted forms of femaleness/femininity.

Vuthsanya is thus not a character who asks us to negate our femininity but who says that, along with feminine qualities and even when positioned as inferior/female, women can be heroic and thus can exist outside and independent of the male/female dualism. She can exist not as *woman* but as a multiple being who incorporates and reconstitutes that which was previously understood as essential to either masculinity or femininity.

Conclusion

Who we are, our subjectivity, is spoken into existence in every utterance, not just in the sense that others speak us into existence and impose unwanted structures on us, as much early feminist writing presumed, but, in each moment of speaking and being, we each reinvent ourselves inside the male/female dualism, socially, psychically, and physically (Davies 1989c). The lived and imaginary narratives that we generate in our attempt to speak into existence a different way of being outside the male/female dualism need to achieve several contradictory purposes. We need stories that are elaborations of existing stories that mark their problematic nature. We need not only to see the problems in rational, didactic terms (though we need that too) but to see freshly the images and metaphors and story lines we have grown up with and to learn to read them against the grain. The desire to read them against the grain does not simply come with knowing what those alternative readings are, however, because the old story lines, through which old discourses are lived out, inevitably compete for our attention. Any reading against the grain implies a detailed knowledge of the grain itself. And who we have taken ourselves to be in the past and in much of the present are known precisely in terms of that which we are trying to undo. As Hollway (1984, p. 260) says of new discourses and new practices:

> Changes don't automatically eradicate what went before—neither in structure nor in the way that practices, powers and meanings have been produced historically. Consciousness-changing is not accomplished by new discourses replacing old ones. It is accomplished as a result of the contradictions in our positionings, desires and practices—and thus in our subjectivities—which result from the coexistence of the old and the new. Every relation and every practice to some extent articulates such contradictions and therefore is a site of potential change as much as it is a site of reproduction.

One of the major contributions of feminist fictional writing has been to invent new images for readings outside the male/female dualism. In the following passage from Wittig (1969, p. 19), a new image of female genitals is created that uses as the grain-to-write-against the old attitudes of shame and the related averted female gaze. The contradictory image that she creates is one in which female genitals are celebrated, not as objects of the male gaze, and thus not inside the male/female dualism, but as signifiers of a power of mythic proportions:

> The women say that they expose their genitals so that the sun may be reflected therein as a mirror. They say that they retain its brilliance. They say that the pubic hair is like a spider's web that captures the rays. They are seen running with great strides. They are all illuminated at their center, starting from the pubes of the

hooded clitorides the folded double labia. The glare they shed when they stand still and turn to face one makes the eye turn elsewhere, unable to stand the sight.

The multiple and contradictory nature of such changes cannot be incorporated in any one linear story. As I have tried here to draw fragments of my own life together with images presented to me by others to make a new kind of story that lends itself to multiple readings, so too our stories need to break their old shapes and burst forth into new ones. That bursting forth is not simply through the creation of images that others can be inspired by and follow. It is also a collective awareness of the power of speaking and writing, both to reconstitute ourselves in ways we do not wish within the male/female dualism and to create a succession of moments in which we know ourselves otherwise, as multiple and whole, encompassing in our beings both sides of any dualism, thus dismantling the dualisms themselves.

References

Althusser, Louis. 1971. *Lenin and Philosophy and Other Essays*. New York: Monthly Review.

Butler, Judith. 1990. *Gender Trouble: Feminism and the Subversion of Identity*. New York: Routledge.

Cixous, Helene. 1981. "The Laugh of the Medusa." Pp. 245-64 in *New French Feminisms: An Anthology*, edited by E. Marks and I. de Courtivron. Brighton: Harvester.

————1986. "Sorties: Out and Out: Attacks/Ways Out/Forays." Pp. 63-132 in *The Newly Born Woman*, edited by H. Cixous and C. Clement. Manchester: Manchester University Press.

Cohen, Patsy and Margaret Somerville. 1990. *Ingelba and the Five Black Matriarchs*. Sydney: Allen and Unwin.

Connell, Robert W. 1987. *Gender and Power*. Sydney: Allen and Unwin.

Cunningham, George. 1989. "'Called into Existence': Desire, Gender, and Voice in Frederick Douglass's Narrative of 1845." *Differences: A Journal of Feminist Cultural Studies* 1:108-36.

Davies, Bronwyn. 1989a. "The Discursive Production of the Male/Female Dualism in School Settings." *Oxford Review of Education* 15:229-41.

————1989b. "Life Sentences." Pp. 196-200 in *Angry Women: An Anthology of Australian Women's Writing*, edited by D. Brown, H. Ellyard, and B. Polkinghorne. Sydney: Hale and Iremonger.

————1989c. *Frogs and Snails and Feminist Tales: Preschool Children and Gender*. Sydney: Allen and Unwin.

————1990. "The Problem of Desire." *Social Problems* 37:801-16.

————Forthcoming. "Agency: A Discursive Practice." *Social Analysis*.

Davies, Bronwyn and Rom Harré. 1990. "Positioning: Conversation and the Production of Selves." *Journal for the Theory of Social Behaviour* 20:43-63.

————Forthcoming. "Contradiction in Lived and Told Narratives." *Research on Language and Social Interaction*.

de Beauvoir, Simone. 1972. *The Second Sex*. Harmondsworth: Penguin.

Edwards, Anne. 1983. "Sex Roles: A Problem for the Sociology of Women." *The Australian and New Zealand Journal of Sociology* 19:385-412.

Farmer, Beverley. 1990. *A Body of Water*. St. Lucia: University of Queensland Press.

Freidan, Betty. 1963. *The Feminine Mystique*. Harmondsworth: Penguin.

Gramsci, Antonio. 1957. *The Modern Prince and Other Writings*. New York: International.

Haug, Frigga. 1987. *Female Sexualisation*. London: Verso.

Henriques, J., W. Hollway, C. Urwin, C. Venn, and V. Walkerdine, eds. 1984. *Changing the Subject: Psychology, Social Regulation and Subjectivity*. London: Methuen.

Hite, Molly. 1989. *The Other Side of the Story: Structures and Strategies of Contemporary Feminist Narratives*. Ithaca, NY: Cornell University Press.

Hollway, Wendy. 1984. "Gender Difference and the Production of Subjectivity." Pp. 227-63 in *Changing the Subject: Psychology, Social Regulation and Subjectivity*, edited by J. Henriques, W. Hollway, C. Urwin, C. Venn, and V. Walkerdine. London: Methuen.

Riviere, Joan. 1986. "Womanliness as a Masquerade." Pp. 35-44 in *Formations of Fantasy*, edited by V. Burgin, J. Donald, and C. Kaplan. London: Methuen.

Rogers, Lesley. 1988. "Biology, the Popular Weapon: Sex Differences in Cognitive Function." Pp. 43-51 in *Crossing Boundaries: Feminisms and the Critique of Knowledges*, edited by B. Caine, E. A. Grosz, and M. de Lepervanche. Sydney: Allen and Unwin.

Sayers, Janet. 1986. *Sexual Contradictions: Psychology, Psychoanalysis and Feminism*. London: Tavistock.

Seidler, Victor. 1989. *Rediscovering Masculinity: Reason, Language and Sexuality*. London: Routledge.

Stanley, Liz and Sue Wise. 1983. *Breaking Out: Feminist Consciousness and Feminist Research*. London: Routledge & Kegan Paul.

Taylor, Helen. 1990. "So What About It, Mr. Menzies? Women's Claims for Citizenship, 1939-41." Paper presented at the "Woman/Australia/Theory Conference," Brisbane, July.

Trinh, T. Minh-ha. 1989. *Woman, Native, Other: Writing Postcoloniality and Feminism*. Bloomington: Indiana University Press.

Walkerdine, Valerie. 1981. "Sex, Power and Pedagogy." *Screen Education* 38:14-24.

———1984. "Some Day My Prince Will Come." Pp. 162-84 in *Gender and Generation*, edited by A. McRobbie and M. Nava. London: Macmillan.

———1989. "Femininity as Performance." *Oxford Review of Education* 15:267-79.

Walkerdine, Valerie and Helen Lucey. 1989. *Democracy in the Kitchen*. London: Virago.

Wex, Marianne. 1979. *Let's Take Back Our Space: Female and Male Body Language as a Result of Patriarchal Structures*. Frauenliteraturverlag: Hermine Fees.

Wilshire, Donna. 1989. "The Uses of Myth, Image, and the Female Body in Re-visioning Knowledge." Pp. 92-114 in *Gender/Body/Knowledge: Feminist Reconstructions of Being and Knowing*, edited by A. M. Jagger and S. R. Borno. New Brunswick, NJ: Rutgers University Press.

Wittig, Monique. 1969. *Les Guérilleres*. Boston: Beacon.

Zweig, Paul. 1974. *The Adventurer*. New York: Basic Books.

PART II

Creating Texts

4

Telling and Performing Personal Stories

The Constraints of Choice in Abortion

CAROLYN ELLIS
ARTHUR P. BOCHNER

To see ourselves as others see us can be eye-opening. To see others as
sharing a nature with ourselves is the merest decency. But it is from the far
more difficult achievement of seeing ourselves amongst others, as a local
example of the forms human life has locally taken, a case among cases, a
world among worlds, that the largeness of mind, without which objectivity
is self-congratulation and tolerance a sham, comes.

Geertz 1983, p. 16

The act of telling a personal story is a way of giving voice to experiences
that are shrouded in secrecy. By finding words to express these experiences
and share them with others, we "attempt to lift the interior facts of bodily
sentience out of the inarticulate pre-language of 'cries and whispers' into the
realm of shared objectification" (Scarry 1985, p. 11). By making intricate
details of one's life accessible to others in public discourse, personal narratives bridge the dominions of public and private life. Telling a personal story

AUTHORS' NOTE: We wish to acknowledge the helpful comments of Michael Flaherty,
Arlie Hochschild, and Ruth Linden on an earlier version of this chapter.

becomes a social process for making lived experience understandable and meaningful.

This chapter presents our personal account of the lived experience of abortion narrated in both the female and the male voices. The events depicted in the narrative were experienced as an epiphany. Denzin (1988) characterizes epiphanies as events in which individuals are so powerfully absorbed that they are left without an interpretive framework to make sense of their experience. During the time period in which these events took place, we were too engaged by what was happening to record our experiences. Two months after the abortion, we independently reconstructed a chronology of the events that took place, including the emotional dimensions of our decision making, turning points, coping strategies, the symbolic environment of the clinic, and the abortion procedure as each of us experienced it (Bochner and Ellis 1992). These separate accounts then were transformed into a dialogic mode of narration that attempted to capture the processual and emotional details of what happened. Other people with whom we had consulted also wrote of their experiences during our decision-making process and thus provided multiple voices for the telling of the story.

We offer this work as an experimental form of narrating personal experience in which "we make ourselves experimental subjects and treat our experiences as primary data" (Jackson 1989, p. 4). Our goal is to lead readers through a journey in which they develop an "experiential sense" of the events (Krieger 1984, p. 273) and thus come away with a sense of "what it must have felt like" to live through what happened (Becker, McCall, and Morris 1989, p. 95; McCall 1991). As a project originating in the context of "emotional sociology" (Ellis 1991b), our inquiry starts from a biographical point of departure that uses systematic introspection (Ellis 1991a) to explore the emotional and cognitive details of our lived experience.

The text was written with the express purpose of being performed so that nuances of feeling, expression, and interpretation could be communicated more clearly (Becker et al. 1989; Bochner and Ellis 1992; Paget 1990). An audience that witnesses a performance of this text thus is subjected to much more than words: they see facial expressions, movements, and gestures; they hear the tones, intonations, and inflections of the actors' voices; and they can feel the passion of the performers. The audience is moved away from the universal and forced to deal with the concrete—particular people in particular places in face-to-face encounters (Conquergood 1990).

The Story

Scene 1: The Pregnancy Test and the Test of Pregnancy

(ALICE FACES AUDIENCE; TED TURNS AWAY)

Alice: I experience it as a ritual, though I have never done it before. I think of the many women before me who have. Some, like me, assuming it will be negative, a false alarm. Some fearing, others hoping. I read the directions carefully, several times, and take deep breaths.

Why am I scared? Of course, I'm not pregnant. I'm 39 and never been pregnant. Ted's 44 and has never had a partner who was pregnant. And, we were careful.

Cautiously, I urinate a few drops into the plastic container, then insert the stick that will reveal the verdict. In about ten seconds, the first dot begins to turn purple. No, that can't be right. I scan the directions, and, according to the picture, there are now two possibilities. Either I have done the test wrong and the next two dots will be white, or I am pregnant and the second dot will be white and the third will turn purple. Feeling my heart rate increase, I tell myself again that I can't be pregnant, but now my held breath and flash of warmth reveal I am no longer so sure. As I wait for the urine to saturate the third dot, I skim the directions again. My eyes focus on the 99% accuracy claim, then quickly move back to the third dot, already taking on a bare shade of pink, then pinker, and pinker, and now a tinge of purple. I compare it with the illustration. Again. "My god, I'm pregnant," I say out loud, softly, matter-of-factly, with no panic, only awe in my voice.

Rushing in are images of the trauma my body will go through. At the same time, mesmerized, my hands and eyes explore my abdomen. I now define the feeling I had thought was my period ready to begin as pregnancy. I want to locate *it* and am suddenly aware that there's something pushing out from inside. I have a baby inside me. My god, what a miracle. I experience *it* as company now, and then I interpret my response as feeling womanly.

Oh, my god, I'm pregnant. I'm going to have to get an abortion, and I hate doctors, pain, and agony.

Then that company feeling returns. I moan, and tears form in my eyes but don't fall.

(TED TURNS TOWARD AUDIENCE, THEN TOWARD ALICE)

> Then Ted arrives and plays with the dogs before he looks at me. He knows I bought the test. Does he suspect that I am pregnant? "Well, what do you want to name it?" I ask, and immediately wonder if this is a good way to tell him. I feel none of the lightness that my words are supposed to convey ironically.

Ted: "What? You are?"

> "Yes."

> "Pregnant?"

> "Yes."

> "Are you sure?"

> "The tests are 99 percent effective."

> "Oh, god. What are we going to do?"

(ALICE TURNS AWAY; TED TURNS TOWARD AUDIENCE)

Ted: I feel myself drifting away. Memories flash quickly through my mind. I recall conversations with former lovers in which I fantasized the birth of a "love child," created during a nearly perfect, mutually orgasmic sexual encounter and nurtured to birth by the compassion and tenderness characteristic of idealistic love. I particularly recall the brief moments during our passionate romance when Alice and I had played with the idea of having a child, more jokingly than seriously, but nevertheless opening possibilities that simultaneously were threatening and thrilling. I remember how easily and innocently we flirted with danger by finding reasons not to use a diaphragm. I conjured up sweet images of fathering that had been buried by the despairing experiences of three childless marriages in which the timing was never quite right or the love never quite sufficient. My head is spinning as I try to concentrate on the immediate circumstances, but my mind is crowded with memories and fantasies. Part of me wants to scream with joy; another part, to howl in agony.

Scene 2: Making the Decision

(TED AND ALICE TURN TOWARD EACH OTHER)

Ted: When I ask Alice, "What are you going to do?" I think I already know the answer.

Alice: "I don't know. I've called an abortion clinic, and I have a call in to my gynecologist. I'm only gathering information. But I guess I want to have an abortion."

(ALICE TURNS AWAY; TED TURNS TOWARD AUDIENCE)

Ted: I am surprised at how quickly she has acted to set an abortion in motion. Suddenly Alice has shifted from "what will we name it?" to "how can we find the right doctor to perform an abortion?" I feel an inner conflict about my own rights and obligations. As father of the fetus, don't I have any rights regarding whether to terminate the pregnancy? On the other hand, don't I have an obligation to defer to Alice's judgment? It's her body changing, not mine. It's in her womb that this life will nest, not mine. She's the one who will be sick in the mornings and who will have to labor in the last minutes or hours of her pregnancy to push a resistant source of energy into the world. I conclude without much hesitation that my obligations far outweigh my rights.

Moreover, I am not very sure about what I want. On the one hand, I'd like to rejoice in the splendor of this moment, knowing for the first time in my life that a woman I love is pregnant with our child.

But my desire to rejoice is counteracted by the obvious strain a pregnancy would place on our relationship, which is only a few months old. I am numbed by the feelings and thoughts rumbling inside me.

(TED TURNS TOWARD ALICE; ALICE TURNS TOWARD TED)

Ted: "The decision will have to be yours. It's your body that will be in pain. You can count on my emotional and financial support. I'll support whatever you want to do."

(ALICE TURNS TOWARD AUDIENCE)

Alice: I am glad for his sensitivity and am suddenly relieved that we are in this together. But I am also afraid that he will want to have the baby. I don't have time for a baby. And, I've only known Ted for ten weeks. I'm just not sure. It would mean being connected through the baby forever.

(ALICE TURNS TOWARD TED)

Alice: "It's hard to imagine having the baby, but there's a real baby in there."

Ted: "I know. Let me feel your stomach again. I want to share the experience with you. If you have an abortion I want to be in the room with you."

Alice: "Oh, I would like that." I am appreciative, yet a little surprised that he would be willing to go through the ordeal.

(TED TURNS TOWARD AUDIENCE)

Ted: But she does not ask me to explain why I want this or how I feel about it.

(TED TURNS TOWARD ALICE)

Alice: I jump when the phone rings but wait to hear the voice of my doctor on the answering machine. "Hello," I say quickly so she doesn't hang up.

"I hear you have a positive home pregnancy test," Dr. Wilson says happily. "I hope this is an occasion of joy for you."

She is antiabortion, I think, and I am embarrassed when I say, "Well, as a matter-of-fact, it's not. I guess I want to have an abortion."

"Are you sure? Have you considered other options, such as adoption?"

Why is she asking this? Does she disapprove of abortion? Or does she feel obligated as a doctor to ask these questions?

"Yes, I'm sure," I say, with confidence, then follow hesitantly with, "I guess I'm pregnant. Is a home pregnancy test accurate?"

"Yes, they are now. Do you feel pregnant?"

Surprised by her question, I reply, "Yes. Yes, I do," as I gently rub my abdomen.

Immediately I call the private doctor she recommends. "I'll make the appointment," I say to Ted. "We can always cancel it." He hesitantly nods. I am glad he doesn't stop me.

"Come in a week from today," the receptionist says. "We'll do a test to make sure you are at least six weeks pregnant. The cost is $350, which must be paid before the test. The whole amount. In cash. That's up front. Then we'll schedule the abortion." When I hang up, the chaos of legal and illegal symbols, ideologies of right and sin, along with my fluctuating feelings of having a baby inside me and a thing that must be gotten rid of, all contribute to my confusion.

(TED TURNS TOWARD AUDIENCE; ALICE TURNS AWAY)

Ted: Alice and I lay on the sofa after the call and recollect when this child was conceived. We agree on the date, the place, and the position we were in when this predicament was created. It was a memorable Saturday afternoon when we had luxuriated in one of the freest and most passionate sexual encounters of our relationship. We walked around later that night under the spell of a halo cast by this loving and intense encounter as if we had been drugged by orgasmic release and stood apart from the rest of the crowded world. There was no way to know whether this was, indeed, the particular occasion on which we had conceived a child. But we seemed contented, perhaps even exalted, by romanticizing our conception this way. We never doubted the validity of the date we fixed for this event. Perhaps it provided an ironic balance to the tragic drama we were about to enact. At least we had experienced a transcendent moment together, however brief in duration and tragic in consequences, that could justify our having thrown caution to the wind.

Scene 3: Dealing with the Decision

(TED TURNS AWAY; ALICE TURNS TOWARD AUDIENCE)

Alice: The next day while I am working, Jeanie calls. She is one of many people I talk to about the abortion. I listen to my telling of the story over and over to work out how I am feeling and to provide opportunities for input from others. Since Jeanie is a sex educator and has had an abortion, I ask her questions. "Did it hurt?"

"No, it was like a pinch." I am relieved, then wonder if she is trying to make me feel better.

"I sort of like it," I say, "like that my body can do it, and the way it feels."

"I loved being pregnant."

"What do they actually do during the abortion?" I ask, realizing how little I know.

Jeanie reads from one of her textbooks: "After the cervical opening is dilated, a thin plastic tube is inserted into the uterus and is connected to a suction pump. . . . Should I go on?"

"Yes," I say, although I feel faint.

"The uterine lining, along with fetal and placental tissue, is then suctioned out."

The imagery is overwhelming. That's a baby, my mind screams. And, that's my body. I lie down on the floor as Jeanie continues reading and I pass out.

(PAUSE, TO INDICATE PASSAGE OF TIME)

(TED TURNS AWAY; ALICE TURNS TOWARD AUDIENCE)

Alice: For the hundredth time, I think through the pros and cons of abortion. Abortion gets rid of the problem. I don't have to make major life decisions, everything continues on the same trajectory, my relationship with Ted is not artificially accelerated, I don't have to be pregnant for nine months. My work won't suffer. How would I meet all the obligations I have taken on? On the other hand, I have to go through the physical and emotional pain of abortion and cope with having killed a living being. It feels wrong, selfish. Why is this happening? Was it meant to be? I'm 39. Is this my last chance to have a baby? Perhaps I would find meaning being a mother that I could not know any other way. Ironically, I think of another advantage of having a baby—I wouldn't have to be department chair. Who would ask a pregnant woman/new mother to be department chair?

But every time I work it through, it comes out to having an abortion. Still, that doesn't make me feel better. Perhaps I have forgotten something, not assigned the right weight to a factor. My decision makes me see myself in ways that make me uncomfortable. Am I a selfish, self-centered, workaholic scared of commitment, willing to kill my baby to live the kind of independent, self-sufficient life to which I have grown accustomed?

Sometimes I fantasize that I am going to have a baby, not an abortion. Then I like the feeling of the pressure on my abdomen. I shake my head so that I don't get carried away with this thought. Then I grieve for the child that I will give up.

(PAUSE)

(TED AND ALICE TURN TOWARD EACH OTHER)

Ted: "You don't have to do this."

Alice: "What?"

Ted: "Have this abortion. I'm with you all the way. I'll do whatever you want."

(PAUSE)

(ALICE TURNS AWAY; TED TURNS TOWARD THE AUDIENCE)

Ted: "Alice is pregnant," I say to Diane, one of only two people I talk to about the pregnancy. I do not want to share my conflicts, be judged, questioned, or challenged. Nor do I want to be pitied or sympathized, but I feel obligated to tell Diane because she knows something is wrong. "I feel foolish about how careless we were. We're not teenagers, although we acted like we were." Then I am distracted by the crying infant and two other young children scooting around the table near us as we finish our lunch.

Diane nods her head in agreement, and later she writes, "I don't recall exactly how Ted told me, although I recall the message being delivered with nervousness in his voice and his eyes diverted from mine, looking beyond me. I do recall my thought (though I don't think I spoke it since it would sound too judgmental and would be better left unsaid): "How stupid; there's no excuse." However, Ted said it just as well, though couched differently: "I know it's crazy, we know better, we're not teenagers," to which I readily agreed.

(PAUSE)

(TED TURNS AWAY; ALICE TURNS TOWARD AUDIENCE)

Alice: I tell Joan about passing out. "No wonder," she says, "look at the imagery—tissue and blood being sucked out."

"And my pain," I add. "Being scared of the pain."

"I'll come over and do some visualization."

I don't know if I believe in visualization, but I agree since I seem to need another way of knowing now. Cognitive and emotional knowing confuse me and leave me in tears, and there is something going on that I can't understand.

In an incense-filled room, Joan and I sit quietly with closed eyes. I am deeply affected by the total context of the experience, more than by Joan's specific words. As soon as I hear her voice, I sob. Joan speaks quietly about my decision to abort the fetus. I feel sorry for myself and the decision I have made as I experience the fetus as part of my body. I am in touch with a deeper, perhaps spiritual world, now, and suddenly I am aware for the first time of something else that is distressing me.

This is a spirit trying to get to earth. What if it's the spirit of my brother who died in an airplane crash in 1982? No, it can't be. How can we know? But what if it is? How can I kill it? How can I be so selfish?

I hear Joan talking about letting go of the fetus. "Embrace it and be with it, and then release it. It may not be time for this spirit to enter the earth. It will come back when the time is right."

I sob and melt into feeling. I am with my baby, experiencing loss, and saying good-bye. I forgive myself for the decision I have made.

Later Joan writes that she remembers "watching Alice soften her mind and body's resistance and struggle as she relaxed into the pure feelings of grief for an entity/organism that was physically indefinable, yet undeniably present to her. She went from conceptual linear mind into what I perceived as intuitive, right-brain 'knowing' beyond reason."

Thankful to have experienced realities other than the cognitive realm in which so much of my life is lived, I am reminded also of the mythical construction of my own reality, where work and independence reign. I feel released now to continue with the abortion.

(PAUSE)

(TED TURNS TOWARD AUDIENCE AND THEN TOWARD ALICE;
ALICE FACES AUDIENCE)

Ted: All of a sudden I see abortion everywhere. Passing a newspaper stand, the headlines shout: "A Chain of Tears: A Doctor and Abortion."[1]

I take the paper home and read: "It is a five-minute medical procedure that has become a battle of extremes. . . ." The caption, "Abortion has been good to me," leads me to believe the article will be affirming and therapeutic, that it will further alleviate any lingering and unspoken doubts about the moral decision we have reached and any remaining fears about the severity of the medical procedure. I read aloud to Alice:

"A woman who is pregnant. A room beyond the protesters' reach. And a doctor."

"On this day, at a clinic in Houston, the doctor is Robert Crist. To the woman on the examining table, he is a stranger. Just as mysterious to her is the procedure she is about to undergo. But to Crist, who has been performing abortions since 1968, it is routine."

"You're going to feel a pinch and a cramp," he says, just before beginning. The woman, who is ten weeks pregnant, stares at the ceiling. The pinch, which is an injection of anesthesia, comes and goes. The cramp begins to swell.

"OK, you're going to hear the machine."

"Now the woman's eyes close. A low rumble fills the room as the suction machine comes on and the embryo is vacuumed from the uterus. The vacuuming lasts less than a minute."

"Then: 'All done.' "

Totally unprepared for what is to follow, I continue at the top of the next column.

"And that's it. In all, four minutes have gone by. The woman opens her eyes and stares again at the ceiling as Crist examines what he has removed."

Ted: I see the words on the page and hesitate to continue. A rush of emotion bursts through my cool facade as I stammer to get the words I am reading out. "He sees a hand. He sees a foot. He sees the tissue of the head."

(ALICE TURNS AWAY)

Ted: Immediately, with no forewarning, my emotional shield is shattered. I am overcome with grief and sorrow. My pain is expressed in a loud and tormented groan. "Oh, god," I scream. The pain feels unbearable. Help me. Somebody, please help me, I think. I can't bear the horror. I can't hide from the images of hands, and feet, and a head. The grief is overwhelming. I have tried to bury the moral dimension of our tragic decision, to conceal it by echoing platitudes about choice and acting deferent to Alice's rights, as if I could escape any moral responsibility of my own. The burden of my denial is heavy. I now stand face-to-face with the terrifying reality of our decision. We are going to end a life before it can begin. These parts we call a body will never become a person. I have been walking around as if the pain were not there, as if I could pass through this experience without suffering any emotional loss or self-contempt. Now, without warning, I cannot control the pain of my loss, the fear of committing a diabolical act, the panic of losing control. I feel the tears streaming down my face.

(ALICE TURNS TOWARD TED)

Ted: Alice is crying too. We clutch each other tightly, but do not speak. I cannot express what I am feeling. Words fail me. The pain is unsharable. Now that I have felt the pain, I want it to go away. I am breathless and tired. My muscles ache. We go to sleep for several hours. When I awaken, my pain is under control. I cannot bring myself to finish the newspaper article.

(TED TURNS AWAY; ALICE FACES AUDIENCE)

Alice: The image of killing a baby with hands and feet breaks through the boundaries of my decision. And, while I know I am not going to change my mind, I'm tormented by what we are about to do. For the first time, I experience the depth of Ted's agony along with my own as I hold him close and feel the physical wholeness of our sobs take us over. Soon, my emotional agony and my fear that he will try to change my mind lead me to say,

(ALICE AND TED TURN TOWARD EACH OTHER)

"They're talking about ten-week abortions, not six-week ones."

Ted: "Yeah, you're right."

(PAUSE)

(TED TURNS TOWARD AUDIENCE; ALICE TURNS AWAY)

Ted: Jeanie has been emotionally supportive of Alice and comes to visit prior to the preabortion procedure. When she sees me, we embrace. She hugs me affectionately, kissing me on the lips. "I appreciate," she says, "how supportive you are of Alice and how helpful you have been." She says this as if she had not expected me to be this way.

I have an ambivalent reaction to Jeanie's physical and verbal messages. Her affection is sympathetic and benevolent, what I would expect from a close friend. It feels genuine and I like it. At the same time, however, I feel some resentment. She has not asked me how I feel about the abortion; she does not sense that I am suffering a loss of my own, connected to but also independent from Alice's loss. I am not comforted by the realization that Jeanie's affection toward me is based entirely on my actions toward Alice.

Jeanie experiences this episode differently, as she writes later in a response to Alice: "I was at your house one day and Ted was there, and I gave him a big hug and said that I knew he needed support too, and he was very receptive. I was glad that he was being so there for you, and glad that he was also willing to 'let me in,' which helped strengthen my feelings of bondedness with the two of you as a couple."

(PAUSE)

(ALICE TURNS TOWARD AUDIENCE; TED TURNS AWAY)

"What's wrong?" a female colleague asks the day of the preabortion procedure.

Alice: "I'm pregnant and going to have an abortion," I confide.

"I've had five," she responds.

"Holy shit," I say, irreverently. "You must be fertile." I think, but do not say, that she must not know much about birth control. From then on, I am amazed that almost every time I talk about my abortion, there is a woman present who talks about hers.

Scene 4: The Preabortion Procedure

(ALICE TURNS AWAY; TED FACES AUDIENCE)

Ted: The clinic is a large, attractive building, clean and polished. It gives no appearance of a place where dreams have been shattered. There are no marching protesters screaming bloody murder, no placards depicting abortionists as scumbags, no guards to protect the building from bombs or from vandalism by antiabortionists. This is a place where abortions are the exception, not the rule. I feel conspicuous among the other 15 patients here. All are women. Pictures of babies and children line the walls and literature about childbirth and child care are on the tables. I feel hatred and disdain from the others in the room. They must know why I'm here.

I want to share this experience with Alice. I need to suffer some of the pain and humiliation of witnessing the consequences of our decision firsthand. Pro-choice is no longer a political ideal or theoretical abstraction. I cannot accept the notion that Alice's disclosure of her experience of the abortion to me will be the extent of my experience. I don't want a concept, an image, or a fantasy. I want to experience for myself what we are doing, what it feels like, and what it means. I already have a mental image of what is going to happen. Unless I am physically present, this experience will always remain disembodied.

(ALICE TURNS TOWARD TED)

"Remember I want to be with you," I say to Alice when she goes back for the blood test.

(TED TURNS AWAY; ALICE FACES AUDIENCE)

"Is this for a pregnancy termination?" the nurse asks.

Alice: "Yes," I respond. Um . . . Pregnancy termination. I like that phrase. It seems value neutral, while abortion seems so judgmental. From then on, I have that descriptor to use on insurance forms and for talking to other doctors and receptionists.

"We'll need $350 in cash," states the nurse.

"I know, they told me, several times. Do you get cash for your other procedures?"

"No, just this one."

"Is this because people are often in distress when they want an abortion and you're afraid they won't be able to pay?"

"It's just the way we've always done it."

"It feels strange," I say as I count out the money. The visions of illegality, coat hangers in back alleys, and sin loom large.

(ALICE AND TED FACE AUDIENCE)

Ted: I have had to fight to be with Alice. Now I hold her arms as she lies back on the examining table. She spreads her legs, placing her feet in the stirrups. The doctor tells her that he is going to insert seaweed to dilate her cervix overnight. "You will feel a little pain, like a cramp, but it shouldn't last long," he says.

Suddenly, I am aware of the importance of the frame of this interactive encounter. I am holding the hand of the woman I love while another man—a stranger to me—prepares to enter her vagina. I will not stop him. Indeed, I am expected to thank him. How absurd. He's going to hurt her physically. We will not call it abusive. Indeed, we are paying him to do it. She's a patient, not a victim; he's a doctor, not an oppressor. This is medical, not sexual. We are pro-choice and this is the choice we have made. It's time to feel the terrifying constraints of our choice.

On the way home, we drive through a torrential rainstorm. The roads are flooded and the driving is hazardous. While I concentrate on driving, Alice vomits in the car.

Scene 5: The Abortion

(ALICE AND TED FACE AUDIENCE)

Alice: "But we want him with me," I say to the nurse, repeating the same scene as the day before. When Ted insists, I am encouraged, and grab his hand defiantly as we walk to the room located in the very back of the building.

"You have to rest and be quiet. It's important," the nurse says, defeated.

Alice: "We will. We won't talk," I respond. Finally, she shrugs her shoulders and says to Ted, "You'll have to leave when the doctor arrives."

Another nurse comes to give me a shot of Demerol. "Now you must rest. No talking," she instructs, and turns off the lights. Soft music plays.

Ted sits beside me and I hold his hand in my cupped hands near my pregnant belly.

Ted: "I guess this is it. The end is near," and then we don't talk. I put my head down on the examining table near Alice's breast and close my eyes.

Alice: "Yes, it's time to say good-bye."

Ted: Tears well as I feel sadness overcome me. I feel momentarily like I am drowning and cannot breathe. I become weary and drift into a druglike slumber.

Alice: It is a wonderful 20 minutes. Relaxed from the drugs, I am ready for what is about to happen. I let my mind wander and feel connected to Ted. This is not the time to be alone, for either of us.

Ted: Suddenly, I am aroused from my slumber by the sound of other voices approaching. I open my eyes and see the lights above us come on. The medical procedure that will terminate this pregnancy is ready to begin. The doctor motions me to stand behind Alice, who places her hands above her head so I can reach and hold them. From above her, the position of her legs and arms looks unusually symmetrical.

Alice: The doctor puts on his gloves, moves the light over to the table, and asks me if I am relaxed.

"Yes," I say. Ted moves behind me. We lock hands to wrists. When the doctor says nothing, I realize that he will let Ted stay. I hope Ted will be OK and that he won't be able to see the blood and tissue.

"I am removing the laminary now," the doctor says. My cervix feels strange, open for the first time ever. "I am numbing your cervix now," I hear the doctor say. "You'll feel a little pinch." I'm scared of the pain and hope this means there won't be any. I feel the pinch.

Ted: The action speeds up rapidly. The assistant hands the doctor an instrument that I can't see but I assume is a pair of forceps. He reminds Alice that she is going to feel a pinch and perhaps a cramp. Alice is prepared for the worst. After yesterday, I think she expects it. From my angle, I cannot see what he is doing, but I know from Alice's reaction when he has reached inside her. She begins to moan and groan and move her upper body. He tells her to breathe. She squeezes my hand tighter as the intensity of her pain mounts, and her groans become progressively louder. The sounds in the room are chaotic and intense now. He tells her to hold on just a little longer. "It's almost over," he encourages.

Ted: Suddenly I hear the rumble of the suction machine and I feel a vibration pass through Alice's body as the machine extracts the last remnants of the fetus. I see the blood and am repulsed by the horror of this crude technological achievement. I want to look away, but I can't. I am face-to-face with the terror of creation and destruction. Alice has a firm hold on my hands. I cannot turn away. She cannot escape the physical pain; I cannot feel it. I cannot evade the horror of what I see in front of me; she cannot witness it. My ears are ringing from the frenzied sound created by the simultaneous talking and screaming and rumbling that is engulfing the room. The action is fast and furious. Alice's ferocious cries submerge the sound of the machine. "Hold on, baby," I say. I clutch her hands as tight as I can. Her breathing intensifies, growing louder and louder. "Oh, god," she screams. "Oh, my god." Ironically, her cries and screams echo the sounds of orgasmic pleasure she released the afternoon this fetus was created.

Alice: The suction machine is turned on. I tighten my grip on Ted's wrists, he tightens his. I feel excruciating pain. I moan and scream. Everything speeds up. The nurse yells, "Deep breaths. Deep breaths." I try to, but the screams get in the way. Ted's face is now right next to mine. I hear his voice, sense his encouragement. I don't know what Ted is saying, but I'm glad he's here. There is confusion. I hear the suctioning noise, and then they're pulling out my whole uterus. I bear down, my nails sink into Ted's wrists. Then I am in the pain, going round and round like in a tangled sheet. I feel *it* being sucked out of my vagina. My god I can't stand the pain. I hear gut-wrenching screams. Then the doctor's voice, "Five more seconds, just five more seconds, that's all." I am comforted and know that I can stand anything for five seconds. I feel I am with friends. The nurse continues yelling, "Breathe. Breathe." And I try as hard as I can to breathe as I imagine one should when having a baby. Ted is encouraging, gripping. Then I feel another cutting as the doctor does a D and C to make sure nothing was missed. The pain takes over my full consciousness.

Ted: Then, abruptly, with no forewarning, the machine is turned off. Alice lies still, out of breath, quiet. The doctor's assistant whisks away the tray of remains covered by a bloody towel.

Alice: Then quiet. The machine is turned off. "That's all," the doctor says. A nurse puts a pad between my legs and I have visions of blood gushing from my angry uterus. Ted's grip eases. I relax, but the leftover pain continues to reverberate through my body.

Alice: This is going to be awful, I think. I am spent—emotionally, physically, spiritually. I moan and my body reflexes into the fetal position, just as the nurse says, "bend your knees, it'll feel better." And it does. Now I need to protect myself from feeling and from these people who know. I feel sinful, unclean, totally done in, helpless. I have no dignity. Is it then, when the pain eases, or later, upon reflection, that I feel my womanhood has been jerked out of my body? And I have been raped—gang raped—at the same time for my sins. Held down by a person I love, raped by the doctor, who was encouraged by the nurse. Go get her, she deserves it, a just punishment for a baby killer.

The doctor comes back in. "I'm sorry we had to hurt you," he says tenderly, looking me in the eye.

I am thankful for the human contact, the kindness. "Thank you, thank you so much," I say, and I am thanking him as much for treating me like a human being as for having performed the abortion.

I am stripped at the moment of all my status, position, and prestige. I am a nobody, the word *sinner* comes to mind. Perhaps I have not cast off the demons of my moral Christian upbringing. Perhaps the right-to-life ideology has infiltrated my soul.

And then it is just Ted and me. "A wet cloth," I moan, "for my head." I am sweating, dopey. I feel I have no right to ask for anything. Ted hurries to get the cloth, seems glad to be able to do something for me. He still cares, even though I killed our baby. I am relieved. Then I realize through the fog that we did it together. But it was of my body, and I have internalized the sexism that makes me feel more responsible.

Almost instantly, the physical pain disappears.

Ted: There is silence again. It is quiet. The calm after the storm. The abortion is over; only the memory remains.

Alice: When my body is hit by the sunshine, I feel free, released. It's over. My relief makes me feel I have done the right thing. I have no regrets, only guilt. Thank god for pro-choice. Life can now return to normal. Normal?? What does this mean for my relationship with Ted? It's hard to imagine ever wanting to have sex again. But I can't wait to be cuddled in his arms, and feel safe.

Epilogue

> It is because we all live out narratives in our lives and because we understand our own lives in terms of the narratives that we live out that the form of narrative is appropriate for understanding the actions of others. Stories are lived before they are told—except in the case of fiction. (MacIntyre 1984, p. 212)

This project is an attempt to encourage sociologists to recover what Jackson (1989, p. 3) refers to as the "lost sense of the immediate, active, ambiguous 'plenum of existence' in which all ideas and intellectual constructions are grounded." Abortion is a subject so steeped in political ideology and moral indignation that its experiential side can be forgotten or neglected. What do real people feel during an abortion crisis? How do they experience the physical and emotional pain? What is their point of reference for knowing how to act? What is it like to live through an experience that potentially places you in a muddle of uncertainty, doubt, contradiction, and ambivalence? In the discourse on abortion, these questions are overshadowed by political and moral considerations, and the lived experiences of the women and men who face these choices play a minor role in pro-choice/pro-life debates (McDonnell 1984).

In the United States, approximately one out of five women of reproductive age has had an abortion (Forrest, Sullivan, and Tietze 1979; Henshaw and O'Reilly 1983). For these women, abortion is not an abstract possibility; it is a concrete reality. Every year, thousands of women face a situation in which they must make a tragic, dilemmatic choice. Confronted with rival and incommensurate claims upon them, these women find themselves immersed in a situation where choosing does not exonerate them from the authority of the claims they spurn. We know little about the details of the emotional and cognitive processes that are associated with living through this experience. The stories that are told are primarily about illegal abortions performed in back rooms or dark alleys, couched in generalities, and disclosed many years after they occurred (Bonavoglia 1991; Messer and May 1989). These confessional tales serve the useful purpose of redefining illegal abortion as a bad deed done *to* rather than *by* unfortunate women (Condit 1990). But they do not allay the anxieties and conflicts associated with abortion. Indeed, the coexistence of numerous contradictory messages—pro-choice and pro-life rhetoric, symbols of illegality embedded within legal practices, political correctness, and moral servitude—only make the choices more confusing and paradoxical (Wasielewski 1990; Zimmerman 1977).

Recognizing that the literature rarely reflects the meanings and feelings embodied by the human side of abortion, we wanted to tell our story in a way that would avoid the risks of dissolving the lived experience in a solution of impersonal concepts and abstract theoretical schemes. We have tried to be faithful to our experience, but we understand that the order and wholeness we have brought to it through the narrative form is different than the disjointed and fragmented sense we had of it while it took place. Perhaps this is the way in which narrative constitutes an active and reflexive form of inquiry. Narratives express the values of the narrators, who also construct, formulate, and remake these values. A personal narrative, then, can be viewed as an "experience of the experience" intended to inquire about its possible meanings and values in a way that rides the active currents of lived experience without fixing them once and for all. Understanding is not embedded in the experience as much as it is achieved through an ongoing and continuous experiencing of the experience.

Rosaldo's (1987) serendipitous understanding of rage in Ilongot headhunting is a classic example in which the death of his wife helped him to frame a new experience of the experience of headhunting. The vignettes of our narrative function in a similar way. They act back on us, emotionally and cognitively, evoking new feelings, ideas, and constructions of our experience. They also are intended to evoke responses from readers or audience members. As one woman who witnessed a performance of our narrative said in a letter: "Narratives unfold with flesh and blood . . . encouraging empathy, identification and a humanization of content" (K. Slobin, personal communication, February 1991). But identification and empathy are not the only reactions or necessarily the most desirable ones. Readers are put in the position of experiencing an experience that can reveal to them not only how it was for us but how it could be or once was for them. They are made aware of similarities and differences between their worlds and ours. It becomes possible for them to see the other in themselves or themselves in the other among other possibilities.

Performing the narrative extends the process of inquiry by introducing another form in which one experiences the experience. Turner (1986, p. 81) has argued that performing narratives and ethnographies is a mode of inquiry that operates reflexively to reveal ourselves to ourselves in two ways: "The actor may come to know himself better through acting or enactment; or one set of human beings may come to know themselves better through observing and/or participating in performances generated and presented by another human being." As narrators and performers of this story, we gained a perspective on our experience and a sense of what it meant that we did not have before. The responses of others to our performance strongly suggest that they have been moved to feel and think about themselves and others in new and important ways and to grasp and feel the ambivalence, confusion, and pain associated with experiences of abortion like ours.

As part of our life history, this story has significance and value for us, but it is also an act of self-presentation. Why should such an intensely personal story be transformed into an intersubjective or public one? It has not been our aim to draw attention to ourselves. Our decision to attach different names to the characters in our story is an attempt to focus on the experience instead of the particular persons in it. Many aspects of what occurred seemed unique initially, but we have become convinced by the stories others have shared with us that our narrative may be only a replaying of events experienced by many other people. As Abraham (1986, p. 49) says, "Experiences happen to individuals and therefore sometimes are to be regarded as idiosyncratic; but these very same occurrences might, under other circumstances, be usefully regarded as typical." No doubt, other persons who have faced abortion have felt the sense of not knowing how to feel about or interpret what was happening to them. Others surely have been as bruised as we were by the contradictions and ambivalence associated with the constraints of choice. The absence of personal narratives to detail the emotional complexities and ambivalence often attributed generally to abortion (Francke 1978; Petchesky 1990; Wasielewski 1990) may be only the result of people feeling forced to accept these blows of fate passively or being subjected to taboos against expressing these disturbing feelings openly. Because abortion may still be deemed immoral (Zimmerman 1977), it can become nearly impossible to find the words to talk about what happened. Making public and vivid some of the intricate details of abortion may break the barriers that shield public awareness and prevent marginalized voices of both women and men from being heard (Black 1982; Langellier 1989).

"Lived experience," writes anthropologist Michael Jackson (1989, p. 2), "accommodates our shifting sense of ourselves as subjects and as objects, as acting upon and being acted upon by the world, of living with and without certainty, of belonging and being estranged." In the spirit of postmodern ethnography (Tyler 1986), then, we offer this work as an experiment in formulating narrative as a mode of inquiry that should be judged not so much against the standards and practices of science as against the practical, emotional, and aesthetic demands of life (Jackson 1989).

Note

1. From " 'A Chain of Tears': A Doctor and Abortion," from the *St. Petersburg Times,* Sunday, June 3, 1990, by David Finkel; used by permission.

References

Abraham, R. 1986. "Ordinary and Extraordinary Experience." Pp. 45-72 in *The Anthropology of Experience,* edited by V. Turner and E. Bruner. Urbana: University of Illinois Press.

Becker, H., M. McCall, and L. Morris. 1989. "Theatres and Communities: Three Scenes." *Social Problems* 36:93-116.

Black, P. 1982. "Abortion Affects Men Too." *New York Times Magazine,* March 28, pp. 76-94.

Bochner, A. and C. Ellis. 1992. "Personal Narrative as a Social Approach to Interpersonal Communication." *Communication Theory.* Vol. 2 (in press).

Bonavoglia, A. 1991. *The Choices We Made: Twenty-Five Women and Men Speak Out About Abortion.* New York: Random House.

Condit, C. M. 1990. *Decoding Abortion Rhetoric: Communicating Social Change.* Urbana: University of Illinois Press.

Conquergood, D. 1990. "Rethinking Ethnography: Cultural Politics and Rhetorical Strategies." Paper presented at the Temple Conference on Discourse Analysis, Temple University.

Denzin, N. 1988. *Interpretive Interactionism.* Newbury Park, CA: Sage.

Ellis, C. 1991a. "Sociological Introspection and Emotional Experience." *Symbolic Interaction* 14:23-50.

———1991b. "Emotional Sociology." Pp. 123-145 in *Studies in Symbolic Interaction.* Vol. 12, edited by N. Denzin. Greenwich, CT: JAI.

Forrest, J. D., E. Sullivan, and C. Tietze. 1979. "Abortion in the United States." *Family Planning Perspectives* 11:329-41.

Francke, L. 1978. *The Ambivalence of Abortion.* New York: Random House.

Geertz, C. 1983. *Local Knowledge: Further Essays in Interpretive Anthropology.* New York: Basic Books.

Henshaw, S. and K. O'Reilly. 1983. "Characteristics of Abortion Patients in the United States, 1979 and 1980." *Family Planning Perspectives* 15:5-16.

Jackson, M. 1989. *Paths Toward a Clearing: Radical Empiricism and Ethnographic Inquiry.* Bloomington: Indiana University Press.

Krieger, S. 1984. "Fiction and Social Science." Pp. 269-86 in *Studies in Symbolic Interaction.* Vol. 5, edited by N. Denzin. Greenwich, CT: JAI.

Langellier, K. 1989. "Personal Narrative: Perspectives on Theory and Research." *Text and Performance Quarterly* 9:243-76.

MacIntyre, A. 1984. *After Virtue: A Study in Moral Theory.* Notre Dame: University of Indiana Press.

McCall, M. 1991. "The Significance of Storytelling." In *Studies in Symbolic Interaction.* Vol. 11, edited by N. Denzin. Greenwich, CT: JAI.

McDonnell, K. 1984. *Not an Easy Choice: A Feminist Re-examines Abortion.* Boston: South End.

Messer, E. and K. May. 1989. *Back Rooms: An Oral History of the Illegal Abortion Era.* New York: Simon & Schuster.

Paget, Marianne. 1990. "Performing the Text." *Journal of Contemporary Ethnography* 19:136-55.

Petchesky, R. 1990. *Abortion and Woman's Choice: The State, Sexuality, and Reproductive Freedom.* Boston: Northeastern University Press.

Rosaldo, R. 1987. *Culture and Truth: The Remaking of Social Analysis.* Boston: Beacon.

Scarry, E. 1985. *The Body in Pain: The Making and Unmaking of the World.* New York: Oxford University Press.

Turner, V. 1986. *The Anthropology of Performance.* New York: PAJ.

Tyler, S. 1986. "Post-Modern Ethnography: From Document of the Occult to Occult Document." Pp. 122-40 in *Writing Culture: The Poetics and Politics of Ethnography*, edited by J. Clifford and G. Marcus. Berkeley: University of California Press.

Wasielewski, P. 1990. "Post Abortion Syndrome: Emotional Battles Over Interaction and Ideology." Unpublished paper.

Zimmerman, M. 1977. *Passage Through Abortion: The Personal and Social Reality of Women's Experiences.* New York: Praeger.

5

The Reflexive Self Through Narrative

A Night in the Life of an
Erotic Dancer/Researcher

CAROL RAMBO RONAI

Listen to my voice; it is a blend of many voices. I am a graduate student, a wife, a daughter, an erotic dancer, a friend; the quantity of potential identities extend into infinity . . .

* * *

Let these three asterisks denote a shift to a different temporal/spatial/ attitudinal realm.

* * *

In this chapter, I examine lived emotional experience. I demonstrate the difficulty in extricating a researcher self from other selves while involved in participant observation, and I convey to readers the conflicts in assuming the identity of an erotic dancer. The perspective of "emotional sociology" and

AUTHOR'S NOTE: Special thanks to the editors of this volume and my husband Jack Ronai. I would also like to thank Danny Jorgensen and Hernan Vera for their comments on former drafts of this chapter.

the technique of "systematic introspection" assist in achieving these goals. Ellis (1991b, p. 126) refers to emotional sociology as "consciously and reflectively feeling for our selves, our subjects, and our topics of study, and evoking those feelings in our readers." Dilthey (quoted in Hodges 1944, p. 122) similarly discusses a "transference of the subject's own self into a given complex of expressions." Out of this transference "arises the highest form in which the totality of mental life can operate in understanding—that of reproducing or reliving." Like Dilthey, Weber's (1962, p. 36) "verstehen" is an explanatory, interpretive understanding of behavior based on "a grasp of the context of meaning within which the actual course of behavior arises."

Ellis (1991a, 1991b) calls for the use of one's own emotional experience as a legitimate object of sociological research to be described, examined, and theorized. In this perspective, focus on researchers and their feelings during research situations in the field is of particular interest. Because researchers have fluctuating levels of absorption and emotional involvement in their work on any given project, this view offers significant insight into how various participants in settings might be emotionally experiencing their social worlds.

Finally, Ellis (1991a, 1991b) encourages sociologists to use "emotional narratives" written from a biographically subjective point of view for evidence on how emotions are experienced within the context of everyday life. One may produce one's own narratives by consulting one's experience and/or examining other narratives. Using these as data to theorize and abstract from, one produces an emotional sociology that describes, interprets, and embodies lived emotional experience.

The following is an introspective narrative that examines my emotional experience while rejoining the strip bar setting as a dancer/researcher and the lived experience of writing about it. Introspection is conscious awareness of itself, a social process of self-examination involving conversation with oneself. "It is active thinking about one's thoughts and feelings; it emerges from social interaction" (Ellis 1991a, p. 28). In my narrative, I use multiple layers of reflection—a layered account—shifting forward, backward, and sideways through time, space, and various attitudes in a narrative format.

As an undergraduate, I danced to finance my bachelor's degree. In 1987, I danced again to gather data for my master's thesis. During that time, I used participant observation techniques, systematic self-introspection, and interactive introspection. As a participant observer, I observed the behavior of others, recorded conversations, and described the setting and interactions among participants using systematic introspection, and I focused on and recorded my thoughts and feelings while dancing. Interactive introspection involves working back and forth with others to produce emergent experiences that can be examined. During the study, I interacted with two professors for the purpose of producing these circumstances.

The data presented here come from field notes I took during and after my experience of dancing. They blend events from several nights into a typical "night in the life of a dancer." The participant observer role is never clearly separated from that of being a dancer, a wife, or the other roles I enact. These materials will give the reader a perspective on becoming a dancer/researcher, writing about the experience, and the impact of multiple identities on my "self" as a participant observer. It is my hope that readers will live their own experience while reading about mine and have an understanding of my lived experience as a result.

*   *   *

God dammit! Another rewrite. The amber letters on my computer screen have engraved themselves on my eyeballs. Every time I look away from the terminal, yellow-brown letters float with me in space. Is this the "real" lived experience, my typing this right now, this very second? This is silly. I reflect and start typing, and the reflection is already replaced by the typing experience.

Childlike, I regress into endless digression, a snake chasing my own tail and swallowing it until I finally disappear into absurdity. This prose dually articulates my opinion of my ability to capture the lived experience as well as stalling on the rewrite. When one describes one's experience, the text is always transformed by the telling of it; clearly demarcated, linear story lines cannot be used to convey lived experience. Instead, the telling of it is a circular process of interpretation that blurs and intertwines both cognitive and emotional understandings (Denzin 1984). The writing style I use here—the layered account—is designed to convey the blurred and intertwined quality that writing about the lived experience of dancing entails.

*   *   *

According to one editor, I'm having a problem with my "voice." She tells me it is not clear who is speaking at various points in the text I have produced. I need to clarify when the dancer is speaking and when the researcher is speaking. Here's the problem. My voice is cracking as I write this. My identity is fracturing as I spill my guts while trying to produce in my audience an emotional knowing of my experience as a dancer/researcher. I cannot smoothly switch hats and write, "Here is how the dancer in me feels, and

here is how the researcher feels, and here is how the wife feels, and so on."
It is dishonest and contrived to sort out separate influences and label them,
though occasionally one voice will speak loudly and clearly. My perception
of my "self" incorporates influences from these roles, but the end result is
not compartmentalized around them. The self produced in this text is emergent from the interaction of those roles.

*   *   *

My night (nightmare?) starts when I pull into the parking lot of the strip
bar. Exiting the car, I step out of my mind and into a surreal horror flick, my
black spike-heeled shoes awkwardly clacking their echo across the parking
lot pavement toward the strip bar entrance. Already, I'm assaulted by the
roaming eyes of drunk patrons as they exit the bar. "Hey, baby, are you the
show tonight?" one yells at me as I pass by.

I cringe. I'm not into this. I hate that I'm already perceived as a dancer,
and treated accordingly, even before I get into the bar. I put on a cardboard
smile. "Ain't we all the show here," I respond, more as a statement than a
question. He laughs. The moron doesn't even know I'm implying that he's
as much a part of this freak show as I am. For a moment, I hate him for being
what he is, for facilitating the existence of this place. I next turn the hate in
on myself, the hypocrite. How easily I judge these characters when I'm
here too.

Next, I try to rationalize away my emotional outburst. I'm here for research
purposes; I'm not trapped by this but here voluntarily, I say to myself. I get
off on the idea that I have enough guts not only to dance topless but to share
the experience with others. For most people, this event would be a dark
hidden secret, better left that way. It is in my self-concept that I'm tough,
less influenced by what people think of me than the average person. I dare
anyone to disparage me personally for having been a dancer.

Reacting to the characters in this setting cheapens me, whittles away at
my resolve, demonstrates that in fact I'm not totally shielded from their
opinions. I must straighten up my attitude, be objective, realize that they are
acting in the only way they know, and be above reacting emotionally to their
actions toward myself or other women in the bar.

Regardless of my cognitive desire to be the intrepid sociologist, braving
new frontiers, going where most women dare not tread, my dread of the
coming night imposes its presence on my reality in the form of a tightness
in my chest that constricts my breathing. The tightness is paralysis. My heart
rebels, beating a mad tempo against the constraints of my thoracic cavity.

I imagine the pulse forcing the vasoconstriction to loosen up and dilate with the rush of blood. This sudden looseness is perceived as butterflies in my gut and I am nauseated, afraid I will throw up on the spot. I'm so scared, I almost cry.

My efforts at control barely succeed. The criterion for success is to put one foot in front of the other until I hit the front door. Stark terror lurks below the surface, waiting for a weak millisecond to attack and take hold again. I want to hide and cry and run away, in no particular rational order. I extract a sadomasochistic delight from the image of fleeing the bar, defeated by my fear, into reassuring (male?) arms. "Now don't you know better than to try and go into a place like that?" my fantasy male chides me, asserting his mastery over me and my situation even as he offers salvation and comfort.

Get a grip, damn it, it's only a fucking bar, I mentally slap myself, finding my desire for dependence both attractive and repulsive. I get a charge of machismic satisfaction from not giving in to these emotions. To divert my attention, I again seek my enthusiasm for my research, but it's not there. The closer I get to the door, the more I don't want to dance.

*   *   *

My body always knew better than my mind how much I hated dancing. Every "first" night at a new bar produced hives on my face and/or swollen eyes and lips. After dancing for a week, I inevitably ended up with the flu. Often I quit dancing when I had been sick for a while. Once I quit, recovery was around the corner. I can rationalize all I want but something inside me controlling the show hates doing this. I should probably listen to it, shut it up, or integrate it.

*   *   *

If I am quiet and do not distract myself with the inane details of living life; if I just listen, but not for words; if I just let go and feel for a second, then there is a tightly wound, densely compressed emotion that wants to leap out of my chest—bypassing my mouth and my brain—and scream.

*   *   *

Bury it. I can't listen to that and get anything done. My self is torn into little pieces that must be reassembled into a self that will survive the night. I am Carol, researcher, and wife, yet I am also Sabrina (my stage name), cock-tease, and hustler. My master's thesis topic is tough to legitimate to myself and others. This world I desperately want to understand assaults my reality system and my identity. The roles—dancer, wife, and researcher—often clash with one another. Things become muddled when I try to explain why I am willing to disrobe in front of strange men in the name of research. What is it with me that I am able to do this when others in my culture find the concept untenable? Good wives certainly don't do this to their husbands. Or am I in fact just another dancer with a good line of bullshit, playing the marks?

The self who is all of this is a processual dialectic, emergent from the interaction of all the demands that society places on individuals acting in their social worlds (Blumer 1969). I supposedly have a self that is a whole, neatly divided up into parts or facets that act to fulfill the tasks of particular roles. But, in reality, each facet exists only because my culture demands I frame each separately from the others regardless of the clashes and overlaps that result from the demands of the roles. The self exists as a process in a constant state of transformation and flux; it is the dialogue between the facets. There are no hard and fast answers to what the situation "really is." The answer changes as quickly as I can reflect on it because the situation is constantly in motion. Self is fleeting.

I am frightened. I have total responsibility for what is happening. Sabrina is not a separate self, nor some kind of alternate identity to be blamed, like one of the faces of Eve, but is a culmination of all my dark potential. There is no safely isolating this, cordoning it off from the rest of my identity. Having been/being a dancer is part of what I am. The need to understand these processes compels me finally to open the door.

* * *

I often feel like I'm not a "real" dancer. I use the line "I am going to school" to legitimate my dancing to myself and others and to provide a disclaimer as to why I am there. This backfires sometimes, as I seem to have a talent for getting into trouble with other dancers and customers. One customer, trying to get revenge on me for not giving him a hand job, told two dancers that I said I had more class than they did because I attended college. For the rest of the night, the dancers shoved me around whenever they could get me alone, and said things like, "You don't have to go to class to have class, bitch," and "What have 'you' got stuck so far up 'your' ass!"

One dancer took me aside and asked what I said to the customer. Upon hearing about my refusal to deliver on the hand job, and discussing with her the aforementioned general character of what I tell customers about why I'm in the bar, she told me, "You know, I bet none of us feel like we are 'really' dancers, at least I don't. I'm just doing this for my kids."

Another spoke up, "I've got steep car payments."

And another said, "I want to get enough money together so that I can get my kids back with me again. Their dad got custody because I'm broke." Perhaps believing that you are not really a dancer is part of being a dancer. Maybe I am a "real" dancer after all.

*   *   *

Tobacco smoke and loud music belch from the orifice that is the bar's entrance. The red inner walls are coated with a dank brown nicotine sheen that glistens when the outside lights hit it just so. Inside the tunnel-like hallway, the place is filthy. Trace odors of alcoholic-vomit breath, sweat, feminine musk, and stale smoke sour my stomach. In combination, these qualities inescapably suggest entering a cold, rank, infected womb. This kind of thinking is not productive so I shut down my thoughts to steel myself against the onslaught of confusing stimuli. The dark innards of the bar together with the loud music and colored lights generally leave me disoriented and unable to see for about 45 seconds. The cumulative effect of entering the bar is that of crossing the boundaries of "the real world" to enter a more ethereal, alternate reality.

Sure enough, I step behind and startle two guys waiting for their eyes to adjust before they start navigating the bar's floor plan. They quickly part to let me pass, then follow me to the front desk, where they are left, leaderless, to fend for themselves. They are not regulars; regulars would not be so passive. The bouncer informs me that I am sixth on stage, following a girl named Sunshine.

I negotiate my way to the dressing room, saying hello to a familiar customer who promises to buy me a drink. I swing my hips in a wide rapid arch to barely avoid the groping hands of a man who swears, "I have died and gone to heaven. Momma you're built! Come to me baybeee!"

The tone of his drunken whine pisses me off. I put a smile on my face to disguise my wrath. As if acting the coquette, I smack his hands as hard as I can and whine, "Get a life, baybeee," mocking his tone back to him.

"You're a feisty little cunt, aren't you baybee," he yells, laughing, as I pass him.

A whisper in my head tells me, You needn't have said anything to him; you just escalated the situation. Why did you strike out at him like that?

Another voice answers: His weakness is disgusting. If he has to paw people and whine like that he deserves what he gets. Fuck him.

For god's sake, can't you be a little more above it than that? Besides, what he said was the first hurt of the night. It's so early in the night for hurt feelings or for a bad attitude.

The badder, the better, I think to myself, annoyed with this wimpy voice so easily upset by some silly ass calling me a cunt. I fake a sardonic laugh to myself at the childish exchange of body part names and move on to the dressing room.

Having never met Sunshine, the dancer I follow on stage, I ask around in the dressing room to see who she is. After a bit, a woman in front of the mirror with a butchered haircut and attitude speaks up. "Yeah me, I'm Sunshine. What of it?" Damn, I think to myself, I'm not up to a showdown this early in the evening.

Rapidly, I reply, "I needed to see you so I'd know who to follow on stage."

With an upward stroke, she traces her lower eye lid in an obnoxiously thick black line, while watching me in the mirror. To my relief, she smiles and says, "You scared me. I don't need to be in trouble with management already."

Now I understand her aggressive attitude. She is new. Jocularly, I return with, "Yeah, you're fined a hundred bucks, hand it over." We laugh and the tension eases out of my body. I'm grateful I'm not going to have to fight. Sunshine holds out her hand, and I shake it. Her dry palms and abrupt gestures during the handshake reflect her brusque defensiveness. I decide I like her.

The dressing room is deceptively cheery, lit with bright fluorescent bulbs and feminine chatter. At shift change, about 30 women must cooperate with one another to change clothes in a space designed to hold 10. Tempers flare around the dressing room as half-dressed women step over each other and bags of costumes and makeup to reach differing destinations such as the mirror, locker, electrical outlet, sink, or toilet. Conversation is generally about men, money, or who is feuding with whom these days.

I try to make my space as small as possible, doing all my changing in front of my locker. To save time, I put on makeup and style my hair before I leave home. I'm privately smug that I get ready faster than everyone else and am generally one of the first dancers to "hit the floor." Sometimes, though, I extend my stay in the dressing room to eavesdrop on a good conversation. Tonight, however, my nerve is shot; the man who called me a cunt got to me. I don't feel as cocksure as I need to in order to "be a dancer." Like being thrown from a horse, I have to get out on the floor as soon as possible or else I will have a bad attitude for the rest of the night.

*   *   *

When a dancer has a bad attitude, she is failing to act out the role of "dancer" because she has failed to control her outward display of emotion. Like the airline attendants in Arlie Hochschild's (1983) work on the commercialization of emotion, dancers must "work" on their negative emotions so that customers in the bar will feel like they are in a "friendly and convivial setting."

Fear, for instance, inhibits a dancer from contacting customers or dancing well on stage. If a dancer appears frightened, customers are generally turned off. As one informer put it: "I'm not here to scare the girls. I'm here at least for the illusion that they like me. When I see a scared new dancer, I feel like the boogie man."

Another bad attitude is overt belligerence. One manager was discussing an older dancer he claimed was suffering burnout: "I actually watched her hit a customer on the arm, stick out her hand for the money, and tap her foot on the ground like it was just too much trouble to stand there and wait for him to tip her. She walked off and didn't even say thank you when the customer handed it over." The customer complained to the manager and left the bar. In this situation, the dancer was refusing to get into the part of being concerned for her customer. Like airline attendants suffering burnout, this dancer "may refuse to act at all, thus withdrawing her emotional labor altogether. Since the job itself calls for good acting, she will be seen as doing the job poorly" (Hochschild 1983, p. 188). If a dancer comes in the dressing room claiming to have a bad attitude, it is general knowledge that she means she is not making money because she can not force herself to "act" right.

*   *   *

With all the confused emotions I have about dancing, even dancing for my master's degree, I wonder as I write this why I put myself through it if I hate it as much as I claim? Making large amounts of money and getting a great deal of attention are motivations, but they do not get at the heart of the attraction of dancing.

I become something that is other than what my "self" normally is. The environment elicits behavior and attitudes from me that in nondancing everyday life I would not have a chance to experience. My idea of who I think I am shatters in the face of what I become in the bar. Sabrina, the dancer, does not fit with Carol, the student, and wife. I am forced to reevaluate myself and consequently everything around me. It shakes me out of the lethargy of my daily life and stimulates me for a little while.

*   *   *

Exiting the dressing room, I notice a regular customer I neglected the night before because another customer asked me to sit with him first. Deciding to hit on him, I say flirtatiously as I approach his table, "Dick, I'd like to talk with you when you have the time."

"If I'm in the bar later, then maybe," he replies. It is obvious that Dick's feelings are hurt from the night before. Scorned customers are hard to win back. I walk past Dick and seat myself at a nearby table, leaving him the option to join me while not forcing myself on him. After a while, when Dick does not approach me, I walk toward three men sitting in the corner and ask them if they would care for some company. Once Dick sees me "with other men," he leaves the bar. Dick, in my opinion, is too sensitive and too much into the illusion of being wanted by these women. I get angry at his gullibility for a second, then stifle it. I have other things to think about.

One of the three men, a customer in a silk suit, with two gold rings and a Rolex watch, responds to my overture and asks his more casually dressed companions to move over so that I may be seated. He promptly orders a drink for me, asks my name, and introduces himself as Tom. After introducing his friends, Fred and Harry, Tom asserts, "Coming to this bar was Fred's idea. I want to show these guys a good time, and if this is what they want to do, this is what they are going to do."

Silently, I am amused at Tom's condescension toward Fred and Harry. Tom haughtily continues, "A girl like you, can't you do better than a place like this? I could get you a decent job."

"Where?" I ask. "Doing what?"

"I could get you a job at one of the nursing homes I own. You could work in the kitchen or with the patients. Do you have a valid Florida driver's license?" I think to myself, Sir Galahad wants to take me away from "all of this" so that I may respectably scrub the halls of his nursing home.

Annoyed, I tell him, "I appreciate the thought, but I am doing fine." I give him a pitch about how I am working my way through college, so I won't be stuck doing this the rest of my life. He buys it and pontificates for a while about the importance of college.

Later, I ask, "Would you care for a table dance?"

"No," he responds, "I don't go in for that sort of thing. Tell you what though, why don't you do one for Harry?" I am beginning to realize I am not going to make much money off Tom. He is buying plenty of drinks but acts uninterested in anything more than entertaining his friends.

*   *   *

The Table Dance

> Clothed in a bra-like top and full panties or other revealing costume, the dancer
> leaned over a seated patron, her legs inside his, and swayed suggestively in rhythm
> to the music playing in the bar. Theoretically, customers were allowed to touch
> only the hips, waist, back and outside of a dancer's legs. Many men tried and some
> succeeded in doing more. (Ronai and Ellis 1989, pp. 275-76)

$*$ $*$ $*$

During the next song, I stand and dance for Harry, who slides himself all
the way down to the end of the chair so that my leg brushes his crotch. I back
up an inch or two from him and continue to dance, but turn my backside to
him so that I can regain my composure. Harry places his fingers beneath the
elastic leg openings of my panties, attempting to trace an inward path to my
crotch. I reflexively jerk away from the gesture in part because it tickles and
because the idea of him reaching his goal is repulsive. The snap of the elastic
reverberates loud enough against my ass so that his compatriots are aware of
what he is up to. I look to either side of me at both men. They are amused,
grinning ear to ear. For a split second, the thought of hitting them with a
closed fist enters my mind. It would be great to mangle them, to shatter their
jaws, to permanently wipe those asinine smiles off their smug faces. I think
about the potential money, I think about my role as a researcher, I take a deep
breath, and I turn around to face Harry again.

"God, what a body," Harry says. "You stick with ole' Tom over there, he's
loaded. We're in from Chicago, and we have a condo out on Treasure Island.
We would love to have you out to visit. Five hundred dollars for a private
party."

"What do I have to do at this private party for five hundred dollars?" I ask.

"Anything goes baby, anything," is his reply.

I have difficulty keeping Harry's fingers out of my panties. Every time I
turn around to face him, he attempts to put his fingers in my crotch. "Hey,
be cool about that," I say, "I'll get in trouble with my boss."

"Just havin' some fun baby," he replies.

No one is going to sympathize or give a shit about how this guy is treating
me. I asked for this because I picked this job. I knew what I was getting into
when I chose this as my research topic. Why should I expect anything
different? I'm the type of woman who would take this kind of job, so I am
getting what I deserve. It all becomes my fault.

Sometimes, the whole thing strikes me as absurd, and I laugh. Other times I feel like crying. In the past, I have left customers to go cry. This night is new, however, and my strength fresh. I'll get through this dance.

Afterward, Harry says, "Seriously, think about that five hundred dollars, and stick with Tom."

Later, Tom asks me to dance for Fred, and warns, "Fred offended a girl earlier by putting his hands where they don't belong."

Armed for battle, I approach Fred, who says, "I cannot be held responsible for my actions. I am a dirty boy, and I like to have a good time."

I say, "Momma will keep the dirty boy in line." We laugh. I get him to talk dirty to distract his hands from action.

"Tell me about your favorite fuck," I ask, while dancing.

"Oh, I like it all kinds of ways," he replies. "I'd love to get you in the sack." He sticks his tongue out at me and waggles it.

"Bad boy, are you propositioning me?" I ask.

"It's my duty to proposition you, my duty as a red-blooded horny American male."

"You may need to be disciplined, bad boy."

"Oh, please, don't hurt me." We laugh.

"Did you know I can lick my eyebrows?" he says.

"That line is as old as the hills on my grandmother's chest, and older than the line I just fed you," I reply.

"I swear, sweetheart, I may be old, but you are missing out on the best damn fuck you would ever have," he retorts.

I picture fucking this old buzzard and lose control of my face. I have to turn around and dance with my rear near him, so that he can't see my disgust. I get the buzzard image out of my mind, pull my face together, and turn back around.

"Triple O baby," he says, "I bet I could give you a triple orgasm."

I look at his face and, instead of picturing this activity, I watch his bushy eyebrows go up and down and see him as absurd. I think to myself, this rotting carcass of wrinkled flesh is no threat. Just keep your shit together until the dance is over.

"I could fuck the living daylights out of you, if you would only give me the chance to show you," he says, intruding into my thoughts. At this point, I find the distance I need to tolerate his routine. Thinking of him as silly is doing the trick. I'll never have to screw that. Additionally, my routine is working—he hasn't laid a hand on me through the whole dance.

At the end of the dance, he tells me he wants his friend Tom to loosen his tie and relax. "I'm concerned for anyone wound that tight," he says with conviction.

I exclaim, "How nice of you to be concerned. Even perverts have their good side."

"Get moving along and entertain Tom," Fred says, swatting my butt.

Because it is my turn to dance on stage, I leave the trio. My dance is listless, distracted, and uninvolved because there are few men in the bar. Two drunks with puke breath each tip me a dollar. I avoid kissing their stench by rapidly getting up from my kneeling position. They look piqued, but I ignore them. Dealing with all this grossness is starting to take its toll. Anger spawned of helplessness creeps around the fringes of my consciousness, providing a steady backdrop to the evening's mood.

After my main act, I dance on the side stage. One of the men there appears to be retarded, or at least his demeanor seems strange. With glazed blue eyes peering out beneath an enlarged forehead, and a slack, narrow jaw, he takes an unusually long time, clumsily tipping a one dollar bill to the woman on the main stage. At the side stage, he tips me a ten. My first impulse is to tell him he made a mistake, but I say nothing. I think to myself, would the other girls give him back his money? Hell no! Every guy who walks in here is a potential source of money. I would take the money from a drunk, so why not from him? After all, I'm here for the money. Perhaps he even intended to give me the ten because he liked me a lot and wanted to get my attention. Probably not. I keep the tip, not recognizing the significance of how far my researcher role is losing focus in my thoughts.

*   *   *

My decision gnaws at me much of the night. What a fucked-up society. Who lets retards spend their free time in titty bars? He didn't have the ability to know what he was giving me as a tip. I should have given it back. Should we give IQ tests to all the guys who walk in here? Who the hell teaches these people values anyway? Who taught me mine? It is difficult to justify how easily I can change my behavior when I am working as a dancer. Inside the confines of the establishment, I feel free to take their money from them in any manner I can, short of outright theft. Outside, I judge the same acts as wrong. A "real" dancer, though, would take the money. But would a "real" dancer feel bad about it later?

*   *   *

With my stage acts completed, I hang up my dress in the dressing room, put on a push-up bra and panties, make a note to ask some dancers what they would do in the situation with the retarded guy, and return to Tom's table. When he asks me if I will meet him at the Hilton, I get royally pissed and say, "I'm not allowed to date the customers." He gives me a napkin with his home address and telephone number on it. "I'm not allowed to take phone numbers; I am not a prostitute," I state emphatically.

He begs me to see him. "You just have to go out with me. I don't think of you as one of these women. Wouldn't you please consider it?" His slight inebriation lends a weepy quality to his voice, and it is getting on my nerves. I have not made enough money off him to justify putting up with this bullshit. I decide to leave Tom holding his drink.

Merril, the customer I approach next, walks with a limp and a cane. He has long blonde hair braided to his waist, tanned skin, and is short but stocky like an amateur body builder. He says right up front, "Don't worry about me, I'm full of shit." I should have taken him seriously.

"I've been coming to this bar for years, and I've dropped a lot of money in here. I make a lot of money so I don't have to work."

He says he used to be a biker, at one time played in a rock and roll band, and fought in a war.

I ask, "What do you do these days?"

His response is, "I get tan." I ask him if he wants a table dance. He smiles and says, "Here goes the routine."

Once we are seated, he says, "I eat real good pussy. I bet you've got a fine one. I love pussy. I can eat that all day. I knew a chick once who could eat better pussy than me. She was wild."

Trying to tune in to the tone of his bullshit, I ask him, "What do you consider to be the criteria for a fine pussy?"

He looks at me with what I take to be mock shock and says, "Well, now, I didn't expect you to be so nasty."

I say, "You brought it up, now answer the question."

"What the hell?"

"Answer the question for Christ's sake, or do you feel guilty?"

He slams his beer on the counter and says, "I don't feel guilty about nothing. Do you feel guilty about something?"

"No," I state. "I just heard you say something, and I want to know what you meant by it. Hey look, I ain't ever had a woman or nothing, right? I just wanted to make some interesting small talk."

"Well, shit," he declares, "I ain't never had a woman neither."

We both laugh at this. "Man, but I ain't used to women being just as vulgar as me!"

I get into these moods where I love to fuck with these guys, deriving a perverse pleasure from pushing a point entirely too far. I say, "So do you feel guilty for bringing it up? Is that why you won't answer the question?"

"Guilty!" I love it that this is bugging him. "Shit, I don't feel guilty about nothing, woman. I want to eat your goddamn pussy and fuck you, and if you think I'm gonna feel guilty about all of this, you are full of shit." He calms down, turns to me, and says with a sly smile, "Why do you ask questions, do you feel guilty about maybe wanting me to eat your pussy and fuck you?"

"Nope," I say, trying to conceal my shock at how adept he is at turning the bullshit back on me, "Just trying to understand where you are coming from."

"I'm comin' from here," he says as he grabs his crotch. Then he says, "No, I'm serious, you and me, let's get together. Would you play with me? Do you fool around?"

I am intimidated by how quickly the conversation has shifted in his favor; that is, he is now controlling the subject matter. "I'm not going anywhere with you," I say defensively.

"Why not?"

"Do you really expect someone you met in here to go out with you?"

"Get away from me with that bullshit," Merril says, jerking his body away from my side of the table, "Don't hand me that crap."

"You're not being fair," I say. "See this from my point of view. I would be dead by now if I dated every guy who wanted a date from me." The conversation is now in my control again. I'm running one of my regular routines on him. He cannot win in this interaction. The worst I can do at this point is to fail to sell him a dance. But I know he will buy one. How else will he "prove" to me he is an OK guy?

"But you're not considering my side of things," he says.

"What is your side?"

"It's frustrating, 'cause there ain't no way I can get you to go out with me. The only reason you give is that you're chicken. You don't grab life and go for the gusto do you? You stay safe."

The routine continues through four fairly innocent table dances. I suggest to him that I need time to get to know him before I would consider going out with him, and he buys dances as an excuse to spend time with me, until it is my turn to dance on stage again. I collect my money and leave.

Approaching the main stage, I become furious but swallow it. Why do these assholes act this way? Why can't they treat me like a person? Why must they turn me into a thing? Why do I care so much about it? Why can't I simply be above it? After all, I am here for research purposes. Why do I act the way I do? I feel the anger as I swing myself out into space and onto the stage, twirling a mad entrance just a little too fast for the music.

As I accept a tip, someone attempts to French kiss me. I keep my mouth shut tight against the attack. You can do anything you want to the outside of me, but I won't let you inside. The only thing I can't protect myself from is the words that get in my ears and seep into my brain. I feel the residue from his spittle. When I accept a tip from the next customer, I feel the moist drops of saliva on his moustache and know their germs are mingling. I am hopeful that I have transmitted some horrible mutated disease to this second asshole who is trying to French me also. How dare these men be so stupid in the age of AIDS and other venereal diseases, hell, even the flu? Now I must concentrate on not licking my lips until I can get to the dressing room to wash my mouth. The next customer turns his cheek to me. I use his cheek as a place to wipe off the germs and moisture. This is gross to be going through. Why am I doing it? I keep getting angrier and angrier. It escalates exponentially now. But I must act nice, pretty, and pleasant or I am not doing my job.

Nasally, I take a deep breath, inhaling the electric guitar power chords belting out at me from the speakers. It's a song by a heavy metal band. The singer cries out he doesn't know how to say he's leaving, with emphasis on the word *leaving*. He repeats this in melancholic melodrama, this time with the emphasis on the word *how*. The refrain is followed by an excellent power riff reminiscent of Neil Young's "Cinnamon Girl" or "Rust Never Sleeps." I abandon my body to the music, the guitar energizing me, wailing out my soul. What a great song to play the last set of the last day you dance, ever in your life, I think to myself.

*   *   *

There is another reason I like the song. A dancer named Sheila used to play it every day as her opening number. On stage, she would move her hips from side-to-side in automaton fashion, her hands clasped over her head, her face deadpan—its only redeeming value the piercing ice blue eyes. Everyone stayed away from Sheila because she was "creepy." I would sit and watch her, wondering why she looked so empty, so vacant. She could have been a drug abuser, but I secretly feared (self-centeredly concerned for my own outcome) that she was burned out on dancing.

One day Sheila wasn't around any more. I asked some of the women if they knew about her. They did not know and did not care. "She's trouble," one told me. "She's an ex-con. Got out not too long ago." The others agreed it was best that she left.

I will never know why she liked that song, but now I imagine that Sheila was reliving leaving prison when she played it. She was singing to all the guards, and all the inmates, and the warden, maybe even the governor himself, "I don't know how to say I'm leaving." In my melodramatic fantasy of her fantasy, she even has an electric guitar that she is playing in peak form, offending everyone with its wailing abrasiveness. Fuck 'em all honey, you got out. Good for you.

When I reflect on this in a particularly upbeat mood, I imagine (hope) that she left dancing, realizing that it too is a type of prison (probably not). Many songs I hear on the radio will make me think of a certain dancer, but I decided to use this song myself because I stupidly avoided Sheila like everyone else and want to pay some kind of homage to her to assuage my guilt, and also because I hope to "leave" one day too.

* * *

Stepping up on the edge of the counter that surrounds the stage, careful of my foot placement so that I do not knock over a drink or step on a patron seated there, I stare directly at the strobe, undulating precariously, and I reflect on the fact that *I am leaving*. Here I am, topless, wearing only black pasties, dancer briefs, spike-heeled shoes, and a bow tie, dancing in front of a bunch of screaming, clapping, strange, drunk men, and I don't care. The audience is not real. It's a TV picture with the sound turned off and the stereo cranked up. They are part of my show. The only thing that is real is my hate—a hate so tangible it is a pure, steady, high-pitched tone that rings through my ears above even the guitar. I feel calm set in. It is an empowering high, a meditation on hate—Zen and the art of hate. Perpetual Pollyanna, the girl in me trying to understand everything, the woman who looks to rationalize, is gone. Being nice against your will sucks. Being nice to manipulate, to control, is the point!

* * *

The voices are all talking at once, droning. I can't hear any individual voice unless I stop and strain to single out one. They are many, yet they form one voice. That swarming, screaming confusion is myself, unsettled, frustrated, and thus angry, looking to act on circumstances to control them and to soothe the disordered identity that is the conglomerate noise. I am high on my hyperacute awareness of reality; every stimulus is an irritant. I must not give myself over to the conforming drone, the soothing sellout. I am in danger of falling into the void it forms forever. Staying angry would solve the problem; I'd never be hurt again.

*   *   *

I walk to the dressing room when I am through dancing and wash my face. Next, I use mouthwash to clean around my mouth. Finally, I gargle. Ha! Ha! You bastards are always trying to get inside me with your fingers, your tongues, your dicks. You didn't make it this time did you? I have, of course, deceived myself. They are always inside me. I give them their "bastard" status. They are in me because I have feelings about them.

The mirror reveals my red-rimmed eyes, my blotchy complexion. I look like hell. I breathe deeply, the sound of the running water from the faucet hypnotizing me, harmonizing with the confusion in my brain. I exhale, then gag on an unlabeled, undefined, emotional release that rises up as far as my throat before I catch it by clamping down on it with my epiglottis. To let it escape is to relinquish control of my emotional affect. I focus on the running water, actively trying to regain the drone by merging the sound with my memory of the droning sensation. How am I going to make up my face to disguise how bad I look?

I stare into the mirror, into the blacks of my eyes, imagining I can see the cords that wire my eyes to my brain. I am trapped in here, this body I see, this situation I'm in; there is no escape. The reflection is not really me though, but a flat, two-dimensional representation. The mirror behind me casts its reflection on the mirror in front. I see my face and my slightly oversized behind reflected back at me in an infinite exchange of reflections, creating the illusion of two three-dimensional corridors that disappear at some vanishing point on a horizon.

My image within this is still flat, even with two viewpoints. I am reminded of the video arcade shooting game that appears to have depth except when one focuses on shooting the objects. They are either near, midway, or far, nothing in between, two-dimensional in a three-dimensional space. I am also trapped in the reflection, its prisoner. I can only know myself through reflection, yet any one reflection is never totally accurate. It always depends upon the surface, the context. But I assure myself that the greater the variety of reflections I am able to experience, the better I will understand.

*   *   *

A buzzing, high-pitched, swarming drone sets in again, calm and rapid motion all at the same time. My anger is something to ride, something to use, rather than something that will ride and control me. It is a strange adrenaline calm that has suffused my being. It could eat me up, because it pretends to be calm when it really is an inferno; it is welcome because I don't feel tired, vulnerable, frustrated, or fed up any more.

Now it is time for my side stage performance. My dancing is confident, every step well placed. I set my jaw and cop an attitude. Dancing in my anger, indeed reveling in it, I lose touch with my surroundings. Belligerence pulses through my body to the beat of the music. I no longer have to think about the act of dancing; I am no longer self-conscious. I am at one with the game.

The song playing feeds my anger to a self-righteous frenzied peak. It is about a woman whose mate has had an affair. It is obvious this man has ripped the soul right out of her body as she pleads with him emotionally to realize that she loved and needed him. But then the tone of the song becomes cold, a monotone, calculating, mocking. This man has cheated on her and is no longer worthy of her love. His feelings no longer concern her, and the rest of the song is delivered in the spirit of revenge as she informs him she is looking for a new love, "*baby*." Men always cheat, I think to myself. Look at all these jerks out there with wives and girlfriends, they are all cheating or trying to.

The song is transformed as it weaves into my reality. It is now about all men and all women. All men are using all women. Well fuck you all, because I've found a new love baby—power, control, and money. Use me and I can find a way to use you, manipulating the very thing you are using me for. I feel vindicated for fucking with these guys. The more I take their money, the better I am serving justice. The question of the retarded guy no longer bothers me. I laugh at the idea that it could even have been an issue.

No longer confused and upset, now I smile a lot, and I'm sassy and wisecracking. Control never waivers for a moment. Anger brings confidence and self-assurance. These men have proven to me they are not people but objects that deserve to get burned or even animals that must be treated roughly to be controlled. I don't worry about them any more. I can't.

* * *

Later, as I leave for the night, my anger travels with me outside the bar. I am convinced all men see all women as pieces of ass. Go fuck yourself Mr. Nice Guy. You don't really exist except as some sort of trick to get me into the sack with you. I'm not buying it. At home, my unfortunate husband (a Mr. Nice Guy) is transformed into "one of the assholes," even though he isn't selling anything. He suggests a late night restaurant outing to Denny's or Village Inn, and I silently question his motives, wondering what he is "really" up to. I ask him to wait until I take a shower.

Similar to Hochschild's airline attendants, I am sometimes unable to turn off "the act" when I leave the bar. My dancer self becomes fused with my other selves in such a way as to make it difficult to step out of the role when leaving the bar, so the shower is very important to me. First, I suds up from head to toe and rinse the foreign touches, foul odors, sweat, and grime from my body. After I consider myself squeaky clean, I make the water as hot as I can stand, and rotate slowly under the shower, making the temperature hotter still. The burn is purifying. The purification would not be as sincere if I were to turn the water up when I was still dirty; I must be clean. Some of the night's sins go down the drain with the water. Upon exiting the shower to the cold contrast of the air-conditioning, it occurs to me that it is considerate of my husband to wait up this late and be willing to let me shower before taking me out.

Later still, after several arguments have started by my making the worst of everything my husband says and returning home from the meal, I fling raw emotion at my computer keyboard, pelting out the hate and the tears. The act of writing seems to dissipate more of the hate high, as if having to rationalize what I feel enough to write it gradually brings me back to "outside the bar" reality. I finally decide that my husband isn't an asshole.

*   *   *

After awakening at 1:00 p.m. the same day, I call Danny, one of my professors. "Danny," I say tentatively, "I fucked up again."

"What do you mean by saying that?" Danny patiently responds.

"I turned into a dancer again last night, I was there only for the money at the end, and I'm having a hard time maintaining my objectivity. I'm not even sure what that is any more, or if it is ever possible."

"So what did you get down?" he asks.

"Nothing but a bunch of head fucks," I reply.

"Tell me about it," he says. In this manner, conversing about the data, Danny reels me in. Soon we are talking about "becoming the phenomenon," "emotion work," and "negotiation strategies." Danny and I talk for a couple of hours while I take notes. By the end of the conversation, my "researcher" identity has been reestablished to some extent. I'm not sure I'm happy about it though, because soon it will be time to dance and it would be nice not to have to go through this process again.

*   *   *

After two days of participant observation, a friend noted a marked differ-ence in my outward demeanor. I was walking with her in the mall, when suddenly she pulled me into one of the stores, looked me up and down, and said, "All the men are staring at you, Carol. You'd think you were wearing something really sleazy, the looks you're getting." I was wearing a T-shirt and jeans.

My silent reaction was, of course they are. I was not concentrating on acting a part, but I was aware of inhabiting my body differently. I am normally self-conscious about my height of 5'9", and I have poor posture as a result. It was the most natural thing in the world, however, to hold my shoulders back, my head up, and put a little bounce in my step during the times I was dancing for a living. It was not an act but part of my reassembled self; the self formed in an attempt to resolve the role conflicts that arise in interactions both in and out of the bar. When I have not danced for a while, this act is impossible for me to manufacture believably.

*   *   *

Just like striptease dancing is a form of exhibitionism, this form of writing is an emotional striptease. Using participant observation and systematic sociological introspection (Ellis 1991a), I make my experience as a dancer/researcher the object of study. Using the layered account, I construct an emotional narrative (Ellis 1991b) that depicts the difficulty of maintaining a researcher self in the face of other role demands.

The layered account demonstrates that the impact of participant observa-tion on the researcher's identity is not always the simple problem of "going native" and "becoming the phenomenon" (Jorgensen 1989; Mehan and Wood 1975). The various role conflicts and multiple levels of absorption discussed here cannot be described in terms of a place on a two-dimensional continuum marked *researcher* at one end and *native* at the other. Nor can it be described in terms of being a nonparticipating observer versus a fully participating member (Adler and Adler 1987). Even as a total observer, the researcher interacts with her subject every time she thinks about the data, thus contributing her own influence (style of thinking, biases) to the report.

When I reflect on my ideas, revise them, and rewrite several drafts of a paper, differing levels of absorption at each point in the process contribute to the production of the paper. According to Myerhoff and Metzger (1980, p. 99):

All single reflections are distortions. True reflections can only come from many images, a selection offered from among which one chooses, discards, makes corrections. Only in maturity, with multiple images, is greater accuracy possible.

The layered account is deliberately structured to resemble what Schutz (1970) termed the *duree,* by which he means the stream of consciousness as it naturally flows in the lived experience. Although it is not possible to capture the lived experience, the layered account as a form allows me to express the multiplicity of identities I embody when making a report. Research is plagued with all the emotionality and uncertainty of any human behavior. The layered account reveals my values and position in the frame as well as the situationally embedded contexts out of which my emotions and other behavior arise.

During an exposition on the journal as genre, Myerhoff and Metzger (1980, p. 98) argue that "the necessity for analytic, critical presentation required by academic convention destroys the message. Even the words freeze the contents." Any literary form imprisons lived experience; yet, without form or structure, it would be impossible to convey any experience. The layered account is a structure that organizes and conveys knowledge normally unrelated to classical scientific and/or ethnographic reporting methods.

Emotional sociology (Ellis 1991b) allows readers to incorporate the cognitive/emotional experiences of the researcher into their own stock of knowledge (Berger and Luckmann 1966), thus gaining a resource that may be consulted in the future. This layered account provides the essential elements to readers so that they may read, and vicariously live, an experience through the medium of the text provided by the author. The knowledge from living the experience of interacting with the narrative is an emotional, precognitive apprehending that is sublime, unstructured, and nonverbal in nature. The layered account is an attempt to invoke in the reader the emergent experience of "being" and to use many voices to induce in the reader a comprehension of an alien voice while at the same time fostering the understanding that we all are processual, emergent, multivoiced entities living different situations yet sharing similar lived emotional experiences.

References

Adler, P. A. and P. Adler. 1987. *Membership Roles in Field Research.* Newbury Park, CA: Sage.

Berger, P. and T. Luckmann. 1966. *The Social Construction of Reality.* New York: Anchor, Doubleday.

Blumer, H. 1969. *Symbolic Interactionism.* Berkeley: University of California.

Denzin, N. 1984. *On Understanding Emotion.* San Francisco: Jossey-Bass.

Ellis, C. 1991a. "Sociological Introspection and Emotional Experience." *Symbolic Interaction* 14(1):23-50.

————1991b. "Emotional Sociology." Pp. 123-145 in *Studies in Symbolic Interaction.* Vol. 12, edited by N. Denzin. Greenwich, CT: JAI.

Hochschild, A. 1983. *The Managed Heart.* Berkeley: University of California Press.

Hodges, H. A. 1944. *Wilhelm Dilthey: An Introduction.* London: Routledge & Kegan Paul.

Jorgensen, D. L. 1989. *Participant Observation.* Newbury Park, CA: Sage.

Mehan, H. and H. Wood. 1975. *The Reality of Ethnomethodology.* New York: John Wiley.

Myerhoff, B. and D. Metzger. 1980. "The Journal as Activity and Genre: On Listening to the Silent Laughter of Mozart." *Semiotica* 30:1-2.

Ronai, C. and C. Ellis. 1989. "Turn-Ons for Money: Interactional Strategies of the Table Dancer." *Journal of Contemporary Ethnography* 18(3):271-98.

Schutz, A. 1970. *On Phenomenology and Social Relations.* Chicago: University of Chicago Press.

Weber, M. 1962. *Basic Concepts in Sociology.* New York: Citadel.

6

The Consequences of Poetic Representation

Writing the Other, Rewriting the Self

LAUREL RICHARDSON

This chapter is consciously self-revelatory, but my purpose in writing it is sociological, not confessional. Almost axiomatically, interpretive social scientists assert that our work has consequences for others and ourselves. Sometimes we write about the consequences to others, but less often do we reflect upon the consequences to ourselves. Even more rarely do we consider those consequences in terms of subjectively felt experiences. This chapter joins the growing genre of research, however, that does take as its subject matter the lived experience of the researcher (see Denzin 1987, 1989; Ellis 1991, 1991b; Ellis and Weinstein 1986; Reinharz 1979; Richardson and Lockridge 1991).

Interpretivists have a particular set of norms and values regarding what should be studied and how it should be studied and communicated. Like other social scientists, interpretivists inherit an academic culture that holds a traditional authority over them. That culture suppresses and devalues its members' subjective experiences. For example, we are expected to write papers in prose, reference others, place our work in a lineage, objectify the topic, and focus on the expressed topic rather than on the self-as-producer

AUTHOR'S NOTE: I thank Amber Ault, Carolyn Ellis, Mike Flaherty, and Ernest Lockridge for their careful readings of an earlier draft of this chapter.

(see Richardson 1990a). Like other cultural groups, academics fail to recognize their practices as cultural/political choices, much less see how they are personally affected by those practices (see hooks 1990; Levine 1985; Richardson 1991a; Smith 1990; Van Maanen 1988). Although there are textually marginal places, such as appendixes and prefaces, for social scientists to ponder their lived experience, making that experience the centerpiece of an article seems Improper, bordering on Gauche and Burdensome. I have not, I hope, ventured beyond Improper.

I have breached sociological writing expectations by writing sociology as poetry. This breach has had unexpected consequences for my sense of Self, which may be of sociological and methodological interest to others struggling with alternative forms of representing the sociological. By violating the norms of sociological production and dissemination, I have felt the power of those norms, their role in suppressing lived experience, and the exhilaration of writing nonalienating sociology.

In other papers, I have discussed the production (1991b) and reception (1991a) of this poem. In this chapter, I touch briefly on those topics but focus on the unanticipated consequences to my self of breaching qualitative writing norms by constructing a sociological interview as a poem.

The Project

One evening, as part of a larger project on unmarried mothers, I interviewed Louisa May. I transcribed the tape into 36 pages of text and then fashioned that text into a three-page poem, using *only* her words, her tone, and her diction but relying on poetic devices such as repetition, off-rhyme, meter, and pauses to convey her narrative. Poetic representation plays with connotative structures and literary devices to convey meanings; poetry commends itself to multiple and open readings in ways conventional sociological prose does not.

For sociological readers, the poem may seem to omit "data" that they want to know. But this is Louisa May's narrative, not the sociologist's. She does not choose, for example, to talk about her educational level or her employment. The questions the poem raises for readers about Louisa May thus reflect their own particular subtexts, not universal texts. If they wonder, for example, how Louisa May supports herself, are they tapping into stereotypes about "unwed mothers"? If they feel they cannot understand her unless they know about her schooling, are they telling us something about their own relationship to education, its meaning in their own lives? More generally, have the concepts of sociology been so reified that even interpretivists cannot believe they "know" about a person's life without refracting it through a sociologically prescribed lens?

Here is "Louisa May's Story of Her Life," a transcript masquerading as a poem/a poem masquerading as a transcript.

LOUISA MAY'S STORY OF HER LIFE

i

The most important thing
to say   is that
I grew up in the South.
Being Southern shapes
aspirations   shapes
what you think you are
and what you think you're going to be.

> *(When I hear myself, my Ladybird*
> *kind of accent on tape. I think, OH Lord,*
> *You're from Tennessee.)*

No one ever suggested to me
that anything
might happen *with* my life.

I grew up poor in a rented house
in a very normal sort of way
on a very normal sort of street
with some very nice middle-class friends

> *(Some still to this day)*

and so I thought I'd have a lot of children.

I lived outside.

Unhappy home. Stable family, till it fell apart.
The first divorce in Milfrount County.

So, that's how that was worked out.

ii

Well, one thing that happens
growing up in the South
is that you leave. I
always knew I would

> I would leave.
>> *(I don't know what to say . . .*
>> *I don't know what's germane.)*

My high school sweetheart and I married,
went north to college.
> I got pregnant and miscarried,
and I lost the child.

>> *(As I see it now it was a marriage*
>> *situation which got increasingly horrendous*
>> *where I was under the most stress*
>> *and strain without any sense*
>> *of how to extricate myself.)*

It was purely chance
that I got a job here,
and Robert didn't.
I was mildly happy.

After 14 years of marriage,
That was the break.

We divorced.

A normal sort of life.

iii

So, the Doctor said, "You're pregnant."
I was 41. John and I
had had a happy kind of relationship,
not a serious one.
But beside himself with fear and anger,
awful, rageful, vengeful, horrid,

Jody Mae's father said,
"Get an Abortion."

I told him,
"I would never marry you.
I would never marry you.
I would never.

"I am going to have this child.
I am going to.
I am. I am.

Just Go Away!"

But he wouldn't. He painted the nursery.
He slept on the floor. He went to therapy.
We went to LaMaze.

> *(We ceased having a sexual relationship directly*
> *after I had gotten pregnant and that has never again*
> *entered the situation.)*

He lives 100 miles away now.
He visits every weekend.
He sleeps on the floor.
We all vacation together.
We go camping.

I am not interested in a split-family,
her father taking her on Sundays.
I'm not interested in doing so.

So, little Jody Mae always has had a situation which is normal.

Mother—bless her—the word "married" never crossed her lips.

> *(I do resent mother's stroke. Other mothers have their mother.)*

So, it never occurs to me really that we are unusual in any way.

No, our life really is very normal. I own my house.
I live on a perfectly ordinary middle-class street.

So, that's the way that was worked out.

iv

She has his name. If she wasn't going to have a father,
I thought she should have a father, so to speak.

We both adore her.
John says Jody Mae saved his life.

OH, I do fear that something will change—

v

(Is this helpful?)

This is the happiest time in my life.

I am an entirely different person.

With no husband in the home there is less tension.
And I'm not talking about abnormal families here.
Just normal circumstances. Everyone comes home tired.

I left the South a long time ago.
I had no idea how I would do it.

So, that's the way that worked out.

(I've talked so much my throat hurts.)

The Lived Experience

Why did I choose to breach the norms governing sociological interview writing? Why did I not simply paraphrase Louisa May's life, write it as case study, or quote her words as evidentiary text? What happened when I read and discussed the poem in different discursive sites?

I wrote her life as a poetic representation for several reasons known to me and surely for many that are not. First, for several years, I have been wrestling with the sociological representation of lives (1988, 1990b), which resulted in a monograph on writing qualitative research (1990a). In that book, I looked at the sociohistorical separation of science and literature, the literary devices used in science writing, narrative structures, and strategies for staging texts for different audiences. When we write social science, we use our authority and privileges to talk about the people we study. No matter how we stage the text, we—the authors—are doing the staging. As we speak about the people we study, we also speak for them. As we inscribe their lives, we bestow meaning and promulgate values. I concluded that the ethically principled solution to issues of authority/authorship/appropriation required using my skills and resources in the service of others less beneficially situated. My conclusions were satisfying as rhetorical, aesthetic, and philosophical abstractions; but how to write substantive sociology that pleased me was still elusive.

Second, upon reflection, I realized there were few substantive (not theoretical or methodological) sociology texts that I enjoyed reading or could point to as models for my students (see Brown 1977 on "style"). Even when the topic was ostensibly riveting, the writing style and reporting conventions were deadening. Nearly every time sociologists broke out into prose, they tried to suppress (their own) life: passive voice; absent narrator; long, inelegant, repetitive authorial statements and quotations; "cleaned up" quotations, each sounding like the author; hoards of references; sonorous prose rhythms; dead or dying metaphors; lack of concreteness or overly detailed accounts; tone deafness; and, most disheartening, the suppression of narrativity ("plot," character, event). Unlike literary literature, which I read for the experience of reading, which could touch me emotionally, sociological texts were either skimmable—the cream risen to the top in abstracts or first sentences of paragraphs—or dreary.

Third, I had signed a book contract about voluntarily single adult mothers. Although I had collected the interviews and the manuscript was overdue, I could not get myself to write the book. I found myself clutching at my own throat at the thought of writing "straight" sociological prose.

About this time, a part of me that I had suppressed for more than eight years demanded attention: the part that writes poetry. Writing poetry is emotionally preoccupying; it opens up unexpected, shadow places in my self. As a kind of time-saving/snaring-two-birds-with-one-net strategy, I decided to fashion material from an unmarried mother interview into a poem. That, I thought, would get me started on the contracted book, acknowledge my need for poetry/play, and maybe—just maybe—provide a new strategy for resolving those horrid postmodernist writing dilemmas. Once uttered, however, the idea of the union between the poetic and the sociological was compelling. Like a charismatic idea, it developed a life of its own. It proffered sociological life writing that was endearing, enduring, and endurable—bounded and unbounded, closed and open—sociological writing that I would want to read and write.

During my off-duty quarter, I enrolled in an intensive, advanced poetry workshop at the university. I was fully immersed in poetry for three weeks: every day, three hours in seminar, three hours writing poetry, and another hour or so reading it, and only it. No sociology. I felt adventurous.

Of all the available interviews, I chose to work on Louisa May's not because she was intrinsically more interesting than other women I interviewed but because the literary and sociological challenges were great. If I could "do" Louisa May, I felt, I was onto a "do-able" method.

Because I had decided, for sociological veracity, to use only the words spoken by the interviewee in the construction of the poem, Louisa May posed a difficult literary problem. For the most part, her speech was bland and unconcretized, almost entirely devoid of images, metaphors, and poetic language. She used some literary devices that I felt captured her "poetic essence." For example, she characteristically used large words (e.g., "extricate") and complex sentences, and she had a distinctive "hill-southern" rhythm in her speech. In renarrativizing her story, she told it through dialogue and conversations. Like the Ancient Mariner and the Wife of Bath, Louisa May used the literary device of weaving the listener into her story.

Sociologically, the task of empathic understanding—feeling that I was "getting it right"—was difficult because Louisa May and I differed in many ways: she was an unmarried mother; southern; rural; Christian; from a poor "broken" family. Not only did she belong to different sociological "categories," she positioned herself differently than I did, emotionally and ideologically: Things "turned out" for her, she didn't "make" them happen; her life was "normal"; she liked being "middle class"; she had succeeded in escaping from her background; she had distance from but not disdain for her child's father; she spoke no guilt. I was born and raised in Chicago, into a cultural/religious/class mixed marriage. My father, an attorney, was from a mainline Episcopalian DAR ("Daughters of the American Revolution") family but reared by Christian Scientists; my mother, a graduate of the eighth grade, was a Russian Jewish immigrant. I have seen myself as having "agency" in the world: Things don't just "turn out"; I make them happen. I experience my life as far from normal; yet, I do not choose to escape my background, nor do I think, finally, I could, despite all my claims to agency and independence. I am comfortable on the (intellectual, sociological) margins.

Louisa May was then in many ways my "Other." Her language stylistics, her sociological background, and her fix on the world were near opposites to mine. Could/should I write from this "Other" subject position? Here I was careening fast again into an emotional and pragmatic struggle with the same postmodernist issues of "authorship"/authority/appropriation that I had sought to escape through the poetic representation of the sociological. Challenged, I chose to write through my perplexities.

The poem went through innumerable computer screen revisions, nine hard copy drafts, two critical readings by the professor, and two critiques by workshop participants before becoming the version published here. Writing the poem took the better part of four weeks. During that time, Louisa May moved into my psychic interior in a way that no interviewee of mine ever had. She moved in the way poetry does. She's not yet moved out.

I have presented "Louisa May" to diverse audiences—sociologists, poets, feminists, lay-listeners, poetry bar habitués, women's studies and poetry students, oral historians, and mixed disciplinarians with postmodernist leanings. The responses have been unexpectedly strong, sometimes stirring up heated controversy. Poets have responded with sociological analyses of how "normalness" is constituted as well as discussion of genre boundaries and authorship/expropriation. Poetry audiences, identifying with Louisa May, have tearfully requested I pass on words of encouragement to her. General audiences have discussed implications for family and child policy. Academics have had diverse responses: Oral historians have noted that the poem captures "essence" in the way prose does not and that there are methodological lessons here for them; women's studies audiences have discussed the poem as a method for revealing conventional forms of reporting "findings" as patriarchal strictures—with poetry "feminizing" the product and its production; and postmodernist theorists have discussed the work as an important turn for both theory and research on social scientific writing. Some interpretivists have welcomed the breach as an opportunity to rethink sociological representation. Other social scientists have challenged the "validity" of the poem, demanding to see the transcript although not to hear the tape, see a videotape, or talk directly to Louisa May. Some feminist social scientists have assumed that I am Louisa May. I doubt if the very existence of Louisa May would have been challenged had I reported it conventionally.

Thus I have been variously accused of exploiting Louisa May, of fabricating her, and of being her. But, I also have been applauded for writing Louisa May's "core"; for touching an emotional center in the listener; for showing how patriarchal strictures have controlled the writing of social science

"findings"; for problematizing interpretive methodological practices; and for
providing policymakers with a different slant on "unwed mothers."

Because of the unexpected hold on my psyche stemming from the creation
of the poem and because of the unexpected and intense receptions of "Louisa
May," Louisa May has changed my life. Through writing "Louisa May," I
am rewriting myself.

Consequences to the Self

I have identified five ways the experience of producing and sharing
"Louisa May" has changed my life.

First, I find myself using Louisa May's words in my daily discourse. I find
myself saying—even more so, feeling—"so that's the way that turned out."
Louisa May's words enforce an acceptance of that which cannot be changed.
When my younger son missed a family holiday, I validated his decision with
the mantra, "that's the way that turned out." Sometimes, I say her words with
a touch of irony, amusement. When my department put forward an unworthy
candidate (in my mind) for a prestigious honor, I saw this as an ironic "turn
of events" rather than as a "plot."

Second, speaking Louisa May's words has had a transformative effect on
deeper, more spiritual, parts of my self. I speak her point of view not as hers
but as mine. A dramatic example of how speaking Louisa May's words has
transformed my point of view happened in a favorite place, the Shenandoah
National Park, an area close to Louisa May's heart too. My husband and I
planned an easy day hike, the 7.5 mile Hoover-Laurel loop. During the hike
out, I thought and talked about death, about how quickly and unexpectedly
death can happen, just one wrong turn. We don't know how things are going
to turn out—only, as Louisa May would say, that they will. Therefore, I
reasoned, this is the time in our lives, as is any time in any life, as Joseph
Campbell would say, "to follow our bliss."

We reached Laurel Prong, but a new trail had been blazed with the old
color, which we guilelessly followed. Trail ran into gravel road, but gravel
road dead-ended at groves of trees, half-century high. Nothing made sense.
Dark fell. We "slept" that night in the woods, with one windbreaker jacket
between us, a full moon, six ounces of water, no guarantee of finding our
way back, visions of Laughing Wolf gently pulling the blanket, Night, over
us, and, as we discovered the next day, 22 miles of wilderness hiking under
our boots and 12 more to go before we left the area, called since before the

Civil War and to this day, "The Wilderness," inhabited by some 400 bear, each a night roamer with a 20-square mile territory.

We survived for me to tell how things turned out, including how my internalized sense of life had altered; how I now find the apparent paradox of simultaneously succumbing to life's turns and taking charge by "following one's own bliss" as compatible, complementary visions.

Third, I feel more integrated. The suppressed "poet" and the overactive "sociologist" have found each other. The two separate writing "voices" were united in Louisa May's poem. This is a union I have desired and avoided for nearly two decades while I wrote sociology as "Laurel Richardson Walum" and poetry as "Laurel Richardson" and "Alexis Tyrrell." About a decade ago, I named myself "Laurel Richardson" in both writing arenas; but only now do I bring the two *forms* together. One tangible outcome is that I have returned the advance and contract for the book on unmarried mothers, because I cannot write (at least at this time) the kind of conventional sociology that the contract (and my own proposal) called for. I do not know where the integrated self is heading, but the energy for writing (living) is immense.

Fourth, I am better able to step into the shoes of the Other, as well as into the Other's body and psyche. I am more attuned to lived experiences as subjectively felt by the Other. This has affected my willingness to know myself and others in different ways. For example, in multicultural class-rooms, I have been more willing to risk potential conflictual situations by "modeling" listening to and then speaking from nondominant positions, even if those positions undermine the grounds of my authority within the class-room. My positionality is subject to critique. Similarly, I ask my feminist theory students to critique and rewrite their work from an Other's position. My research interviewing, on the one hand, requires less effort because it is easier now to "travel" unencumbered by my own baggage to the Other's world (see Lugones 1987); but, on the other hand, it is more difficult to choose to do interviews, because I am more cautious, more contemplative, about what "doing research" means.

Fifth, Louisa May brings me to different sites and allows me to see familiar sites in new ways. Disillusionment is one of the outcomes. When, for example, a symbolic interactionist conventioneer asks me to "prove" Louisa May exists by showing him the transcript of my interview (as if transcripts were real), or when my feminist postmodernist reading group wants to know about the "validity" of the poem, I experience deeply the hold of positivism on even those I consider my allies, my intellectual companions. In the chasm,

I experience isolation, alienation, and freedom, exhilaration. I want to record what they are saying; I want to do fieldwork on them. Science them. My romanticized vision of a postmodernist sociology shaken, I seek alternative sites for sharing sociology. Louisa May's life takes me to poetry bars, literature conventions, women's studies classes, social work spaces, and policymaking settings.

I take pleasure in feeling I am a sociological revolutionist in community with others who are questioning how and for whom we write sociology. My feminist mission has intensified. I desire to problematize sociology's concepts and methods by grounding sociology in lived experiences; to write sociology as "windows on lived experience." I struggle now with ways to unite people's subjective experiences with my sociological utterances. I strive for forms in which sociology can be an effective and affecting discourse, a nonalienating practice.

Representing the sociological as poetry is one way of decentering the unreflexive "self" to create a position for experiencing the self as a sociological knower/constructor—not just talking about it, but doing it. In writing the Other, we can (re)write the Self. That is the moral of this story.

I am indebted to Louisa May.
And that's the way
    this has turned
Out.

References

Brown, Richard. 1977. *A Poetic for Sociology*. Cambridge: Cambridge University Press.

Denzin, Norman. 1987. *The Alcoholic Self*. Newbury Park, CA: Sage.

———1989. *Interpretive Biography*. Newbury Park, CA: Sage.

Ellis, Carolyn. 1991a. "Sociological Introspection and Emotional Experience." *Symbolic Interaction* 14:23-50.

———1991b. "Emotional Sociology." Pp. 123-145 in *Studies in Symbolic Interaction*. Vol. 12, edited by N. Denzin. Greenwich, CT: JAI.

Ellis, Carolyn and E. Weinstein. 1986. "Jealousy and the Social Psychology of Emotional Experience." *Journal of Social and Personal Relationships* 3:337-57.

hooks, bell. 1990. *Yearning: Race, Gender, and Cultural Politics*. Boston: South End.

Levine, Donald N. 1985. *The Flight from Ambiguity: Essays in Social and Cultural Theory*. Chicago: University of Chicago Press.

Lugones, Maria. 1987. "Playfulness, 'World'-Travelling, and Loving Perception." *Hypatia* 2:3-19.

Reinharz, Shulamit. 1979. *On Becoming a Social Scientist*. San Francisco: Jossey-Bass.

Richardson, Laurel. 1988. "The Collective Story: Postmodernism and the Writing of Sociology" (North Central Sociological Society Presidential Address). *Sociological Focus* 21:199-208.

————1990a. *Writing Strategies: Reaching Diverse Audiences.* Newbury Park, CA: Sage.

————1990b. "Narrative and Sociology." *Journal of Contemporary Ethnography* 9:116-36.

————1991a. "Interrupting Discursive Spaces." Paper presented to the Midwest Sociological Society Meetings, Des Moines, IA, April 12.

————1991b. "The Poetic Representation of Lives." Pp. 29-38 in *Studies in Symbolic Interaction.* Vol. 12, edited by N. Denzin. Greenwich, CT: JAI.

Richardson, Laurel and Ernest Lockridge. 1991. "The Sea Monster: An Ethnographic Drama and Comment on Ethnographic Fiction." *Symbolic Interaction* 14(3):335-40.

Smith, Dorothy. 1990. *Conceptual Practices of Power: A Feminist Sociology of Knowledge.* Boston: Northeastern University Press.

Van Maanen, John. 1988. *Tales of the Field.* Chicago: University of Chicago.

PART III

Experiencing Subjectivity

7

The Erotics and Hermeneutics
of Temporality

MICHAEL G. FLAHERTY

It was 1966, and Susan Sontag wrote an essay about art. From our standpoint, it had the seemingly seditious title "Against Interpretation." Perhaps it was derived from the spirit of that era, but she was profoundly concerned that, in our preoccupation with recognizing the "meaning" of art, we had lost sight of its primary significance as a feast for the senses. Her (1966, p. 14) conclusion was as elegant as it was partisan: "In place of a hermeneutics we need an erotics of art."

Analogous comments can be directed toward the sociological study of time. Surprisingly little of the sociological research on temporality involves meticulous consideration of what time *feels* like to those who are experiencing it.[1] Instead, research has centered on the social organization of time. While we do not lack analyses of clocks, calendars, and schedules (Melbin 1969, 1978; Zerubavel 1977, 1979, 1981, 1982, 1985), insufficient attention is paid to those processes whereby subjective dimensions of temporality are shaped by characteristics of the social situation (Flaherty 1987a).

It is, of course, tempting to give ourselves over to the sensuous presence of phenomena, but total commitment to a one-sided description of sensation is no more satisfying than interpretation that is divorced from the actualities of human experience. C. Wright Mills (1959) cautioned us to steer between

AUTHOR'S NOTE: I am thankful for the helpful comments of Carolyn Ellis, Gary Fine, Gretchen Flaherty, Keith Irwin, and James MacDougall. I am also grateful for the assistance of Linda O'Bryant and Lloyd Chapin.

the equally dangerous seductions of grand theory and abstracted empiricism. In that same spirit, this chapter addresses both the erotics and the hermeneutics of temporality. Here, the word *erotics* refers to the lived experience of time, while the word *hermeneutics* refers to theoretical interpretation of that lived experience.[2] A salutary synthesis is intended. The goal is to formulate a theoretical interpretation that confronts and ultimately accommodates the full range of variation in the lived experience of time.

Variation in the Erotics of Temporality

Temporality is most clearly manifest in human consciousness as the feeling of duration. Indeed, an intimate awareness of one's own continuity is intrinsic to mentality. We are cognizant of ourselves enduring change; we perceive the continuation of our experience. More to the point, we are aware of time because we sense its passing as an aspect of our own existence (Heidegger [1927] 1962).

There is a tendency for sociological students of temporality to gloss over the basic fact that what feels like minutes for one person may feel like hours for another person. This offhand treatment is remarkable because even cursory reflection indicates that variation in the experience of time does not occur because there are different kinds of people but because people find themselves in different kinds of circumstances.

This variation is evident despite our common socialization to an intersubjective structure of standard temporal units, such as hours, minutes, and seconds. Each of us, now and then, feels that time is passing quickly or slowly. Therefore we can conceptualize three points along a continuum representing the lived experience of temporality. Ordinarily, our perception of time is roughly synchronized with the flow of standard temporal units. In other words, ten minutes as measured by the clock *feels* like approximately ten minutes from the perspective of lived duration. But, under certain circumstances, there are two other possibilities: Ten minutes as measured by the clock may feel like a much longer or much shorter length of time.

Temporality is typically an unconscious facet of social interaction (Hall 1983), but extraordinary circumstances give rise to abnormal temporal experiences, and the latter bring time to the surface of consciousness. So it is that, if you search for stories of lived duration in previously published sources, what you find are only instances of deviant temporality. More specifically, you find almost nothing but accounts of unusual situations in which time was felt to slow drastically. To date, we have assembled 326 of these texts, and, following Goffman's (1974, pp. 14-15) example, they are drawn largely from "the press and popular books of the biographic genre." With an eye toward more control over the resulting records, we also conducted semistructured, open-ended, life history interviews with 316 students so as to elicit comparable stories of incidents in which time was felt to slow dramatically.

Of our 642 stories, 2 are presented within the format of this chapter. These exemplary texts have been purposefully selected because, by themselves, they illustrate the sensual possibilities that must be accommodated in any thoroughgoing interpretation of lived temporality. The first of these texts is taken from Arthur Koestler's (1960) *Dialogue With Death*. This book is a memoir of his solitary confinement after being captured by loyalist forces in the Spanish Civil War. During the course of his imprisonment, he becomes obsessed with the elasticity of temporal experience (1960, pp. 119-20):

> The astonishing thing, the puzzling thing, the consoling thing about this time was that it passed. I am speaking the plain unvarnished truth when I say that I did not know how. I tried to catch it in the act. I lay in wait for it, I riveted my eyes on the second hand of my watch, resolved to think of nothing else but pure time. . . . I stared at the second hand for minutes on end, for quarters of an hour on end, until my eyes watered with the effort of concentration and a kind of trance-like stupor set in. . . .

> Time crawled through this desert of uneventfulness as though lame in both feet. I have said that the astonishing and consoling thing was that in this pitiable state it should pass at all. But there was something that was more astonishing, that positively bordered on the miraculous, and that was that this time, these interminable hours, days and weeks, passed *more swiftly* than a period of times has ever passed for me before. . . .

> I was conscious of this paradox whenever I scratched a fresh mark on the white plaster of the wall, and with a particular shock of astonishment when I drew a circle round the marks to celebrate the passage of the weeks and, later, the months. What, another week, a whole month, a whole quarter of a year! Didn't it seem only like yesterday that this cell door had banged to behind me for the first time?

Koestler's ruminations reveal a complex range of variation in the sensation of temporality. From moment to moment (that is, current experience), his time in solitary confinement seems to pass slowly, but, upon reflection (that is, with hindsight), it seems to have passed quickly. Furthermore, both of those feelings provide implicit contrast with the normal, nearly unnoticeable synchronization between lived duration and the passage of standard temporal units.

Through the ordeal of imprisonment, Koestler stumbles upon a central paradox in the study of lived duration. A single period of time can be experienced as passing slowly in the immediacy of the present yet also be experienced as having passed quickly in retrospect. There is a folk theory that claims that busy time goes by quickly while empty time goes by slowly. The severe limitations of this folk theory are illuminated by a second paradox in the study of lived temporality: both objectively eventful *and* objectively uneventful situations can produce the feeling of interminable duration (Flaherty 1991). This is evident in the following text taken from John Van Maanen's (1988, pp. 113-14) *Tales of the Field*. Let us examine the end of one story, in which Van Maanen gives a first-person account of his participation in the pursuit of a stolen car by the police:

> Except for the sergeant still sitting in the Mercedes, the accident scene empties quickly. I start the car and drive away, slowly realizing that I don't have a clue how to handle this mobile example of police high tech.
>
> The radio seems to be screeching at me to do something. The lights and siren, to my astonishment, somehow come on. The demonic shotgun is no longer secure and bounces around the front seat. The power brakes feel awkward and almost toss me through the [windshield] at the first stop sign. To complicate matters, I have no idea where I'm going.
>
> As I round a corner near the Interstate, the ticket book, the clipboard, the logbook, the portable radio, David's hat, and God knows what else go sliding out the passenger door I'd forgotten to fully close and onto the street. The shotgun would have gone too had I not grasped the stock of the weapon with a last-second, panic-stricken lunge. Shamefully, I pull to the side of the road to gather up my litter.
>
> Luckily, I was not unobserved by the police. Two Southend officers, looking for something to do, had come up to assist in the chase. . . .
>
> They drive up as I'm puzzling over what switch controls what function of the machine. . . . Between chuckles, they give me remedial instructions on how to operate a prowl car and direct me to where I am next to appear.
>
> When I eventually arrive at the firehouse, David is standing on the corner chatting with another officer. Maybe ten minutes have passed since I left the section sergeant fondling the Mercedes, but of course it seems like years. William James is right about time stretching out when events conspire to fill it up.

Van Maanen gives us a detailed description of a busy social context that evokes within him the feeling that time is passing very slowly. But, if "James is right about time stretching out when events conspire to fill it up," then how is it that Koestler reports the same feeling of protracted duration in a setting of solitary confinement that he calls a "desert of uneventfulness"? In part, the foregoing texts were chosen to underscore the fact that, from the perspective of outside observers, 41.1% of our 642 stories depict situations that are unusually uneventful and 58.9% depict situations that are unusually eventful. According to James, *all* of these texts should have been unusually eventful because all of our stories are instances of protracted duration. And there is another problem: If James is "right," why do people in everyday life employ a folk theory that asserts that busy time passes quickly while empty time passes slowly?

To summarize, then, both eventful and uneventful periods of time can seem interminable. Yet, busy intervals also can seem to pass quickly, and empty intervals can seem to have passed quickly in retrospect. Finally, much of the time, our inner sense of duration is roughly synchronized with the passing of standard temporal units, and we do not feel time passing quickly or slowly. The erotics of temporality confront us with an intimidating range of variation.

The Hermeneutics of Lived Duration

Our analysis must accommodate the tripartite distribution of lived duration: time that seems to pass slowly, synchronicity between lived duration and standard temporal units, and time that seems to have passed quickly. A theoretical interpretation is called for that explicates this distribution of temporal sensations. Through the use of analytic induction, we have formulated a conceptual explanation that does encompass the full range of variation in the experience of temporality. We will consider each of the three sensations in turn, beginning with time that seems to pass slowly.

Protracted Duration

First, there is a context that can be described as *extreme circumstances.* Situations that engender protracted duration fall into one of two categories: those with unusually high levels of overt activity, and those with unusually low levels of overt activity. These situations are not as different as they might seem to the casual observer. They share an underlying unity that results in their common effect on the perception of time. Solitary confinement and police pursuit of a stolen car share the characteristic of extremity. That is, people in either context must deal with some degree of departure from the familiar patterns of everyday life (Flaherty 1987b).

Second, people who are faced with extreme circumstances have an increased *emotional concern* for making sense of their situations. They find themselves positioned in a setting that is quite problematic. Strange occasions create anxiety in human beings because such circumstances undermine their taken-for-granted faith in routine forms of understanding (Turner 1988, p. 49). As a result, there is a powerfully felt need to account for one's immediate conditions. Schutz and Luckmann (1973, p. 24) have described this emotional response to unfamiliar situations as a "shock" that accompanies the transition from one realm of being to another.

Third, the individual amplifies self-consciousness as well as perception of the setting in response to new and unusual circumstances. One's subjective involvement with definition of the situation varies according to the nature of the occasion (Goffman 1974, p. 345), but, typically, concentration on the establishment of meaning "is deep only when there is sudden trouble to avoid." At such times, individuals become caught up in special subjective "effort" to collect that information that will allow them to fathom their novel conditions. There is, consequently, a great increase in one's *cognitive engrossment* with self and environment.

Fourth, heightened attention toward one's own subjectivity and surroundings generates *stimulus complexity* even if the setting is characterized by very little overt activity. The sensation of temporality is affected by stimulus complexity, but the latter is not solely a function of the situation's objective qualities. On the contrary, embedded activity is conditional on the intensity of involvement among those individuals who enact the episode. No one can ever hope to perceive everything that is available in a given situation (Neisser 1976). Situated involvement determines whether one takes in more or less of these immediate possibilities, and this governs the actual quantity of stimulus complexity experienced by the individual. In other words, as perception and information processing intensify, so too does embedded activity, albeit of a tacit or subjective form.

Fifth, the increase in stimulus complexity fills standard temporal units with a *density of experience* that is higher than their normal volume of sensations. According to the clock, every minute is the same, but the experience of lived time is one of variation in response to involvement with immediate circumstances. Like the gondola cars of freight trains, standard temporal units are identical to one another in structure but open on top so that they can be filled with an unspecified amount of ore. In the same fashion, a minute can be "loaded" with an enormous quantity of experience or very little, but, whatever the volume, it is not simply determined by the objective events that occur during a particular interval. Where human experience is concerned, cars that look empty to the outside observer may actually carry a great deal of freight. From an objective standpoint, little is happening when we are forced to wait, but, by paying more attention to time itself than is ordinarily the case, we burden standard temporal units with a mass of subjectivity that makes the interval seem much longer than it really is (Schwartz 1975, p. 168).

The sensation of *protracted duration* is produced by the five elements of the foregoing sequence. Under such conditions, the individual perceives lived time to expand as standard temporal units become saturated with the dense experience of subjective stimulus complexity. One has the impression that temporality is hugely, even infinitely, magnified. The situation may seem endless, and the act-to-act flow of gestures may have the molasses-like viscosity that is evident in slow-motion replay of videotape. Objectively "full" and objectively "empty" episodes have the same impact on the individual's perception of time. We cannot resolve this paradox without acknowledging that subjective involvement is crucial to our understanding of protracted duration.

When one listens closely to people describe periods of "empty" time, it quickly becomes clear that such intervals are not as empty as they appear to those who tell us about them. With more careful analysis, these intervals turn out to be quite full—not of visible activity in an objective sense but of perception, emotion, cognition—in a word, *involvement* with the situation however uneventful it may seem to be. Observing Koestler's solitary confinement, an outsider could be excused for seeing little of consequence. Ironically, our respondents themselves, when asked about "uneventful" episodes, reported that "nothing" was happening even though, like Koestler, their own descriptions belie that conclusion. There were, in fact, a multitude of things transpiring and, again, like Koestler, much of what the respondents attended to was of their own making. Put differently, so-called empty time is nothing of the sort, but not because a passive subject is bombarded by overt, external stimuli. On the contrary, that which is misapprehended as time free of embedded activity is, in actuality, filled with the thoughts and feelings of those people who are tacitly, actively, and self-consciously involved with their circumstances, despite (indeed, because of) the seeming uneventfulness.[3]

Synchronicity

Normal perception of the passage of time emerges from social situations that the individual finds familiar and comfortable. The conditions of these settings are not troublesome, and the individual is conducting regular forms of interaction. To be more precise, these situations are located in the middle ranges of two dimensions: from the standpoint of objectivity, there cannot be too much or too little embedded activity, and, from the standpoint of subjectivity, the experience cannot be so customary that it is boring or so unusual that it is challenging. In short, the stimulus complexity provoked by the setting is neither extremely high nor extremely low.

As a result, the people who enact these situations experience relatively modest emotional concern for the meaning of what transpires. Goffman (1974, p. 8) has shown us "that when individuals attend to any current situation, they face the question: 'What is it that's going on here?' " In keeping with his formulation, we can postulate that, during one's waking life, one is nearly always experiencing some level of "framing anxiety." Typically, however, the individual's framing anxiety is tempered by the fact of routine behavior in a conventional setting. This reduces the relevance of framing anxiety to such a degree that it becomes an unconscious facet of one's usual attention to situated proceedings. In this regard, Schutz and Luckmann (1973, p. 3) have pointed out that the "natural attitude" of people in everyday life is the suspension of doubt, which is accomplished by taking for granted one's provisional understanding of events.

When there is moderate salience for framing anxiety, there is an equally moderate salience for cognitive involvement with one's circumstances. Some minimal degree of situated involvement is nearly always necessary, if only to control the direction of one's gaze as well as other aspects of adaptability to the flow of events. The individual is expected to avoid all manner of faux pas, recognize his or her turn in conversation, and in general be aware of the numberless exigencies that make for ordinary wariness and sociability. Still, this interactional regimen would be much more demanding than it is were it not for the prevalence of what Schutz and Luckmann (1973, p. 18) call the "pragmatic motive" in everyday life. Only modest cognitive involvement is requisite if one takes an instrumental attitude and desires nothing beyond a practical level of interactional competence.

With subjective involvement of modest intensity, a temperate amount of stimulus complexity is generated by the individual's relatively lenient attention to self and situation. Both consciousness and the senses contribute to the production of stimulus complexity because the latter reflects cognition and emotion as well as perception. Due to the systematic quality of interpersonal relations, we gradually become well acquainted with the modal quantity of experience (including thoughts, feelings, and perceptions) that is carried by standard units of temporality. In part, this modal quantity of stimulus complexity is governed by the social structure of activity: habits, schedules, and so forth. But, given the socialization of subjectivity, consistency in the amount of experience per standard temporal unit is also conditioned by that which Cicourel (1974, p. 11) has termed "interpretive procedures."

An individual must use interpretive procedures to maintain an approximate synchronization with others. A rough synchronization is critical to the etiquette of interaction, which stipulates that encounters not be too short or too long in duration. This is only possible if, as Goffman (1961, pp. 39, 80) argues, the individual modulates his or her subjective involvement in light of conventional "rules for the management of engrossment," because "too much is one kind of delict; too little, another." And, as we have seen, one does not control subjective involvement without also controlling the stimulus complexity of the situation.

Consequently, there is a routine consistency in the density of experience per standard temporal unit. This consistency is not a naturally occurring phenomenon but is an artifact of structuring processes that are both external and internal with respect to subjectivity. From the outside, the individual is entangled in a web of habits, schedules, calendars, seasons, and other socially defined regularities. From the inside, the individual draws from the lessons of primary socialization to employ interpretive procedures in the self-conscious management of situated involvement. Goffman (1974, p. 345) has demonstrated the elaborate codification of rules regulating subjectivity: "All frames involve expectations of a normative kind as to how deeply and fully the individual is to be carried into the activity organized by the frames." If, therefore, temporal eccentricity is typically avoided, this is attributable to the socialization of subjectivity and the fact that societies provide recurrent things by which to be engrossed. As a result, the individual learns the ordinary correspondence between the density of experience and standard temporal units. It is knowledge of this correspondence that enables one to translate experience into standard units of temporality, and vice versa.

So, given the usual conditions, an individual's perception of the passage of time is approximately synchronized with that intersubjective time that is measured by clocks and calendars. The normal adult under normal circumstances can estimate, with fair accuracy, the elapsed time of an interval by taking into consideration the amount of experience he or she has processed in the course of that interval. Young children are not yet adept at this skill, and it should come as no surprise that they are notorious for their impatience. As we have witnessed, however, even subsequent to socialization and mastery of that particular skill, the vicissitudes of social interaction still confront the individual with variation across the spectrum of lived time.

Temporal Compression

Time flies. For centuries, this has been one of the stock phrases in Western cultures. But, on occasion, we are struck by the sense that time has passed even more quickly than is usually the case. This is to say that, under certain circumstances, it feels like less time has elapsed than has actually been measured by the clock or calendar. Whether the relevant interval is ten hours or ten months, it seems to us that a much shorter length of time has gone by. Therefore we can refer to this sensation as "temporal compression."[4]

One of the most crucial insights to emerge from our studies is that temporal compression is a phenomenon of retrospection. In contrast to protracted duration and synchronicity, both of which are primarily phenomena of the present, temporal compression is only characteristic of the past. Like Koestler's reaction as he circled the chalk marks on the walls of his cell, temporal compression manifests itself as a shocked look backward, and this is evident in those questions that are common forms of its expression: Where have the hours (days, months, or years) gone?

Given what we know already of protracted duration and synchronicity, we should search for temporal compression in situations that make standard temporal units carry less conscious experience than is ordinarily the case. Unfortunately, in response to the intellectual currents of his day, Mead (1934) exaggerated the role of consciousness in human conduct. And, with the exception of dramaturgical treatments of "deep acting" (Goffman 1959, pp. 74-75; Hochschild 1983, p. 49), his followers have continued to neglect the unconscious processes of mind (Stryker and Statham 1985; Turner 1988). So it is that we must look outside of sociological social psychology to find thoroughgoing conceptualization of unconscious processes.

Ashcraft (1989, p. 68) and other students of cognitive psychology have noticed a recurrent trajectory in the learning of new skills:

> Most mental processes begin at a conscious level. That is, they require conscious attention and processing resources at the outset. With extensive practice, however, it also appears that at least some of these mental processes can migrate toward the automatic end of the continuum. Thereafter, the mental activity can routinely happen at a very automatic, effortless level under normal circumstances, requiring little if any attention. If the situation changes dramatically, however, then some greater involvement of conscious processing may be required temporarily.

Although the tendency is movement from conscious attention to automatic processing, once the latter degree of skill is achieved, there is oscillation between the two poles of this continuum, and this oscillation is determined by whether the situation is relatively routine or relatively problematic. Habitual circumstances allow one to operate with largely automatic processing, but, as we saw earlier, difficult situations "capture attentional resources," because one "must revert back to more conscious control . . . under unusual circumstances" (Ashcraft 1989, p. 68).

Automaticity plays a significant part in temporal compression, although it has not heretofore been associated with research on the perception of time. If the passage of time is perceived to slow when the density of experience per standard temporal unit is greater than usual, then the passage of time is perceived to have accelerated when the density of experience per standard temporal unit is lower than usual. This is the case with automaticity because the individual is not guiding his or her conduct with conscious attention to the details of experience.

Support for this interpretation can be found in Gary Fine's study of chefs and their management of the rush period in restaurants. He (1990, p. 107) notes that "cooks prefer evenings when they discover that it is much later than they thought." Put differently, it is desirable that the time seem to have passed quickly, but temporal compression is experienced only if the rush goes smoothly. Although the rush may seem chaotic to one who lacks the requisite skills, the chef is actually performing habitual tasks within the context of an utterly routine situation. Thus Fine (1990, p. 109) gives this summary of his interviews: "Several cooks remarked that their reactions are 'automatic' in that they do not consciously plan or control their emotions or the behavior resulting from the demands made of them." It does not seem coincidental that variations on the words *automatic* and *unconscious* appear so frequently, as Fine and his informants try to articulate the temporal compression that occurs in the rush when everything goes smoothly.

Nevertheless, things can go wrong, and one of Fine's (1990, p. 109) cooks observes that this possibility creates two kinds of rush: " 'When you're all set and you're ready for it, it can be great. When things are happening that aren't supposed to, it can be a nightmare.' " These two kinds of rush have very different impacts on the perception of time. With the routine rush, lived duration collapses in on itself as automaticity produces the retrospective sensation of temporal compression. On such occasions, chefs ask themselves where the night has gone. With the problematic rush, unanticipated difficulties and resulting emotional concern prompt an extraordinary amount of conscious attention to self and situation. This increased subjective involvement generates stimulus complexity, bloating standard temporal units with a density of experience that far surpasses their usual volume. On such occasions, the night seems like it will never end.

We are now in a position to resolve the paradox that centers on the contradiction between Van Maanen's experience of protracted duration in the police chase and the folk theory arguing that busy time passes quickly while empty time passes slowly. There are not just two kinds of restaurant rush. In the broader or more generic sense, there are two kinds of busy time: routine complexity and problematic complexity. The folk theory is based solely on the first, while the second is applicable to the police pursuit of a stolen car, which, at least for a novice like Van Maanen, is anything but routine.

Automaticity is the first of two factors that produce the sensation of temporal compression, and it is peculiar to those situations that are characterized by an extraordinary amount of routine complexity. The second factor that leads to temporal compression is the loss of memory over time, and this is the more common of the two. While automaticity is manifest in our memory of the near past, forgetfulness is more apparent in our memory of the distant past.

Each person's past differs, yet almost everyone remarks on how the past seems to have gone by quickly. The homogeneous manner in which time corrodes memory makes for a nearly uniform impact on the lived duration of the past: All of us are subject to the fact that time begins to erode memory almost as soon as events have transpired.[5] What is more, the responses of those we interviewed indicate that, the further back you go, the more intensely felt is the effect of temporal compression. Hence it should come as no surprise that, the older one is, the more quickly time seems to have passed.

As a general rule, the loss of memory over time shrinks the quantity of experience that was carried by each standard unit of temporality. The past is constantly contracting in our memories, and the speed at which it seems to have transpired quickens as each quantum of experience is forgotten. Lived duration is perceived to have accelerated when standard temporal units carry less experience than is ordinarily the case. From this perspective, the impact of forgetting fits the emerging interpretation perfectly. The past is perceived to have passed quickly and, moreover, is perceived to have passed at an increasing rate, as loss of memory erodes remembered experience per standard temporal unit.

And here, finally, we see a resolution of Koestler's paradox: How can the same period of time be experienced as having passed slowly in the present but quickly in retrospect? As he endured solitary confinement, Koestler filled his time with intense contemplation of his predicament. The duration of his sentence was burdened with perceptions, feelings, and thoughts but not deeds or outward accomplishments. Memory and the relating of memories are both oriented toward tales of overt behavior. What can Koestler say about his imprisonment, save its objective length? He has few stories to tell, he has few stories to remember, and the ravages of time reduce still further what little there is to recall. Standard units of temporality that, at the time, were bloated with the intangibles of subjective involvement now appear almost empty in hindsight. The experience seems to diminish more, and the sentence seems to have elapsed more quickly, with each passing day.

Conclusion

Protracted duration, synchronicity, and temporal compression are three points along a continuum representing the lived experience of duration. Having systematically confronted their empirical complexities, we have fashioned a theoretical interpretation that accommodates the full range of variation in the perception of time. This theoretical interpretation enables us to see that there is an underlying unity that is masked by surface heterogeneity in the experience of temporality. Ultimately, it is the dynamic interplay of self and situation that conditions the individual's perception of the passage of time.

Notes

1. There have been attempts at conceptualization, however (Denzin 1982; Lewis and Weigert 1981), as well as empirically driven studies (Lopata 1986; Maines 1983).

2. When people are asked to relate stories about situations in which time seems to have passed slowly, they frequently finish by saying something like, "I know it only took a few minutes, but it *felt* like forever." Strictly speaking, one does not "feel" time passing, but people speak as if they do, and the "erotics" metaphor is meant to express something of this tendency.

3. Here, it is helpful to remember that the individual's involvement with his or her circumstances is, in this instance, a response to an unusual absence of overt activity, as when one is held in solitary confinement.

4. Temporal compression is not synonymous with that which Csikszentmihalyi (1975, p. 182) has termed "flow." His work concerns the subjective and situated conditions for enjoyment, and he finds that "people who enjoy what they are doing enter a state of 'flow': they concentrate their attention on a limited stimulus field, forget personal problems, lose their sense of time and of themselves, feel competent and in control, and have a sense of harmony and union with their surroundings." The experience of temporal compression occurs not only in enjoyable circumstances but also in unpleasant circumstances, as evidenced by the passage from Koestler's autobiography. Indeed, a majority of the people in our narratives are not enjoying themselves.

5. In general, one's memory of specific events or experiences erodes with the passage of time (Ashcraft 1989, p. 241). There are, however, other kinds of memory that are impervious to the effects of aging.

References

Ashcraft, M. H. 1989. *Human Memory and Cognition.* Glenview, IL: Scott, Foresman.

Cicourel, A. V. 1974. *Cognitive Sociology.* New York: Free Press.

Csikszentmihalyi, M. 1975. *Beyond Boredom and Anxiety.* San Francisco: Jossey-Bass.

Denzin, N. K. 1982. "On Time and Mind." Pp. 35-42 in *Studies in Symbolic Interaction.* Vol. 4, edited by N. K. Denzin. Greenwich, CT: JAI.

Fine, G. A. 1990. "Organizational Time: Temporal Demands and the Experience of Work in Restaurant Kitchens." *Social Forces* 69:95-114.

Flaherty, M. G. 1987a. "The Neglected Dimension of Temporality in Social Psychology." Pp. 143-55 in *Studies in Symbolic Interaction.* Vol. 8, edited by N. K. Denzin. Greenwich, CT: JAI.

————1987b. "Multiple Realities and the Experience of Duration." *Sociological Quarterly* 28:313-26.

————1991. "The Perception of Time and Situated Engrossment." *Social Psychology Quarterly* 54:76-85.

Goffman, E. 1959. *The Presentation of Self in Everyday Life.* Garden City, NY: Anchor, Doubleday.

————1961. *Encounters.* Indianapolis, IN: Bobbs-Merrill.

————1974. *Frame Analysis.* Cambridge, MA: Harvard University Press.

Hall, E. T. 1983. *The Dance of Life.* Garden City, NY: Anchor, Doubleday.

Heidegger, M. [1927] 1962. *Being and Time.* Translated by J. Macquarrie and E. Robinson. London: SCM Press.

Hochschild, A. R. 1983. *The Managed Heart.* Berkeley: University of California Press.

Koestler, A. 1960. *Dialogue with Death.* New York: Macmillan.

Lewis, J. D. and A. Weigert. 1981. "The Structures and Meanings of Social Time." *Social Forces* 60:432-62.

Lopata, H. Z. 1986. "Time in Anticipated Future and Events in Memory." *American Behavioral Scientist* 29:695-709.

Maines, D. R. 1983. "Time and Biography in Diabetic Experience." *Mid-American Review* 8:103-17.

Mead, G. H. 1934. *Mind, Self, and Society.* Chicago: University of Chicago Press.

Melbin, M. 1969. "Behavior Rhythms in Mental Hospitals." *American Journal of Sociology* 74:650-65.

————1978. "Night as Frontier." *American Sociological Review* 43:3-22.

Mills, C. W. 1959. *The Sociological Imagination.* New York: Oxford University Press.

Neisser, U. 1976. *Cognition and Reality: Principles and Implications of Cognitive Psychology.* San Francisco: Freeman.

Schutz, A. and T. Luckmann. 1973. *The Structures of the Life-World,* translated by R. M. Zaner and H. T. Engelhardt, Jr. Evanston, IL: Northwestern University Press.

Schwartz, B. 1975. *Queuing and Waiting.* Chicago: University of Chicago Press.

Sontag, S. 1966. *Against Interpretation.* New York: Farrar, Straus & Giroux.

Stryker, S. and A. Statham. 1985. "Symbolic Interaction and Role Theory." Pp. 311-78 in *Handbook of Social Psychology.* 3rd ed. Vol. 1, edited by G. Lindzey and E. Aronson. New York: Random House.

Turner, J. H. 1988. *A Theory of Social Interaction.* Stanford, CA: Stanford University Press.

Van Maanen, J. 1988. *Tales of the Field.* Chicago: University of Chicago Press.

Zerubavel, E. 1977. "The French Republican Calendar: A Case Study in the Sociology of Time." *American Sociological Review* 42:868-77.

———1979. *Patterns of Time in Hospital Life.* Chicago: University of Chicago Press.

———1981. *Hidden Rhythms.* Chicago: University of Chicago Press.

———1982. "Easter and Passover: On Calendars and Group Identity." *American Sociological Review* 47:284-89.

———1985. *The Seven Day Circle.* New York: Free Press.

8

Wild Life

Authenticity and the Human Experience of "Natural" Places

GARY ALAN FINE

As Erving Goffman (1974) trenchantly emphasized throughout *Frame Analysis*, not all realities have the same weight. We experience the world as a function of the keys that we select for deciphering it. For Goffman, the critical feature that determines how a situation could be interpreted is the frame, the sense of what it is that is happening, and this frame does not emerge directly from the situation but is a construction of the social actors who are parties to it. This provides a means by which the context that an actor operates within can be aligned with other, comparable contexts that an actor had experienced or known about, establishing the grounding for action (Fine 1992).

For his analysis, Goffman focuses on what occurs within the setting. The behaviors of actors provide the critical cues as to what is happening. While this understanding is both true and valid, it has the effect of downplaying the effects of the surround (the *Umwelt*)—the ultimate reality of place. Yet, the backdrop of interaction is a powerful force in generating meaning. Although the interpretive significance of place does not derive from the noumenal reality of the location as a physical space, meaning does become attached to place so strongly that it becomes firmly linked and unquestioned by actors.

My argument about the effects of the lived experience of place, and hence its capacity for generating meaning, can be applied to all types of places. To achieve analytic focus, however, I shall explore the elements of one special sort of place: those physical arenas that we term *nature*. I argue that "being in nature" provides a lens for experiencing "reality," a *deep reality*. This experience is cognitive, affective, and behavioral.

Most people believe cognitively and feel in their "gut" that nature and culture are different kinds of "things," separate realms, and then act accordingly. For better or worse, we moderns are born within a social world that we consider cultural, created by design, and only occasionally do we step outside into "nature," separate from ourselves. Our cocoon is spun by human hands.

Three Visions of Nature

It seems like a simple question: What is nature? Not so. Like all spheres of existence, humans attempt to understand the natural environment by means of metaphors. The question therefore becomes not "What is nature?" but "What is nature like?" To understand this question, I present three competing perspectives—visions—of nature. These are social constructions that emerge and change over time, affect our experiences of "nature," and influence what we are willing to countenance being done to our planet.

An Imperial Vision: Nature as Usufruct

A common, "preenvironmentalist" view of the relationship between humanity and nature postulates what Donald Worster (1977) terms the "Imperial" vision. This sees a sharp differentiation between culture and nature, suggesting that nature is to be used for human purposes. A recent articulate and visible advocate of this vision was James Watt. This perspective gives no special moral weight to nature, except, in some versions, as defining nature as needing to be "tamed." The turn-of-the-century supporters of nature preserves were frequently business leaders, who saw no contradiction between their capitalist ventures, often dependent on the extraction of natural resources, and their support of environmental preserves. Humans had the legitimate right to dominate nature and to make choices as to its place and boundaries.

A Protectionist Vision: Saving Nature From Ourselves

In contrast to an imperial vision, other models award "nature" a special position. While these views have been lumped together as "environmentalism," this lumping ignores at least two distinct strands: one an inversion of the imperial vision, and the other an attempt to claim the basic oneness of the planet. Each theme animates current environmental writing and thought. The first approach, which we might term a *protectionist* vision, argues that nature is a special realm—authentic and uncontaminated, fundamentally distinct from the built environment (Hewitt 1984). Such a view implies that nature is a preserve that human beings could easily spoil. We protect nature from our own incursions and instincts. We must set aside wilderness areas, prevent acid rain, and limit the human, "built" environment. This view is evident in the naturalist's slogan that, in nature, "one should take nothing but memories, and leave nothing but footprints." Even the smallest transformation is inappropriate. This view inverts the imperial view of nature that underlines human moral authority over nature. We have the responsibility to restrain our activities to protect nature. As one environmentalist and amateur mushroom collector averred: "Life on earth could exist very nicely without people, a hell of a lot better without people, but it couldn't exist without fungi. Human beings are the biggest threat to nature. . . . We should try to have as little impact on the environment as possible" (Personal interview). Both the protectionist and the imperial view see culture and nature as separate realities. Human activity differs from activities of other beings: The human dam has a different moral valuation than a beaver dam. Whether this attitude is based on the fact that human activities are more complex (depending on a greater array of tools) or more consequential, a differential moral calculus is claimed.

An Organic Vision: Civil Rights for Trees

The other stream of environmental thought, which we might term an *organic* vision, is based on distinct presuppositions. It denies that human beings are separate from nature. From this perspective, human beings are part of nature—part of an organic whole. We reside in a republic of the Earth. A substantial proportion of environmental writers emphasize this argument, even while stressing the primacy of nature. The perspective of natural man residing in the Garden of Eden is a foundation of what Worster terms the "Arcadian" vision, which postulates a pastoral linkage between man and nature while postulating the authenticity of the natural environment. Yet, if human beings are part of nature, humans have no greater need to restrain human action than to restrain the actions of any creature. We can no more condemn the human hunter than the feline hunter, the developer than the nest maker, and the engineer than the beaver. Can we say that, when an animal builds a home, altering the ecosystem, that is natural, and, when humans do the same, "nature" has been violated. Each is operating on the basis of genetic and material capabilities and on some sense of what is in its interest. This perspective, then, could be used to erase the division between nature and culture, incorporating the latter into the former.

While this argument, as I have presented it here, would be abhorrent to the vast majority of self-defined environmentalists, it is the flip-side of attempts to ensure "rights" for nature, which also erases the conceptual boundary, or at least the legal distinction, between humans and other living things. For instance, Dave Foreman (quoted in Nash 1989, p. 4) suggests:

> We must constantly extend the community to include all. . . . The other beings— four-legged, winged, six-legged, rooted, flowing, etc.—have just as much right to be in that place as we do, they are their own justification for being, they have inherent value, value completely apart from whatever worth they have for . . . humans.

Foreman's argument is a part of the thrust for the expansion of rights that is characteristic of modern social systems (MacIntyre 1984). Yet, rights may cut several ways. If community includes all, we humans, too, have the rights gainsaid by this community of equals. If nature is to be a "protected" class, how and by whom is that protection justified? The answer involves the human perception of the powerlessness of nature. Rights are structured to protect the powerless while demanding that the powerful mitigate the full extent of their control. On the surface, humans have extensive power to alter nature, but the powerlessness of nature with regard to human expansiveness is a moral virtue. From the standpoint of the human actors, nature is among the "oppressed." This virtue is evident in that portion of the environmental movement that can be read as a civil rights movement for trees (see Stone 1974).

We live in an age characterized by an "ethic of tolerance," particularly among intellectual and cultural elites. There is an insistent questioning of the place of elites; a questioning whether the status structure is just and whether there aren't special virtues in the oppressed—what Tom Wolfe (1970) cynically referred to as *nostalgie de la boue*. This is evident in social movements that question the established power structure on behalf of minorities, women, children, and animals. These movements can be read, in making a moral claim for these groups, as demonstrating a purity, a purity that stems from the mix of innocence and exploitation. As Nash (1989) suggests, this circle is now being expanded to include nature. The environmental movement is part of this same bundle of social movements, growing out of the questioning 1960s. Nature has been invested with a peace and innocence that depends for its status on being controlled by more powerful human forces. Loving nature is a luxury in a human culture that so totally dominates it. Fear is only sensible when there is a perceived danger to society and the individuals that constitute it.

Is "Nature" "Natural"?

How "nature" is interpreted is not "natural." It, too, is a part of culture. The meaning of nature is not inherent in the environment itself but requires a human template. We do not come into the world with a sense of nature as natural—all objects, after all, have greater or fewer transformations by human hands. According to the protectionist vision, the question of human transformation is often defined as crucial to what "nature" means. Yet, this view is not without potential challenge, as we attempt to force nature to live up to our expectations of it. In our national parks (e.g., Chase 1987), we actively transform nature to make it feel authentic. An interrelated ecosystem inevitably causes problems for protectionists who wish for "pure" nature.

Most Americans—three-fourths of the population if surveys can be believed—define themselves as environmentalists. The label is a badge of honor. We claim that we "love" nature, but what does this love entail? The idea of "nature" suggests in practice the existence of "culture": In the protectionist vision, the differentiation is overt; in the organic vision, the implicit argument is that humans (as a class) must change their behaviors to be "in tune" with nature and to allow nature a voice in human affairs (the legitimacy of "rights"). In the former vision, human beings are separate from nature *by nature*; in the latter vision, human beings separated themselves from nature and need to adjust to it for their benefit.

We can imagine a world in which a beaver's dam and a human dam could be considered the same sort of construction. Yet, this is not our world. The definitional choice is ours, and we have made it. The "ultimate" meaning of nature is shaped by humans; the idea that nature and culture are not and cannot be ultimately separate in their metaphysical reality is at the heart of an interpretivist approach to human life. In this sense, the nature-culture division is, at its heart, a fraud.

Why do we distinguish between culture and nature? There is a set of social differentiations that have become traditional, unthought, and that humans as symbol users accept without self-reflection. The claim that there exists an autonomous realm of nature is taught by parents from infancy and bolstered by the ideology of schooling and children's books. We learn to treat natural settings differently than cultural settings. Those realms that are (or appear) unsusceptible to human shaping have been lumped into the category of nature. Human beings for millennia have distinguished between nature and culture, which some theorists, such as Lévi-Strauss (1962), suggest, without proof, is a distinction that is inherent in human thought. Whether it is truly inherent, it is a distinction, in effect, between "us" and "not-us"—the basic mode of differentiation. Us and not-us distinctions operate on many levels: from the infant recognizing that the mother's breast is separate from the infant's body, to ethnic groups differentiating themselves from other groups, to gender or racial divisions. To the degree that humans recognize themselves as a species, then a distinction with other species feels self-evident, even though it has been learned. What humans do is seen as qualitatively different than what humans have not done, and nature, defined as untransformed by human action—despite the falsity of that claim—is differentiated from the built environment.[1]

Mushrooms and I

To examine the collision of nature and culture, I focus on a single small corner of environmental interest: people who have joined an organization to collect mushrooms in their leisure time—the Minnesota Mycological Society. I explore how mushrooms are transformed from often unseen objects to meaningful ones.

In most major metropolitan areas (particularly in the Northeast, Midwest, and West), there are a group of amateurs who have banded together for support and community in the fulfillment of their hobby. The Minnesota Mycological Society meets once a week during the prime mushroom-picking months in Minnesota: May, June, September, and October. At these meetings, the president describes the mushrooms that members bring. In addition to these meetings, the club organizes approximately half a dozen forays to state and county parks and private land. I attended most of the meetings, forays, and banquets during a three-year period, writing detailed field notes. These notes were supplemented with a questionnaire I sent to all members as well as in-depth interviews with approximately two dozen members.

I entered the research with very little knowledge of mushrooms and mushroom collecting, never having collected mushrooms in the wild, and knowing no more than two or three species. Like other novices, I had a desire to learn where and how to pick morel mushrooms, which appear only for three weeks in the spring, but had no appreciation of the diversity of fungal species. Most crucially, I had no idea of the range of subjective meanings attached to mushrooms and, like many novices, I was profoundly anxious about eating wild mushrooms, even those that I was assured were prime edibles and entirely safe. I kept expecting to keel over, even days after consuming species that I could not myself identify. Most novices, early in their mycological experiences, go through a period in which they must place their confidence in their more experienced fellows, assuming that their trust will be well placed, for, if not, it could potentially lead to death.

Transfiguring Nature

We must go beyond the recognition that nature is a social construction, for each part of nature is equally a social construction. People attempt to make sense of the world of nature not *in its own terms* but as an extension of human society. Culture is a template to understand the environment. As Blumer (1969, p. 2) maintained, all meaning is generated through social interaction, not through qualities inherent in the objects themselves.

To this point, I have focused on how people come to understand nature as a general concern—as a master concept—without heeding the "micro reality" of the natural sphere. I now turn to this micro reality. When people become "interested" in nature, we choose some corner of what we term the *natural environment,* an environment that in its specifics is opaque, and provide it meaning; we learn about it and make it symbolic. We make others' ground our figure. In the apt phrase of philosopher Arthur Danto (1981), we participate in "the transfiguration of the commonplace." Danto's witty phrase refers to modern art, where, as in nature, the issue is to pull out meanings from objects that many think lack them.

It is surely no exaggeration to suggest that, for most Americans, mushrooms are not a topic that commands much interest. Perhaps mushrooms are considered a nice addition to spinach salad, perhaps they are something that children are warned to avoid, or perhaps they are seen as homes for elves. More typically, for most Americans, mushrooms are out of mind and thus out of sight. What we don't know of and what we don't expect are excluded from our vision. As one prominent mushroomer recalled:

> I can't remember ever seeing a single mushroom in Kentucky [where he grew up], and yet I hiked the hills and spent a great deal of time in the country. . . . I can't remember *one single mushroom.* I wonder how many morels I stumbled over. (Personal interview)

The slogan of the North American Mycological Association, "A world of wonder at your feet," is particularly telling in that a part of the wonder is recognizing that it was at your feet all along.

For novices interested in any corner of nature, and specifically for mushroomers, one of the first tasks is to identify the objects that they come upon—to distinguish them from others of that class, so that everything is not simply a "mushroom." The act of distinguishing objects involves the potential to separate them by their meaning (Stone 1977). People have a strong desire to know, a desire that is often frustrated by the variations produced by weather, age, species variation, substrate, or disease.

In most spheres of meaning, there is a core that is symbolically and subjectively central as well as marginal elements that are seen as profoundly deviant and threatening to that core. When a determination cannot be made as to belonging, these ambiguous, residual objects may be excluded from consideration, because they threaten the collector's competence. In mushroom collecting, those mushrooms that are difficult to identify are often ignored—they are treated as if they were not there and are derisively described as "forest trash" or "lawn litter" or, more generally, as LBMs (Little Brown Mushrooms). The Little Brown Jobbies (LBJs) of bird watchers and the "rock rubbish" of rock collectors suggest that this desire to know is generalizable and that there is an exclusion of what is not knowable.

Knowability is subjectively constructed rather than grounded in "fact." Species categories *could* be created that permit an easier, macroscopic determination (some species *are* known by their visual appearance, even to scientists). Successful identification of any object is rewarding, and LBMs offer few rewards and generate little meaning; they are "out of frame." These mushrooms are ignored in favor of others with more symbolic potency. Even though they are equally "fungal," they do not carry the subjective satisfaction of those that collectors define as more "distinctive."

Understanding nature goes beyond identification; it includes evaluation. In mushroom collecting, the edibility of mushrooms, crucial to many hobbyists, is often translated into a related moral evaluation of good and bad. A "good" one is one you can eat; a "bad" one is poisonous, although some more sophisticated collectors are willing to expand their definition of "good" to include rarity and scientific interest, as in this discussion:

> At a mushroom society meeting Brian comments about a *Psathyrella epimyces*: "This is a mushroom which grows on a mushroom [i.e., a parasitic mushroom]. . . . We are very lucky, very fortunate to find these three meetings in a row. . . . This is good stuff."

A woman asks him: "Is that edible?"

Brian responds: "I don't think so."

The woman says: "Then it's not good."

Brian responds: "It has its place in nature. It's good to see them. It's rare." (Field notes)

For none of the participants is a mushroom simply a mushroom.

An even stronger use of a cultural template to explain the natural environment is personification. Morels, the most popular edible mushroom, are often personified. They are objects of moral value and often are ascribed human-like qualities—blurring the lines between nature and culture. Thus mushroomers claim, jokingly, but significantly, that morels hide or run away. Hunting under the forest canopy with dappled sunlight, it is common to spot a morel, or what one thinks to be a morel, glance up, and be unable to find it again. The assumption here is that the mushroom and the hunter are engaged in a game or challenge. Consider a comment that addresses the fact that, in Minnesota, morels are typically found near prickly ash, stinging nettles, and poison ivy: "Morels like bad company, or at least protective company. Like having an Italian family around you. If you want it, you have to pay for it" (Field notes). Another mushroomer noted: "Sometimes I could almost believe that the mushrooms make themselves invisible, except when they let you find them" (Field notes). Morels are seen both as well-liked friends and as challenging opponents. Mushroomers frequently talk of these fungi *as if* they were human.

Images develop around other mushrooms as well. There is great respect for the "mystical" power of the deadly *Amanita virosa* (the Destroying Angel), a stately white mushroom. One mushroomer states that the *Amanita virosa* is "death masquerading as a virgin bride" (Saiki 1983, p. 5). Another describes it as "spooky." The deadly virosa, like the morel, is a challenging opponent.

A variety of sexual jokes and references are made in response to the spotting of a stinkhorn—*Phallus impudicus,* which looks like what its Latin name implies. The American common name is more discrete than that used by Poles, who call it the "lewd mushroom" (Harper 1985, p. 143). Jokes are made by male mushroomers about planting it on the lawns of women to whom they are attracted. One woman joked that she should send a picture of an erect stinkhorn, bracketed by two stinkhorn eggs, to *Hustler* magazine.[2]

In addition to personification, aesthetic valuation also plays a central role. Mushroomers, like other nature lovers, find their quarry beautiful. On any foray, mushroomers comment to each other about a particularly beautiful specimen or may "ooh" and "aah" at what they have found. For example, the president of the Minnesota Mycological Society pointed out a perfectly symmetrical *Pleurotis ostreatus*: "This is an art form. . . . It's that nifty, a beautiful specimen" (field notes). Likewise, consider this written description of truffles:

> There they were. Big. The size of a man's fist. Black. Like the night sky. And with a thick powerful aroma. The aroma of overripe olives, of sweet old mother earth, of indulgence. (Kasper 1984, p. 15)

Of course, not all mushrooms are given a positive evaluation. One club member described a slime mold—*Exidia glandulosa*—as "yuck on a stick." Another member said of a *Sarcosoma* specimen: "That was the ugliest, slimiest, ugh, thing." A third said of *Lycogala epidendrum*: "It looks like spit."

To outsiders, the identification of mushrooms might seem to be an instance of purely technical knowledge, but the above examples suggest that the knowledge here—and elsewhere in the natural world—has been made moral. The shared investment of meaning gives mushrooms significance beyond what their biological form provides.

Felt Emotion in the Wild

Let us return to our division among imperialists, protectionists, and organicists. Their existence recognizes that spatial reality can be defined and understood in various ways, but they also suggest that the world can be *felt* differently. We can see this division as tapping the variables of "sacred" and "secular." This distinction is, at root, a claim about how the world, or portions of it, are to be experienced. The imperialist view makes nature a secular realm, a realm of resources. In contrast, from the environmental perspective, "nature" is God's preserve (or the mystical equivalent of the divine). This contrasts with man's role. Here the term *man* is quite deliberate, as women have had traditionally something of the same status as nature—wild, unciv-ilized, and uncontrolled (yin, not yang)—to be valued, subjugated, and protected.

Nature, particularly the untamed nature of wilderness, is often defined as a tonic for modernity by those who feel the sacredness of nature. Consider the words of George Evans in 1904 (Nash 1967, p. 141):

> Whenever the light of civilization falls upon you with a blighting power . . . go to the wilderness. . . . Dull business routine, the fierce passions of the market place, the perils of envious cities become but a memory. . . . The wilderness will take hold of you. It will give you good red blood; it will turn you from a weakling into a man. . . . You will soon behold all with a peaceful soul.

Evans's argument is that nature changes the emotional tenor of life: the way that we experience the world. Similarly, Ralph Waldo Emerson ([1836] 1983, p. 11) believed that "the greatest delight which the fields and woods minister is the suggestion of an occult relationship between man and the vegetable." Nature, in this romantic view, represents an unmediated and intensely personal relationship between the person and the natural world (Robbins 1987, p. 593). Through nature, one can learn about life and oneself. As amateur mycologists note:

> In the woods, the wind blows and the leaves fall and one learns to come to terms with life. You see clearly there is a time for being born and a time for dying. (Rosen 1982, p. 25)

> Early in the season, hunting in the cool, magnificent giant redwood forests . . . can produce both many choice edible mushrooms . . . and an exquisite sense of beauty, tranquility and exultation from the deep silence and sheer size of the trees. Right next to a thousand-year-old 300-foot tall giant, you can find tiny, fragile, elegant Lepiotas and Mycenas, which can set your senses of proportion and perspective atingle. (Stickney 1983-84, pp. 27-28)

It is common to hear references to the "mysteries of nature," "the temple of nature," "primal glory," and "sublime solitude." Wilderness is a state of mind (Nash 1967, p. 5)—a lived reality that is felt as different than being located in a built environment. One voluntarily tenders a sense of control in such settings. In the words of John Hewitt (1984, pp. 9-10), nature is "an authentic reality." In this, Hewitt is emphasizing that nature is separate from the built environment, and is felt as "solid, unyielding, fixed and necessary. Nature is construed as a reality that exists and endures on her own terms."

This feeling is most dramatically expressed when nature and divinity are linked and tied to feelings of mystical possession. For instance, Thaddeus Masson Harris (Nash 1967, p. 58) argued in the nineteenth century that "there is something which impresses the mind with awe in the shade and silence of these vast forests. In the deep solitude, along with nature, we converse with GOD." Entering the woods produced "some of the same emotions felt by a devout Christian entering the door of his church" (Rieger 1986, p. 35). As John Muir (Chase 1987, p. 300) wrote after visiting Yellowstone in 1885:

> A thousand Yellowstone wonders are calling. "Look up and down and round about you!" And a multitude of still, small voices may be heard directing you to look through all this transient, shifting show of things called "substantial" into the truly substantial spiritual world whose forms flesh and wood, rock and water, air and sunshine, only veil and conceal, and to learn that here is heaven and the dwelling-place of the angels.

Nature worship is sacralization for the modern man,[3] a quasi religion originating in the early American republic, flowering with Emerson, Thoreau, and John Muir, and expanding in the twentieth century into what Alston Chase (1987, p. 300) termed "a new distinctively American religion." While this bald statement surely goes too far, given the lack of doctrinal, ritualistic, and institutional components of this religion, feelings of awe are present. Truly, we experience nature, share faith with it, as much as "know" it.

Threats and Finds

Where is emotion found in the wild? Turning from the general qualities of emotional response to "nature," I examine the fears and joys of actually being in the field. In this case, I examine how mushroomers respond to particular threats and finds. Lived experience in nature, in practice, can be filled with emotions. Although being in nature does not by itself compel any set of emotions, the symbolic meaning of natural objects, as discussed above, can be translated into felt emotion.

To demonstrate how this operates in practice, I return to my discussion of mushroom collectors to examine their responses to danger and to success, to how particular events and discoveries are felt—not as something external, but internally.

Danger. Mushroom collectors, like all naturalists, face some threats that derive from separating themselves from an environment in which human control is total. They indulge a desire to "go native." Removing oneself from "civilization" is part of the call of the wild. We desire to free ourselves from human chains, but along with this giving up of control comes danger. For mushroom collectors, this danger is exacerbated in that their lack of control is connected to their desire to consume, what are to many, unknown objects. Consider the comments of a mycologist about the fear involved in the consumption of mushrooms as well as other "wild tasks":

> There's . . . a fear element. If you really get into mushrooms, and, like the Japanese blowfish, if you eat a bad one, you die. . . . Presumably within the mycological society, there are people who are pressing the limits. . . . So, there's that kind of challenge in mycology. You really can extend the limits of your knowledge. (Personal interview)

Further, mushroomers, like many nature lovers, are willing to experience uncomfortable experiences, as one comments: "I know of cases of poison ivy contracted during mushroom outings. A young woman in Upper Sandusky once counted 103 chigger bites on her body the day following a foray" (Grimm 1985, p. 39). Most mushroomers can contribute stories about similar mundane troubles. The benefits outweigh the drawbacks but, as the first quotation suggests, some drawbacks may be benefits. Dangerous activities such as rock climbing tend to produce this dangerous satisfaction (Alverez 1988; Fox 1981, p. 338; Mitchell 1983; Walter 1984, p. 74). As Vester (1987, pp. 245-46) suggests, risk can be associated with a feeling of transcendence—making ordinary life into an "adventure." Under such circumstances, people can feel self-actualized. As Elias and Dunning (1986, p. 106) note,

> in leisure occupations, seemingly antagonistic feelings such as fear and pleasure are not simply opposed to one another . . . but are inseparable parts of a process of leisure enjoyment. . . . In that sense, one can say that no satisfaction can be had from leisure occupations without short wisps of fear alternating with flutters of delight, and in some cases, through waves of this kind.

This tension between fear (or, at least, the demand for perceptual clarity) and satisfaction is what Csikszentmihalyi (1975, 1990) labels "flow"—an optimal human experience, an intense focusing of attention. Being in nature, while not inevitably producing feelings of flow, seems linked because of the lack of human control.

Joy. Danger is not the only way in which individuals discover transcendence or self-actualization. Nature is filled with hidden beauties—objects that are figuratively, and occasionally literally, breathtaking. These experiences, known to bird-watchers, rock hounds, photographers, mountaineers, mushroomers, and dozens of other "nature lovers," demonstrate the possibility for emotional response to nature—responses that might make little sense to those outside of the community.

Consider the mushroomer who finds a particularly rare species, one that he has long been searching for:

> I looked for it [a *Vorariella bombycina*] all my life. . . . I have known about this mushroom, and looked for it for years. I mean, there's a picture I have in my mind from Orson Miller's book, and I imagined walking up trails and finding it on trees. For years I imagined this thing. I never found it. Last summer we were riding along on the road, and, as we passed a tree, I knew—I saw—I knew with absolute certainty that that's what it was. . . . First of all, to have that image of searching for it, that energy stored up to look for it. You know, myths kind of accumulate energy anyway . . . and then to have it suddenly discharged in that moment is like a lightning flash. When I picked it and realized what it was, it [was] absolute vindication. (Personal interview)

He relates a sense of triumph, of intense satisfaction that occurs in a blinding flash. Emotions upon finding a cache of particularly valued, rare, or beautiful mushrooms can range from awe to exhilaration to a near religious fervor:

> Finding a *Sparassis* was an experience God bestowed only on the truly deserving. "Here I was, worming along the ground looking at these tiny little mushrooms, when I caught a glimpse of something bright out of the corner of my eye midway along a rotted log. I remember thinking in awed tones to myself, 'I finally found one.'" (Norvell 1987, p. 27)

> Finding buried gold on a treasure hunt could not bring more joy than that felt by mushroom hunters at the discovery of a fine crop of morels. With cries of delight I dropped to my knees on the fragrant leaf mold and the hunt was on. ("Morel Mania," 1985, p. 1)

> Three intense white masses draped over fallen logs stunned me with their brilliance. I held my breath and recounted. I had found three of the much prized *Hericium abietis*. . . . Each cluster was larger than my basket. My heart beat faster, my breath came shorter and quicker. I raced over to the closest one, knife ready. I knelt and cut between the log and fairy mass, the sweet, heady fragrance rising up about me. Placing the delicate sculpture on my lap, I marveled at the weight of it. . . . Gently I turned it this way and that, caught by its iridescence in the sunlight. (Morrell 1984, p. 37)

One should take care in extrapolating from "literary" texts to experiences in the field—lived experience unmediated by the pen. Still, observation of a mushroom foray provides evidence that people are excited or awed by what they capture in the fields and woods. They ooh and aah and call their friends around to experience and validate their good fortune. Later, they will transform their experience into a narrative that they can share publicly.

The relationship between lived experience and narrative is significant. The narration mediates the experience into a social form. As listeners, or even copresent observers, we lack access to the internal emotional responses of the subject. The experience of finding a mushroom is transformed into an exaggerated story, which combines humor and awe—the presentation of an event that could only happen once or, implicitly, could never happen at all. For instance, consider the account of one mushroomer who finds a field full of the very beautiful, reddish-orange *Amanita ceasarea*:

> [I] was slightly embarrassed when coming across one, I thought it was a golf ball . . . golf balls everywhere in the middle of the woods! Excited as we were to find those first few and then seeing the eggs that meant that more were forthcoming, we figured we had had the highlight of the day, but the climax was still to come. After settling in, I went out for another quick walk little knowing that it would turn into a "mystical journey to a land where *Amanita caesarea* ruled elegantly and profusely." So many there were, that I will never quite believe this to probably be a one-time event. We walked on counting one after another one to some hundred-fifty—that day alone, in various stages of development. Oh, there were other mushrooms about, but nothing surpassing the beauty and delight of these "emperors of the woods." We had truly found Caesar's Haven! . . . A few hours that will always be special as I remember all the places and miles I've walked. (Bobersky 1984, p. 5)

Similar stories of great finds are common as some mushroomers joke about needing to cut large mushrooms with a scythe (Rogers 1983, p. 46) or lawn mower (field notes), or, as one Alaska mushroomer recounted: "*Leccinum auranticum* is so thick around the house that some mornings I've got to get out the 4 x 4 and plow the driveway clear of the things before I can go to work" (Sutcliffe 1986-87, p. 11). Stories of sore backs from picking amazing quantities of mushrooms are also common. The public story constitutes the experience and makes it socially real. As Mitchell (1983, p. 72) suggests about mountain climbers:

> As a social phenomenon the climb is not over until the tale is told. The meaning of mountaineering events emerges in the reflective discussion and debate that follow them. Debriefing is the occasion when one's private physical accomplishments become public social topics of interest. . . . The past event is reinterpreted, clarified, and judged.

For this reason, narrators are motivated to present the event and the felt experience of the event in a self-enhancing light. As suggested above, these stories often contain an emotional template, depicting the satisfaction of life in the woods; the emotional reactions are magnified and dramatized. This leads to the assumption, jocular in part, that such stories will be as fictional of those of fishermen. As the president of the Minnesota Mycological Society said after the end of one of their weekly meetings: "We can visit now. That's one of the nice things to do. Swap lies about what you found and where you found it." These "fish stories" have become institutionalized as means of sharing the "joys" of being in nature with others—not only making status claims but pointing to the rich rewards that nature can provide.

Nature Time

I have discussed some of the cognitive and emotional components of human understandings of nature. Yet, this ignores the experienced component of human-nature interaction. What does it mean to be in nature as a subjectively meaningful sensation? While there are many dimensions on which this question might be answered, I shall focus here on a single issue: how time is experienced in the wild. Time is fundamentally a social construct, a creation of social organization, along with the built environment. Examining the reality of time in nature will, I hope, reveal something about nature, about time, and about the way that humans experience the two in conjunction.

To understand the meaning of time in the wild, one must imagine oneself within an untransformed preserve—one must lay aside one's powers of transformation and give oneself to the experience. Time itself seems to have a different quality in a natural environment than it does in a built environment. On the level of the environment itself, time has a different phenomenological reality in nature than it does in a built environment. Clock time is structurally irrelevant in nature, although it is not infrequently depended on by those humans who do not choose to cut the ties to the built environment. The time sequences that have greater centrality are those I describe as meteorological time, lived time, and biological time.

By *meteorological time,* I refer to the experience of the day that results from changes brought about by the rotation of the earth and by changes in weather patterns. What is most dramatic and obvious in this regard is the alternation of day and night—the rotation of the earth, producing the apparent movement of sun, moon, and stars. One responds to nature depending upon the time of day. Watches serve as a surrogate for a close examination of the movement of the sun, but the watches merely symbolize that movement. One may choose to find shelter or return to the built environment depending on one's observations and the clues implied about changes in one's experience of nature.

More subtly, one may react to the natural environment based on changes in the ambient air or in the sky color. Temperatures change, both regularly and unexpectedly. Some people can predict approaching rain through temperature or wind change. A sudden stillness in the air or a change in pressure serve almost as an alarm—a warning that the end of one natural segment is near and another is to begin. While this temporal pattern is not as precise as the hands of a clock in predicting duration, it may be precise in its prediction of sequence.

The second temporal feature of the experience of nature involves *lived time*. As noted, Csikszentmihalyi (1975) speaks of flow, in which an individual is so engrossed in an activity that temporal experience is literally not experienced—one runs on adrenaline and tightly focused attention. While some flow experiences occur within natural surroundings—for instance, when scaling rocks or mountain climbing—the experience of nature is not typically a flow experience in the sense that Csikszentmihalyi uses the term. Temporality is experienced, but one is rarely consciously reminded of it. One is engrossed but not overwhelmed. We might conceive of being in nature the way that Goffman speaks of participation in games in his essay "Fun in Games." Goffman (1961, p. 17) suggests that a lack of "fun" is an adequate excuse for withdrawal. So it is when one visits a natural environment to "experience" it. There is no instrumental rationale for one's presence; the justification is purely expressive. When time becomes noticeable, it suggests that something is wrong. One begins to judge one's satisfaction self-consciously rather than "simply" experiencing nature. In such a situation, one is likely to change one's location or remove oneself from the natural environment. In the case of mushrooming, collectors enjoy the activity, but not without temporal limits. There is a point of diminishing returns for each mushroomer, when one loses interest, can't find additional interesting mushrooms, or desires a change of pace. One becomes aware of the sense of *duree*. No mushroomers, bird-watchers, hikers, or butterfly collectors enjoy these pleasures for unlimited periods. The internal recognition of the passage of time, brought about by intrusive external cues, provides a motivation to alter one's location in the natural environment.

The third form of time in nature, *biological time,* connects to lived time. Certain biological realities exert pressure on the individual if they are ignored for too long. No matter how interested or involved an individual may be in communing with the natural environment, one's stomach or bowels eventually take precedence. One's body and one's physicality have an obdurate reality, and this reality cannot be put aside for long. Being in nature can become uncomfortable, and people respond to those feelings. Walking for hours, by virtue of its temporal duration, and the strain that it places on one's muscles and joints, leads to exhaustion and a desire to rest. Biological experiences have temporal realities, and these realities connect to the subjective experience of time. The body maintains its own biological clock, which the experience of being in nature can alter if we become engrossed but cannot completely overwhelm.

Obviously, clock time is not entirely absent when humans and nature share a space: Modern men and women remain "tourists" when outside of the built environment. They visit such locations rather than reside there: They are strangers in the Garden of Eden and Forest of Arden. Humans typically have obligations outside of this environment. There are other engagements—meals, meetings, work, school—that press, and so most tourists bring a watch and, should they have other obligations, use it. Clock time is a temporal cocoon around the experience of nature.

Frequently, human tourists "give themselves" a certain amount of time to remain in nature (two hours of mushroom collecting, three hours for a hike) and time their activities according to this decision. In these cases, the temporal experience of nature has dimensions similar to the temporal experience of the built environment in terms of the closure of the experience.

Conclusion

The experience of being in nature is potent; an experience that in some regards is more intense, at times, than being in the built environment. As I have emphasized, it is not nature itself that is a different reality; rather, our experience of nature is a consequence of the way in which nature is treated as a social construction—an "authentic reality." This belief in the authenticity of nature has profound effects in attitudes, emotions, behavior, and even in the nature of temporal experience. Nature, whatever this odd construct means as a noumenal reality, is treated as separate from culture, and, so, it is separate from culture. Nature is seen as ultimate and authentic, whereas that side of the world that we humans have organized is often seen as artificial and derivative.

Although researchers have not much examined nature as a scholarly arena in its own right, I hope I have demonstrated that the human experience of an open meadow on a cool spring morning carries as much sociological *gravitas* as the hustle of a factory floor on a sweaty summer afternoon.

Notes

1. Within the nature/culture distinction, there are numerous subcategories. Nature can be divided into forest, meadow, prairie, wilderness, ocean, tundra, and the like. These are second-order divisions: not as basic as that of "nature."

2. The symbolism of this mushroom can even have more dramatic effects, as in the following story ("A Theory About Stinkhorns," 1982, p. 2) cribbed from *The New York Times* of February 24, 1929: "Today at Melun, near Paris, the trial of the 12 religious devotees, ten of them women, who nearly killed the Curé of Bonbon several weeks ago when, with sticks and stones, they tried to drive the devil out of the poor man. Their accusation against him was that when migrating birds flew southward over Bonbon the priest filled them with disease, so that when they passed over Bordeaux, 500 miles away, they caused to grow poisoned mushrooms of lascivious shapes and noxious odor, which gave the residents on the banks of the Gironde shameful diseases in various forms."

3. A large proportion of naturalists were men; it was not until the 1960s that any sizable portion of nature writers were women. Whether women had the same experiences as men is a separate issue.

References

Alverez, A. 1988. "Feeding the Rat." *The New Yorker*, April 18, pp. 99-115.

Blumer, Herbert. 1969. *Symbolic Interactionism.* Englewood Cliffs, NJ: Prentice-Hall.

Bobersky, M. E. 1984. "Caesars by the Dozens: A Postscript." *Ohio Spore Print*, March/April, p. 5.

Chase, Alston. 1987. *Playing God in Yellowstone.* New York: Harcourt Brace Jovanovich.

Csikszentmihalyi, Mihalyi. 1975. *Beyond Boredom and Anxiety.* San Francisco: Jossey-Bass.

———1990. *Flow: The Psychology of Optimal Experience.* New York: Harper & Row.

Danto, Arthur C. 1981. *The Transfiguration of the Commonplace.* Cambridge, MA: Harvard University Press.

Elias, Norbert and Eric Dunning. 1986. *Quest for Excitement.* Oxford: Basil Blackwell.

Emerson, Ralph Waldo. [1836] 1983. "Nature." In *Essays & Lectures,* by Ralph Waldo Emerson. New York: Library of America.

Fine, Gary Alan. 1992. "Agency, Structure, and Comparative Contexts: Toward a Synthetic Interactionism." *Symbolic Interaction* 15: in press.

Fox, Stephen. 1981. *John Muir and His Legacy.* Boston: Little, Brown.

Goffman, Erving. 1961. *Encounters.* Indianapolis: Bobbs-Merrill.

———1974. *Frame Analysis.* Cambridge, MA: Harvard University Press.

Grimm, Dick. 1985. "Eating Wild Mushrooms Is Dangerous." *Mushroom* 3(Fall):39.

Harper, Herbert H. 1985. *Harper's Mushroom Reference Guide & Check List.* Forest Lake, MN: Herbert H. Harper.

Hewitt, John. 1984. "Stalking the Wild Identity." Unpublished manuscript.

Kasper, Bob. 1984. "Truffles Are Here!" *Mushroom* 2(Summer):15.

Lévi-Strauss, Claude. 1962. *The Savage Mind.* Chicago: University of Chicago Press.

MacIntyre, Alasdair. 1984. *After Virtue.* Notre Dame: Notre Dame University Press.

Mitchell, Richard. 1983. *Mountain Experience.* Chicago: University of Chicago Press.

"Morel Mania." 1985. *Mycena News* (Newsletter of the Mycological Society of San Francisco) 34(April):1, 4.

Morrell, Darby. 1984. "Finding Hericium Abietis." *Mushroom* 2(Fall):37.

Nash, Roderick F. 1967. *Wilderness and the American Mind.* New Haven, CT: Yale University Press.

———1989. *The Rights of Nature.* Madison: University of Wisconsin Press.

Norvell, Lorelei. 1987. "Sparassis." *Mushroom* 5(Fall):26-28.

Rieger, John. 1986. *American Sportsmen and the Origins of Conservation.* Rev. ed. Norman: University of Oklahoma Press.

Robbins, David. 1987. "Sport, Hegemony, and the Middle Class." *Theory, Culture & Society* 4:579-601.

Rogers, Maggie. 1983. "Keeping Up." *Mushroom* 1(Fall):46-47.

Rosen, Samuel R. 1982. *A Judge Judges Mushrooms.* Nashville, IN: Highlander.

Saiki, Jessie K. 1983. "Death's Angel (Amanita Virosa)." *Wisconsin Mycological Society Newsletter* 1(Spring):5.

Stickney, Larry. 1983-84. "Mushroom Vagabonding." *Mushroom* 2(Winter):27-28.

Stone, Christopher D. 1974. *Should Trees Have Standing? Toward Legal Rights for Natural Objects.* Los Altos, CA: W. Kaufmann.

Stone, Gregory. 1977. "Personal Acts." *Symbolic Interaction* 1:2-19.

Sutcliffe, Ron. 1986-87. "A Serious Case of Underpick-Alaska Mushrooming." *Mushroom* 5(Winter):11, 13.

"A Theory About Stinkhorns." 1982. *Newsletter: Parkside Mycological Club*, Autumn, p. 2.

Vester, Heinz-Gunter. 1987. "Adventure as a Form of Leisure." *Leisure Studies* 6:237-49.

Walter, J. A. 1984. "Death as Recreation: Armchair Mountaineering." *Leisure Studies* 3:67-76.

Wolfe, Tom. 1970. *Radical Chic & Mau-Mauing the Flak Catchers.* New York: Farrar, Straus & Giroux.

Worster, Donald. 1977. *Nature's Economy: The Roots of Ecology.* San Francisco: Sierra Club Books.

9

The Trail Through Experience

Finding Self in the Recollection of Travel

MARK NEUMANN

The road away from home calls out to many with a different promise. For some, it is a familiar offer of liberation from the routines of daily living. "I am so structured in my everyday life that when I'm on vacation, I'm free to think what I want to think, learn what I want to learn, spit out what I don't want," writes a 32-year-old Massachusetts man. Then, as he reflects on the free space of travel, he curiously adds: "Everyday life isn't very free for me right now, although what I'm doing now is what I want to do most." In a similar way, a 40-year-old California woman describes leisure travel as an opportunity to "recenter" herself. "I always get reflective on trips because the routine is broken," she says. "It seems like I always do a lot of my best thinking then—prioritizing, making decisions about myself and my family, those types of things—and the Grand Canyon was one of those types of trips. It's almost like therapy." A 26-year-old Utah woman recalls several reasons for hiking nearly 25 miles from the North Rim of Grand Canyon to the South Rim. "One of my motivations for this kind of traveling is to be able to say you've done it. It's almost like the work ethic, that the more work you do, the better experience it is. You're doing as much as you can," she says. "If you're going to Europe, you're seeing as much as you can. If you're at Grand Canyon, you're actually hiking it and not going down on some mule. I chose to walk. I think you get closer to the earth."

Their comments remind us that travel offers an opportunity to belong differently to the world for a while. But, in various ways, these recollections of travel also suggest how the promises of being "away" often find relief against the meanings of home. For one person, the meaning of travel straddles an unclear division between freedom and captivity. For another, the break in the routines of everyday life is a moment that prompts her to evaluate and reflect on those same routines. And for the woman who hikes the canyon, her leisure finds meaning as a form of work that provides a closer connection with the earth and as an experience that gains value in stories told at home.

To be sure, tourism is a flight from the routines and practices of everyday life. But it is also a place, as Henri Lefebvre (1979) argues about leisure generally, for critiquing daily life. The world of leisure, he argues, provides an inverse image of daily life. Leisure experience compensates for everyday life in ways that inherently recall and provide a critical stance toward the routine worlds that people attempt to escape. People seek out in leisure what is sometimes lost or obscured in the worlds of work, family, and private life. The world of leisure cannot develop, Lefebvre (1979, p. 137) notes, "without constant reference to everyday life and the changing contrasts implied by it."

Although commonly viewed as a reprieve from the "realities" of everyday living, tourism is a domain of leisure often criticized for its shallowness and inauthenticity. Daniel Boorstin (1961, p. 79), for instance, argues that tourism is filled with "diluted, contrived, prefabricated . . . pseudo-events." In an alternative view, however, Dean MacCannell (1976) suggests that tourists demand authenticity. In contrast to Boorstin, he argues that tourism is a form of pilgrimage where people seek to escape the shallowness and alienation of modern life and discover the "real." Although neither of these views comprehensively addresses the variations that are possible in tourist experience, they suggest much broader concerns about the relationship between society and self and the meaning of leisure in the context of everyday life.

Tourist sites—whether theme parks or national parks—are culturally contrived productions that raise a number of issues about authenticity. But, at the same time, they are places where people find themselves working toward forms of self-realization and meaning, attempting to fill experiential vacancies that run through contemporary life. This chapter examines the struggle of tourists to make meaning of their experience in a specific tourist location, the Grand Canyon region of northern Arizona. Through accounts that give form and significance to experiences sought away from home, people reflected on their travels in ways that produced visions of self and identity found through leisure.[1] While these narratives specifically center on nature tourism, they offer comments that often take much broader strokes at the meaning of travel. My concern in these stories is not with how people traveled on a particular trip or with the truth or falsity of their accounts. Instead, such stories reveal the ways people give structure and meaning to their experience in the moments of their telling (Neumann and Eason 1990). As people assign meaning and significance to their travel experiences, they reveal how culture and identity become incorporated through travel, the kinds of selves people find and lose while away from home, how identities are made as people confront others, and the peculiar and paradoxical ways that everyday life reappears as people seek to escape in their journeys.

Travel Accounts and the Performance of Self

Travel accounts are occasions when people produce the meaning and value of experiences that take place away from home. Karl Schiebe (1986, p. 130) suggests that adventure plays a central role "in the construction and development of life stories, and that life stories, in turn, are the major supports for human identities." For instance, one 37-year-old man recalled "the West was a place to go." Now living in Colorado, he reflected on his first journey west from his home in Connecticut in a manner that suggests the larger promise of the open road and its relationship to a personal biography:

> Some of my friends had gone to the Southwest and when they returned they seemed to have changed, somehow they were different, and I wanted to know what it was out there that had influenced that change. My first trip was in 1973, the Sixties had not quite come to an end and the road, as a place of discovery and becoming, was still a powerful theme among young people. The road represented adventure, uncertainty, and challenge as well as the prospect of personal growth. The road was a place where one could get an appreciation of what it was to be alive and human, and living on the eastern fringe of the continent, all roads led West.

His account describes a quintessential romantic vision of "the road" as a site of dual passages and reminds us that journeys provide the opportunity to acquire experiences that become the basis for discovering and transforming one's self. On the one hand, a journey is a passage from one point to another along a route of travel. The road is a line between the points, and the journey is characterized by a linear dimension with a beginning, a middle, and an end. During the journey, terrain that has been covered appears with a glance back over the shoulder. Before us, it is the horizon we move toward.

But, on the other hand, the movement over land is one through time as well. In this way, the journey identifies another kind of passage, a *temporal passage,* where people undergo experiences and transformations. The interlocking dimensions of time and space make the journey a potent metaphor that symbolizes the simultaneous discovery of a region and its people as well as a self. Journeys not only represent the exploration of an environment "but some redemptive experience occurring not in space but in another dimension, inner or spiritual," observes Janis Stout (1983, p. 13). "It is precisely this capacity for mirroring the inner and outer dimensions that makes possible the 'inward voyage,' an archetypal form in which movement through the geographic world becomes an analogue for the process of introspection."

Journeys provide the opportunity to acquire experiences that become the basis for the production of identity and are revealed through the narratives that emerge from travel experiences. "A journey *makes sense* as a 'coming to consciousness,' " notes James Clifford (1988, p. 167). "Its story hardens around an identity."

Through the performance of narratives, we also witness the performance of self. For many, the meaning and significance of travel assume value in the moment of recollecting for others the experiences that occur away from home. "I knew that it would be an adventure which would make a much more lasting impression for years after the trip," wrote a 45-year-old man from Ohio who took his family to Grand Canyon. "Recall of such experiences, I have found, is one of the true pleasures of the life experience." In a similar way, a man from Utah suggested that the home slide show is a clear indicator of such a desire to place experience on display for others:

> One of the guys that I know takes slides, maybe a hundred each time, so he has thousands and thousands of slides. Whole closets full of slide carousels. For him, I think a real big part of it is to have a slide show of where he's been. So he has like a little cult following of like fifteen or twenty people who come over every time and he gives a slide show virtually every week of where he's just been the week before. He goes to beautiful places, all the big mountain ranges in the west, and everywhere. I think a big important part for him is to take his camera. And he doesn't like prints that you keep more for yourself. A slide show is just that, it's a show.

These comments suggest that the possibility of recollection is a facet of travel that holds importance even before a person leaves home. While "home" may serve as a stable physical marker for the beginning and end of a tour, the experience of travel assumes various levels of conscious reflection that complicate the idea of what it means to be "away." The memory of a trip is a critical dimension of travel that holds a certain attraction and intrinsic reward that materialize in the moments of storytelling. "The pleasure of reminiscence might be just that—a pleasure independent of the environment experienced later," suggests Robert Riley (1979, p. 14), "a pleasure in which the poignance and power come solely from the internal play of memory, the very essence of the pleasure is the fact that it cannot be lived in the real world." As travel accounts provide a domain for performing a sense of self before others, moments of recollection also give structure to a journey that endows it with meaning and becomes a form of self-knowledge. Being a self requires having a story, and having a story requires recollecting ways of experiencing the world.

Tourist sites offer both knowledge about the world as well as an orientation to one's place in that world. Places such as the Grand Canyon are, in many ways, sites of existential performances, places where people can embody different dimensions of existence through self-presentation. These accounts reveal how the tourist site is itself a domain of self-performance, a place where people are at work, creatively making meaning, situating themselves in relation to public spectacle, attempting to order their experience, and composing narratives that provide some coherence between the self and a public world others have made. Storytelling provides a reflexive domain where we "show ourselves to ourselves" as we occupy the stage in our own dramas (Myerhoff 1982, p. 104). In doing so, these narratives mobilize the relationship between individuals and the cultural landscape. They are stories that show how culture moves through people's lives as people move through culture in places like the Grand Canyon (Braudy 1982). In their telling, the tourist site and the individual are integrated through narratives that mutually inform and energize each other.

At the Intersection of Culture and Identity

For many of the nearly 4 million who travel there each year, the Grand Canyon is a site where individuals locate their experience within an emblematic geography of narratives that produces the canyon's cultural value and significance. In addition to the automobiles, jets, buses, and trains that carry them to northern Arizona, canyon visitors ride a current of steady images and stories about the Grand Canyon that have circulated through American culture since the end of the nineteenth century and that have made the canyon a prominent landmark. "I chose to go to Grand Canyon because of its natural beauty and grandeur which I had seen in photographs and movies," wrote a 36-year-old Colorado man. For one 54-year-old Michigan woman, "A trip out West wouldn't seem complete without visiting the Grand Canyon—one of the wonders of nature I've read about and seen in movies and on TV."

Over time, the mass media, as well as personal stories and images, have cast a spell around the canyon. These forces of attraction call people away from home and bring the canyon into their lives. Flowing in the deep current of American cultural life, these images have much to do with the way the experience of the Grand Canyon has been constructed over time and influence how people integrate its meaning into their lives. "I like to travel to Europe, but felt that I should see some of my own country, too," wrote a 45-year-old Massachusetts woman. "The Grand Canyon was my top priority as I felt that it signified America as a natural wonder." For a 71-year-old Connecticut man, the canyon is "one of the great sites—and sights—of our nation. I didn't want to die without having seen it." Here, travel accounts suggest something of the relationship between the representations of the canyon and individual desires to experientially possess the cultural value inherent in those representations. In different ways, the canyon links people with a larger iconography of American experience.

As people move through the geographic, symbolic, dreamlike images produced by tourism, their accounts of travel reveal the equally diverse ways that culture *moves* through individual lives, providing reference points that can identify the biographical coordinates of family, self, and other. In this sense, the canyon is a stage for enacting situations and events that mark the development and meaning of relationships. Specific events are cast within the dimensions of relationships, and the recollections of travel not only emphasize where people go geographically but also the ways a journey tracks how they have been together. For one couple, hiking the canyon every year was a ritual that recognized the durability of self as well as their relationship. A retired 68-year-old Iowa woman said that an important part of her marriage was an annual hike into the Grand Canyon with her 71-year-old husband. "For us, coming back year after year gives us a feeling of confidence in ourselves, exercise and a challenge to keep ourselves in condition to do this hike each year," she wrote. The hike into the canyon not only provides a measure of self-confidence in their physical abilities but also carries itself into the routine of their daily lives as a goal to be accomplished again by keeping their bodies physically fit. Each year, returning to hike the canyon measures not only their physical endurance but is itself a performance that dramatizes their enduring relationship.

Others, as well, suggest how their trips to the canyon were part of a quest for common experiences that functioned to maintain relationships. For instance, a 46-year-old California woman who traveled through the South-west with her daughter emphasized the way the trip anticipated a change in their relationship. "She is away at school and probably won't move back home when she graduates," she wrote. "We had a wonderful time and had time to talk and fun seeing new places together. . . . And now we have this common experience to which we refer often and find photos or news articles to share with each other about places we saw." Although the trip is completed, it carries a memory of an extraordinary and exceptional time that continues to move within the currents of routine life. Another woman described how a series of trips taken with a friend formed a bond that gave depth to their friendship as well as helped to maintain it over time:

> I really feel a strong camaraderie with my friend Katherine and I don't think we'd necessarily be as close if we hadn't done these kinds of things. We have these great common experiences—hiking Grand Canyon and climbing Grand Teton—and they give you a common bond to look back on, to reminisce over. And especially because she was here while I was away on the east coast for about five years and we weren't establishing many new common experiences and things to reflect on, the fact that we had these things that were really physically challenging that we had done were important because they gave us an esprit de corps.

All of these examples suggest how the canyon becomes integrated into lives and relationships as people bind themselves through common experi-ence. But, while the canyon can serve as a symbolic site where people mark time with family and friends, it is also a site where they dramatize visions of self that differ from the familiar forms of identity that carry them through everyday life.

The Discovery of Self Through Travel

The moments of travel provide a context for entering into other levels of being and belonging to the world that activate latent or potential dimensions of self. "My first trip to Grand Canyon in 1984 was different [than other trips to the canyon] because I traveled as a single person for the first time," recalled a 47-year-old Wisconsin woman who has since rafted through the canyon on a number of occasions:

I chose to go to Grand Canyon because the river trip was sponsored by the College of Wooster and a planned, guided trip was the sort of thing I needed on my first solo vacation as a widow. That alone made it important in my life—a landmark of sorts. Because of the inherent dangers in rafting the Colorado River and climbing some challenging side canyons, it was a trip that was by far the most adventurous I'd ever taken. The combination of the emotional and physical impact was strong, indeed. It felt like a life-changing experience at the time and, in retrospect, it truly was.

Travel often provides situations and contexts where people confront alternative possibilities for belonging to the world and others that differ from everyday life. Indeed, part of the promise of travel is to live and know the self in other ways. Many times, the personal stories of travel suggest moments of transformation or transcendence, a witnessing of a moment where the structure, routine, and expectation of everyday life collapse. In such ruptures, people discover something of themselves that reveals alternative forms of identity.

The difficult hike to the bottom of the Grand Canyon is one activity some describe as an attempt to transcend the world of mass tourism that looks over the canyon's rim and to seek out the "real" canyon. Whether they actually do is debatable because hundreds of people daily walk the trails into the canyon. But, as people describe hiking down into the Grand Canyon, many of their accounts often suggest how a new sense of self emerges through the conditions and events experienced on such journeys. Their stories produce visions of self that reveal qualities of personal character, individuality, resistance, endurance, struggle, and accomplishment.

Some accounts testify to a sense of character and goodwill as people choose to describe how they helped others in time of trouble. "While hiking down, we caught up with this older man huffing and puffing and we asked if we could help him carry part of his pack," wrote a 61-year-old New Jersey man. "He asked us to take the whole thing, so we did and carried it the last mile. He made it down by walking backwards because his legs hurt so badly." A 23-year-old man from Germany said that he stopped to help a person hiking out of the canyon. "I gave another person so much of my water that I ran out before I made it to the rim," he wrote. "That was nearly dangerous. I never thought that water was so important." Each of these stories suggests personal sacrifice for the benefit of another. The stories thus become an opportunity to tell of good deeds and the account becomes a performance and display of character and unselfishness.

People also display a sense of character as they describe the endurance and challenges they have gone through in their journeys into the canyon. A 38-year-old woman from California, for example, described her hike to the bottom in terms that highlight an "adventurous," "risk-taking" self:

> We wanted to go down into the canyon because of our adventurous spirit. We had no food nor water and were not prepared to go down. We didn't realize that it could be dangerous hiking down without being prepared. We were willing to take the risk. As we began our journey we had intentions of only hiking a few hours. The closer we were, the more we wanted to continue. We finally decided to go all the way to the bottom even if we didn't have the necessary things to make the trip down safely. . . . I can still remember the feelings I had of excitement as we reached the bottom. Once we were there we decided to sleep there. We didn't have a permit, but that didn't bother us in the least. That night was one of the most memorable ones. The moonlight lit up the Colorado River. If I close my eyes now I can still see the picture vividly. The next day we went back up. We were hungry, thirsty, tired, dirty, and excited all at the same time because we had a fantastic experience.

The "adventurous spirit" that motivated her canyon trip seeks physical challenge and risk. Her account calls attention to a self who resists the park rules (a camping permit) and overcomes physical danger (hiking in the desert without food) in an impromptu pursuit of the river that seems to attract like a magnet ("the closer we were, the more we wanted to continue"). Like many stories about hiking to the bottom of the canyon, this account emphasizes the experience of overcoming obstacles that depicts the self in "heroic" proportions.

Other people also called attention to the inherent dangers that they feel surrounded their hikes into the canyon. "This trip is not to be taken lightly," wrote a 35-year-old Indiana man about his inner-canyon excursion. "People have died in the canyon because they weren't prepared." Another speculated about the potential for personal risk as he noted the circumstances that surrounded his hike into the canyon. "I was quite excited as there was nobody who could help me if I twisted my ankle or something, and timewise I wasn't sure if I could reach the river and make it back to the bus in time," he wrote. These comments embellish the possibility for personal risk and illuminate the sense of personal heroism that individuals may feel on their hikes.

These details become a backdrop for the circumstances that travelers have overcome in their excursions. Rather than emphasizing the destination or scenery, such stories reveal a self who has endured and accomplished something. They are stories of private victories, which tell of persons who possess qualities of perseverance in the face of harsh conditions. "I could just think of putting one foot in front of the other," wrote a 26-year-old New York woman. "It was still worse the next day when we had to hike up. But at the top, it was like a victory. I just made it." Or, for a 28-year-old Ohio woman, her most "significant experience was hiking the entire way and finally reaching the bottom. We yelled, 'We finally made it!' " A number of people chose to describe the difficulties and problems they endured during their hikes. For instance, a man from New Jersey described the physical and mental struggle of hiking to the river. "This is a long, dry trip which turns excessively hot in the afternoon as the sun beats down directly on you," he wrote. "At rest stops I had to crawl under a rock to receive some shade and relief from the heat. It is difficult to judge distance in the canyon. You see glimpses of the river at the bottom and then an hour later you're still not there. It can be frustrating." A 40-year-old Oregon man described his hike as a painful physical ordeal:

> I hiked down the South Kaibab Trail carrying approximately 40 pounds down. It was dusty, not particularly pretty. My big toes hit the end of my hiking boots because I had put an extra cushion in the shoes that elevated my feet too much. I was in a lot of pain and ended up losing both of my big toenails. Because of the painful stress of walking I worked double-time trying to hold back. It was exhausting. Soaked my feet in cold creek water since our tent was on creek side of camp. It helped reduce the swelling some. After I removed the cushions I had no other hiking problems.

These stories all suggest that people find value in their endurance of harsh conditions on the trail. Despite physical and mental stress, these accounts bear witness to the ability of the self to struggle through a difficult time. The extent to which we can call these events "adventures," however, is a matter of personal judgment. The trails described here are well patrolled by park service rangers and many people walk them each day. The idea of "adventure," then, is a relative one and perhaps best revealed as people talk about their experiences as the accomplishment of a great event and the overcoming of major obstacles. The canyon, as it is narrated in these accounts, provides the stage for performances where a person can have great accomplishments that are not applauded by a crowd but that will serve as a basis for revealing a sense of self that may be hidden in much of daily living. Adventures can "restore values which have been worn thin by domesticity," suggests Paul Zweig (1974, pp. 229, 239):

> Sometimes we feel that we have paid too high a price for our comfort; that the network of relationships and names which we have become does not leave us room to breathe. The limits which define us for others then seem like prisons. And we suspect, momentarily, that we live in exile from the best part of ourselves.

Zweig's suggestion of self-imposed captivity casts a subtle doubt and skepticism on the belief that everyday life allows people to live up to their physical and creative potential. Perhaps this is what makes walking into the heat of the desert an appealing challenge. On the trail, hikers may distrust their initial desires to see the river at the bottom that carved the canyon, but, once they return, their accounts celebrate their struggle to exceed the dimensions of self experienced in the routines of daily life.

Escaping the Self: Transcendent Peak Experiences

The stories people tell about travel experiences, in general, attest to the ways they find to shed the skins they inhabit in everyday life and live differently for a while. Extreme instances become moments of self-transcendence—experiences where people lose awareness of self through intense engagement in an activity. Caught in the flow of their experience, people say they find an enhanced connection with the world. A 48-year-old woman who works as a grocery store clerk in California suggested, in a general way, the experiential differences she finds in the worlds of work and travel. "I don't get tired when I'm traveling," she wrote. "I can stay up late and get up early because I'm hyper, trying to see the most I can in my travels. When I'm at [the store] I'm cheerful and a steady worker—but I'm not hyper and sometimes very bored."

People take to the world of travel and nature to flee the routines of work, home, and family and seek out ways of living that involve them in situations where they find they can be closer to some primary and basic mode of life. The river, the trail, and the road are places where the alienating rhythms, routines, and boredom of modern life seem less imposing. They are places where people may find individuality, excitement, flexibility, and freedom. Travel experiences can provide moments of deep connection to experience, even in what may seem like the most mundane settings. "We felt like we were really living," said a 48-year-old California woman, as she described sharing a meal with her daughter on the edge of the canyon one evening.

Clearly, the worlds of travel contain new structures that make demands on people. But, at the same time, many people describe events that suggest a fundamentally different experience of self while traveling. Sometimes, the events are dramatic experiences that, while experientially temporary, are of lasting significance and meaning. For example, a 47-year-old Wisconsin woman described a significant experience she had at Toroweap Overlook near sunset during one of her five trips to the Grand Canyon:

While everyone was sitting around the fire as dinner cooked, I wandered off a bit and climbed on to a huge rock (Supai, my favorite Canyon rock) and sat watching the sun go down and the night come up. We were the only people for miles around and I gradually became unaware of the others, except for my daughter who had come to sit with me. The canyon was before us, the river 3,000 feet below. The sky was every hue from pale pink to deep blue. The stars began to appear and, for a split second, I felt as though I was totally at one with the universe. I felt connected to all the Anasazi who had lived there earlier; I felt no more important than an insect or a tree leaf or a flower. It was an incredible moment which will always be a part of who I am. I have returned to that moment many times in the past years—I treasure it.

This experience of solitude reflects the desires of many who look to nature seeking some primary and natural relationship with the world. Her account is reminiscent of the nineteenth-century transcendental philosophy popularized by Thoreau and Emerson. "I become a transparent eyeball; I am nothing; I see all," wrote Emerson ([1836] 1971, p. 10), reflecting a desire to escape the alienation of social life and find a sense of place and connection with the world. In a similar way, this Wisconsin woman's account reflects a spiritual experience where a sense of belonging to a natural world momentarily eclipses the self who lives detached from nature and inhabits it as a form of leisure. Although the event is fleeting and occurs only for "a split second," the sense of transcendence returns to a stable self as a lasting story and a reminder of the ways that are possible for escape.

Others experience transcendence as the self becomes lost within a sense of "flow." This often occurs as a person becomes caught up in a particular activity or circumstance. Mihaly Csikszentmihalyi (1982, p. 36) argues that "flow" experiences are "to a lesser or greater extent, autotelic—that is, people seek flow primarily for itself, not for the incidental extrinsic rewards that may accrue from it." In the moments of flow experiences, people become engrossed in an activity, and there is a "merging of action and awareness. A person in flow has no dualistic perspective: he is aware of his actions but not of the awareness itself" (Csikszentmihalyi 1982, p. 38). In the preceding account, the transcendence of self-awareness that occurs during a contemplative moment in nature at sunset has some of the elements of the flow experience. For others, a loss of self-awareness occurs as a result of physical activity. A 30-year-old New Hampshire man described a loss of self-awareness as he found himself off of a trail and climbing on a steep canyon wall in a side canyon during a river trip:

The trail sort of ran out and I was on this steep rock surface without realizing how I got there. I really started to get into the climbing part though, and I didn't ever think I was going to go very high up, but I got to this point where I was moving without thinking about what I had to do. It was really weird, almost like something was helping me, pushing me along. It was intense and I had a lot of energy and the holds were just sort of coming to me like they were popping out of the rock and saying "hold on here," "hold on here." And that's not really the best rock to climb on because it's kind of loose in spots and I was just trusting it to hold. I mean the way the whole thing was going how could it not hold? It was great, I'll never forget it. Kind of scary, too, but really fun. Like you couldn't be sure you weren't going to take a fall, but you knew you had the whole thing under control. . . . I finally made it up to a ledge and I was shaky so I rested. When I took a look at what I'd just done, man, I must have been crazy. But it was fun. After that, I was really cautious and took an easier way down.

Here, the loss of self-awareness takes place in an experience that requires unusual physical exertion and concentration. His description of intense energy and the feeling "like something was helping me" reveal the extent to which he became caught up in a dreamlike moment of physical activity. He comes alive in a middle ground that places him between uncertainty and ability. In that space of creativity and risk emerges a sense of self, experienced only for the moment of the activity as a spontaneous and mysterious response to an unfamiliar situation.

This transcendence of self, however, does not occur only in forms of physical activity. The merging of heightened awareness and action takes place in a number of contexts where energy and concentration are applied to meaningful experience (Mitchell 1983, p. 225). For some, the process of passage is itself a different "place." For example, a 35-year-old man from Oregon equated driving and hiking as experiences of focused reflection:

What driving and hiking allow me to do is to take one thought and follow it as far as I want for hours at a time. I find that I don't have the sort of space to do that in other areas and times of my life. It's a different kind of road that isn't asphalt and isn't concrete, and the vehicle is the thoughts themselves. They have their own power and energy and force that move them.

His comments about hiking and driving led him to reflect more generally on how he sought the moments of travel as a way of intensifying the immediacy of his relationship with experience and of achieving an experience of transcendent consciousness.

For me, travel isn't getting from one place to another. Travel is getting from one way of thinking to another way of thinking. The movement facilitates it because I leave behind my home, my work and what I have is some clothes, some fruit, some water and a vehicle. And when I lose all of those things that I've surrounded myself with, it helps me to cleanse sort of an old way of thinking and look at the world through fresh eyes. It's sort of like looking at the Grand Canyon and seeing both the void and the fullness. . . . The Grand Canyon is both full and empty, and that's the paradox. Because it's a void, an empty place, and we go out and stare over a rim and say, "Wow, look at how far down it is . . . look at the void below me that I could fall into." And that is kind of symbolic for me. . . . I choose when I travel to fall into a void, [one] that does not have a future and a past. The Eagles sing about don't let the sound of your own wheels drive you crazy, the constant spinning. So the void represents a place where all of that spinning comes to an end, and there's a sense of here and now-ness.

Driving, hiking, climbing, and contemplation have the potential for transcending the conditions that hold a stable self in check and for providing conditions where another dimension of self emerges. But the difficulty for many is that flow is reached without planning. It is an experience of pleasure and intensity, but it is also ephemeral. Attempts to find it again are typically unsuccessful because there is nearly always a dimension of self-conscious anticipation that keeps the ability to lose self-awareness at bay. Still, the peak experiences revealed in stories are important because they testify to the potential for experiencing the world in profound and dramatic ways. As caught in stories, such moments mark the possibility for experiencing expressions of self often absent in daily life.

Finding the Self in the Face of the Other

Many people say the importance of travel is simply that it is a way to "meet new people and see new things." This is true, to be sure. But, to extend that analysis, the encounter with others and different worlds is a moment where a distinctive sense of self is produced. The previous sections examined how traveling into new worlds provides experiences that fall outside the parameters of life at home. This section considers the way that confrontations with others lead to a production of self-identity. One 26-year-old woman who hiked from rim to rim in the Grand Canyon noted that she liked backpacking because "people are very friendly in those back to nature experiences." In light of the way people seemed open toward each other, backpacking for her was an opportunity to have different kinds of social experiences. "You meet a lot of people," she said, "because you're out of your own environment. In certain instances you're out of your social and class structure and you can meet people you wouldn't normally meet . . . you put yourself in a situation where you have a chance to meet those people who wouldn't come to your environment."

Travel opens people to contexts where the lives of others become a backdrop that reflects back the conditions of their own existence. "Encountering the other, I encounter myself as other and perceive myself through other eyes and ears, thus stepping outside myself, moving elsewhere, to gauge my relation to truth," writes David Patterson (1988, p. 17). "Only by thus placing myself in the position of the other can I return to the truth of myself. Truth is recognized by its power to disturb the one who is its witness, throwing him back on himself and making him noncoincident with himself."

In the Southwest region and at the Grand Canyon, some search for the "other" by looking deeply into the ruins of people from a premodern world. For others, it is the contemporary culture of the Indian reservation that promises a confrontation with an "authentic" other. For one 28-year-old woman who hiked with a friend into Grand Canyon on the Havasupai Reservation, however, such a confrontation with the "other" left her feeling self-conscious. "I felt judged by the Indians. Their gaze is real glassy and I noticed that when I tried to speak with them they'd always try to look past me," she said, describing how she and her partner asked for directions to a camping area near a stream:

> I knew he was thinking "dumb tourist." There was no real interest in us, but there was no real resentment either. Just complete indifference. . . . I guess I felt a little guilty since I am one of these tourists in his eyes even though I like to disassociate myself from the stereotypical tourist. I am to them, though, and I know that. I felt like I wanted to explain or wear a disclaimer on my back.

Despite the fact that they were hundreds of miles from home, it was a feeling of home and belonging she found missing on the reservation. Her account reveals a desire to have "the locals" show an interest in them and, perhaps, be treated as though they belonged on the reservation. The Native American man's indifference toward them becomes an evaluation of their own status as "stereotypical" tourists. The eyes of the "other" gaze upon them and prompt a certain self-consciousness that reveals, despite their inclinations to believe differently, that they, too, are another pair of tourists hiking the reservation. The Native Americans who live on the reservation can call up this self-consciousness because they are an integral part of the environment and a constant reminder that everyone comes from elsewhere to see the canyon.

In relation to other reservation visitors, however, the terms of their identity are mobilized. In contrast to their self-consciousness before the gaze of the Native American man, this couple distinguished themselves from others whom they portrayed negatively as tourists. "We packed all our own gear and food in," she said, "so we were feeling rather superior to the other tourists who were having the Indians carry their stuff down. Like there was one group that had like twenty bottles of Catalina salad dressing in their packs. Stuff like that I can't help but criticize." Her partner agreed with her assessment and noted that their past experience as hikers also distinguished them from the other tourists:

> We're a little bit more purist about it than that. I mean we're used to working hard at it. It seemed like most of the people that went down there were pretty amateur. I mean, we do this a lot and it seemed like a lot of the people who were there were the kind of people that would go on a cruise ship or something.

The distinction between self and "other" here centers on the degree of struggle that is endured. These claims of superiority are founded on this woman's self-sufficiency and practicality. Her partner suggests that it is simply their ability to work hard that separates them from others who indulge their leisure by hiring porters.

Endurance and struggle as markers of identity between people also figure prominently among other hikers. For instance, three friends who hiked to the bottom of the canyon and back out in a single day made continual comparisons between themselves and other people who had gone into the canyon to hike or take a raft trip. "I think part of going down to the bottom of the Grand Canyon is a way of separating yourself apart from the normal tourist," said a 28-year-old California man. "You didn't just see it from the top, but that you're somehow better because you've done that." His hiking partner, a 27-year-old Indiana man, said that it was "the physical challenge of doing something manlier" that prompted him to hike into the canyon. Hiking itself was one differentiating experience that took place inside the canyon.

"There's like this hierarchy where we're trying to put ourselves higher up," said the man from California. "It has to do with the level of physicality involved, the ruggedness of it, how outdoorsy you get and what you have to endure. The one group we couldn't [stand above] were the rafters and the people we passed who were going out for nine days." The third member of their group, a 26-year-old Pennsylvania man, dismissed this distinction between their experience and that of rafters and the nine-day hiking party. He said that "rafting trips are too planned out," and that, while the nine-day trip seemed rugged, "I thought of us doing it in one day and I knew they'd never do what we did with those packs on . . . there's no way you could do the trip we did with the amount of weight they were carrying." In the face of his friends' accounts, his response is an attempt to restore some integrity to their effort.

These comments illustrate how the meaning of experience shifts relationally according to different ways of seeing and experiencing the canyon as it is embodied in the performances of others. For instance, one of the hikers suggested the shifting value of their one-day hike in and out of the canyon during a terrible rain storm. When confronted with the accomplishment of some other hikers, their journey takes on new meaning:

> When we finally got back up I was sitting in the Bright Angel Lodge and feeling good about myself and how we had done this and then these guys started coming in who had done rim to rim to rim, and they had started before six in the morning, and they were coming in. It was like forty miles in one day. And here we were. We had just gone down and up, and they had started in the same place we had, gone to the North Rim and then back to the South Rim. So that kind of changed it for me when I saw these guys.

Faced with the prospect of another group having covered nearly twice the terrain they covered, their one-day hike diminishes in value. When comparing themselves with tourists who never left the rim, they suggested that their hike held value because of the degree of struggle and endurance required. But, compared with other hikers who seemed to have completed a feat of greater difficulty, the importance of their excursion lost some of that value.

The preceding examples all refer to specific ways that Grand Canyon hikers distinguish themselves from each other in the ways they assign meaning to their approaches to travel. Implicit in their comments, however, is a more general distinction between themselves and the others they view negatively as tourists. One canyon hiker from Michigan recalled that he intentionally sought to separate himself from others he saw along the trail:

> I hate feeling like a tourist, so I do things along the way that distinguish myself. One of the difficulties is taking cameras. A camera and taking photographs make you a tourist. The people I distinguish myself from were the kind of people who go on a leisurely walk, go down a couple of miles then head back up. It's also the same with the people on the mules. I think we all kind of made fun of the mule riders. They were humorous. They had bought their hats that you could buy from

the guide leader and stuff. They all looked the same, and it was the easiest way down. But you could tell that some of them looked uncomfortable. I mean I love to see people try to look like a cowboy when they're like from Indianapolis or something.

In addition to making a distinction between himself and the others based on effort, this man recalls a common cultural stereotype of "the tourist" as a person who participates in a structured experience, carries a camera, and generally looks like he or she came from somewhere else. Here, he particularly calls attention to the ways that people from elsewhere fail in their attempts to look like they belong. With gift shop paraphernalia, their attempt to appropriate a portion of regional style becomes a source of amusement.

This man's account alludes to the more general descriptions people offer of who "tourists" are. Quite often, the tourist is defined as a manifestation of a one-dimensional, unthinking, passive, and uneducated member of the mass population. "The tourist," as this description suggests, is framed as a conceptual abstraction that serves as a baseline for suggesting how their experience of travel holds a deeper significance. For example, one woman said a tourist is someone who "travels for pleasure and has experiences mostly of a surface nature." She did not consider herself a tourist because she paradoxically viewed "all experience, including travel, to be enhancements to existence." Another woman wrote that "the term 'tourist' has negative connotations for me—a consumer, a user, often without respect for the places, the people, or other 'tourists.' " She said that, instead, she liked to think of herself as "a traveler, a visitor, an explorer, an adventurer." One man defined the tourist as "someone who hangs around exhibits, spends a lot of time in ticky-tack souvenir stores, thematic restaurants, and likes to have someone else create a show for them [sic]." He suggested that on occasion he considered himself a tourist. "Usually it's when I find myself among a lot of people with cameras, walking into stores, galleries, or exhibits, taking guided tours and the like," he wrote. "But mostly, when I travel, I think of myself more as a Road Warrior on a mission of adventure and discovery, on a search for freedom." Another man described the tourist by using the Grand Canyon as an example:

> A tourist is someone who never ventures beyond the limits of easy access. They visit the gift shops, peer over the edge and occasionally ride the mules to the bottom to stay in a bunk and have someone cook their meals and clean up after them. Rarely do they venture into the "backcountry" where they must be totally "self-supporting."

In relation to their own descriptions of tourists as superficial, disrespectful consumers of ordinary, heavily structured, and seemingly unreal experiences, these people see themselves as self-sufficient explorers in serious pursuit of adventures, freedom, and meaningful experiences.

The Paradox of Modern Escape

Although people often travel to escape the constraints and structures of everyday life, elements of the everyday world often reappear as a basis for the value and meaning of travel. Many of these accounts suggest that the value of experience ambiguously moves between a resistance to a structured world produced by mass tourism and a reconfiguration of conventional and admired American values such as individuality, efficiency, practicality, and the work ethic.

One woman, for example, said that she liked the idea of packing her own food into an area because it made her totally self-sufficient. "It's nice to know that you're only depending on yourself for what you have in there [the backcountry]—and that means blaming yourself, too," she said. For another woman, the ability to backpack with efficiency was an important part of the trip:

Part of what I find enjoyable is the whole process of packing and shopping and seeing how efficient I can be, and how much more efficient I can be than on the last trip. Like if I took an extra pot, I won't bring it this time. As far as food goes, too, I'll buy freeze-dried food and see if I can judge it exactly. Like on this Grand Canyon trip, we ate everything. We wasted nothing, except one bag of tortillas, which is pretty good.

Efficient and practical planning for food and equipment has obvious benefits that are directly related to the amount of effort required for this woman to carry her pack on her back for miles. As she describes it here, however, efficiency is also a pleasurable game that provides evidence of her competence in the art of wilderness camping.

One man argued that the value of backpacking into the canyon, in part, came from the hard work involved in carrying his own equipment into an area. This, he said, is undermined by people who ride horses and have others carry their equipment:

A lot of people were paying for horses to carry their stuff down for them. And you kind of resent that because you're working hard to get down there and your back is sore and your legs are tired, and you're working hard so you can get to this nice place that most people don't get to and here are people taking the easy way in who wouldn't probably be able to do it otherwise. There'd probably be fewer people and you'd have a more solitary experience if there weren't this possibility of horses taking your stuff down. So if people were willing to do a little work like we were, it would be a lot nicer down there. Instead, you have all these people taking the lazy way out. It sort of infringes on our pleasure.

His comments suggest that his efforts should provide a reward of better trail conditions and a more solitary experience. Ironically, his idealized vision of the work ethic is undermined by an economy that allows people to purchase labor. Side by side, on horse and on foot, the value of work holds dual meanings. For the paying visitor on horseback, work at an earlier time allows this moment of leisure. On the other hand, this hiker seeks out a purified form of work that, theoretically, will spawn immediate experiential benefits. As he suggests, working on the trail is simultaneously a kind of pleasure.

In a similar way, others suggest that work is important to the experience of hiking and that it takes a different form than in everyday life. "For one thing it's very physical and your adrenalin is pumping and it feels good to work your body," said one woman. "You can just let your mind go in physical work that's strenuous." Another woman compared the work of hiking with the work she did in her office. "Daily work here is more complicated and you don't always get what you work for. You can be using a computer to do a letter and you can lose it like that. There are headaches and little things that are beyond my control," she said. "But when I'm out in nature and work is only physical, well, I feel like I'm more in control because I'm the only one there."

A traditional notion of a work ethic that promises (but often fails to produce) individuality and personal reward finds redemption in the work of physical exertion that takes place during leisure travel. Where daily work is characterized as alienating and abstracted from any clear sense of value, the world of leisure provides a context where work is transformed into pleasure because it involves control and intrinsic, immediate rewards.

These accounts suggest that leisure-as-work allows people an experience of self that is absent from the daily work they perform that is viewed as distinct from leisure. Such accounts also suggest that a need to be productive permeates the world that people seek in their leisure time. This dual meaning of work is found in leisure situations apart from the trails at the Grand Canyon. For instance, one woman complained that her trips with her father were often organized around some form of productive effort:

Now I want you to know, for your project, that sometimes I like luxurious vacations. But my father says that he really likes vacations where you're doing as much as you can. I mean even in Hawaii we're climbing up the volcanoes and going snorkeling. We were always doing something. I think it has a lot to do with that work ethic. I mean you're taking a vacation, but at the same time it feels like you have to be doing something. I don't know how to analyze my father, but with him it seems like when we travel that we should always be doing something productive and not just "vegging out." . . . As far as these "back to nature vacations" go, I enjoy them somewhat during the trip but usually more afterwards. I really like cultural vacations because I really like art, history, and literature. So for me, I feel as though I'm in my element. And on those luxurious vacations, when I'm luxuriating I usually read. And when I read I never read junk, so I guess I'm almost always doing something productive.

Despite her criticisms of her father's insistence on activity and effort, her comment ultimately reveals that she too is inclined to be "productive" during her moments of leisure. The interplay between work and leisure suggested in these accounts directs us, in a general way, toward the ambiguous relationship between home and away, familiar and strange, and quest and escape that drives much of contemporary travel. Journeys toward something are often journeys away from something as well. As people search for something new, they often become occupied by the problem of escaping the old. Both forces propel people in a paradoxical longing for new experience and self-identity.

The way that the commercially structured designs of tourism surround experience is particularly a problem to those people who fancy themselves to be "explorers" and "adventurers." The explorer and adventurer make their journeys into places unknown and unexplained. As some point out, however, finding such places can be a problem. One woman said that an adventure gave her "the satisfaction of accomplishing or doing something that hadn't already been defined and had an element of risk, but it seems like everything has been discovered by previous explorers and the dangers are all defined." The ideas of "getting away from it all," "experiencing the unknown," and "getting off the beaten track" balance precariously on the margins of the industries that profit from tourists. Finding a way to get off the beaten track is difficult in an age where the machinery for transforming experience into a profitable commodity continually proliferates. One backpacker noted the contradiction he experienced in having to apply for a permit to hike to the bottom of the Grand Canyon. "It's like standing in line to buy a concert ticket or something," he said. "They've got a waiting list every day and if you're lucky enough to get a permit you find yourself camping in designated areas, side-by-side with people. That doesn't feel much like the wilderness." Although the park service issues permits limiting the number of people in one area to prevent excessive environmental damage, the permits are also one way that institutional bureaucracy reappears in a "natural setting."

Another incarnation of the problem of modern escape finds form in the publication of guidebooks. One man noted that the value of adventure was in "not knowing what obstacles are going to be presented or what beautiful things you're going to see." He added:

> That's why I kind of get mad at all these hiking books. Although they've helped us find some new places, they've been disappointing in that they say, "OK, it'll take six hours to get through here," or "after two miles you'll come across this nice pond." They tell you what it's like and how far away it is, and how easy it is to get to, and that takes some of the fun away. . . . It's just real common that everybody finds these places. It's sort of a paradox. I mean you're happy they wrote 'em because you can find some of these places, but so can everybody else. So it makes it worse. And if it's some place that you knew about and other people didn't, and then a guidebook comes out telling everyone about it, then you're actually kind of angry.

In a similar way, one woman was disappointed to learn that a place she thought was unknown was getting publicity. "I'm happy if it's a discovery for us, but angry if it's a place we identified as our own and it gets published in a book," she said. "It just irks me to have there be a great spot that we found and know it's in a tourist guide." Their anger erupts, most likely, because they realize that the possibility for experiencing a seemingly original moment of adventure and exploration has been clawed back into the centralizing mechanisms of tourism.

The good fortune to have an experience that falls outside the defined world of maps and guidebooks carries significance because it allows for a recovery of "sovereignty" over experience (Percy 1989, pp. 46-63). Such discoveries only occur by accident, in moments when "the system" breaks down, when one is lost, or when one makes a mistake. In gaps where structure and knowledge about a place or an event are absent, people may discover something of themselves or of the world that feels genuine in its immediacy and becomes precious for the possibilities of meaning it holds. The possibility of significance for such moments was suggested by one woman who recalled getting lost in the forest that surrounded her campground at the Grand Canyon. "I think part of the fun of getting lost is being able to figure it out, the process of discovering your way back. I figured it out and made my way back there, so I'm an OK person, I'm pretty intelligent after all. And then I told other people how I figured it out and I told 'em, 'Don't take that trail.' " The moment when the trail disappears and she is left on her own is both frightening and exhilarating for the chance it affords her for taking control of herself, for finding a way without guideposts. At the same time, such opportunities for meaningful moments are precarious and never found in the same place twice. Upon finding her way back to camp, she tells others of her adventure as well as warning them. Within moments of her return, the experience takes on definition as story and advice, and the terrain, in the simplest way, begins to be mapped.

As I suggested in the previous section, people define themselves oppositionally in relation to tourism and suggest that their travels are guided by a general resistance against being viewed as tourists. "We never do what a tourist agency would want us to do," said one man. "We sort of pride ourselves on that. I mean everybody looks down on tourists." The strategies of resistance for some are attempts to keep open the potential for spontaneity, chance, and accident. For instance, one woman described herself as an "adventurous tourist." "Like I never make reservations in hotels, that way I stay where I wind up," she said. "If it's the only place left in town and I'm stuck with it, great. That's where you get the adventure." The lack of planning is her hope for adventure. Yet, the idea of calculated spontaneity seems in itself a new paradox that fosters an awareness of groping at the mystery of the unknown. In its own way, anticipation can become a new form of containment that is best described as self-consciousness about being a tourist. One man, for example, recalled telling his wife at the Grand Canyon that "we don't want to look like a typical tourist":

> It's really hard to describe what I do. I guess I'm trying to be me, but that's not very informative. It's mostly defined in terms of a negative, what I'm trying not to be. . . . I guess what you try to do is be cool. You know people stand out there and gawk and say things like "Oh Wow!" and "Oh Neat!" and they say it out loud a lot. So instead you say [calmly] "that's nice." You try to be cool about it. You try to be competent. Like, "I know what's going on." It's being in control.

Like the many who define themselves oppositionally in relation to the "mass tourist," he describes the predicament of trying to be an individual in the middle of a crowd. While he looks at the sight before him, he looks also at his own performance. Despite the fact that he has traveled some distance to stand before something that is remarkably different than his everyday world, he adopts a posture of relative indifference. Although he is away from home, he seeks to feel "at home."

This experiential paradox shines some light on the ambiguous meaning of being "away." In different ways, the ghosts of home tag along behind the station wagon and Winnebago, appearing along the road on occasion as disconcerting reminders of the difficulties that accompany the quest and the escape. While visitors may gaze with disappointment on the numbers who swell the roads and trails, and burgeon around the rim, some travelers find that their suspicions, anxiety, and disappointment with tourism only reveal their own complicity in the gathering crowd. "You find you bring the city along with you," said one man, suggesting the ongoing tension that exists between "home" and "away" that propels people through their travels.

The Road Away From Home

The road, with all of the possibilities for experience it engenders, is where the meanings of selves that have become lost over time may be rediscovered. Some head out to places like the Grand Canyon and look into the empty space in the land for meanings that they have brought there with them. The preceding accounts reveal the complex interaction between geography and individuals. They reveal not only the complex ways that people move through a tourist site but also the way that culture provides experiences that move through them. Travel narratives can recall the simple details of what a person encounters away from home, but they can also become allegories that reveal the place where the physical landscape intersects with the landscape of the mind. "To be on the river for a week was a spiritual experience—a lasting reference point—a metaphor for inner journeying," recalls a 51-year-old Wisconsin man, "going into the depths of things has always been important to me and the trip down the river was a profound metaphor for this downward movement in spiritual, social, and intellectual life." This man, and others like him who travel to the Grand Canyon, remind us of the deep meanings that we inherently know our leisure pursuits hold. "At night I had a chance to sit outside and see the South Rim," writes a man who recalls looking across the canyon from the North Rim. "It was fascinating to see the lights glowing so far away, knowing there was human life in that sea of darkness."

Perhaps such moments are at the heart of travel and are what draw us toward experience and others that, for a moment, may give us omens and clues, make us feel whole, or at least offer us back to ourselves in a new or familiar way. Meeting with others and new environs through travel is an experience centered in ambiguity and uncertainty that finds resolution in the moments of encounter. Travel brings people into a world of unpredictable possibilities that can reveal new ways of knowing the self. In this way, the world of travel exemplifies the possibility for "authoring" one's self through a confrontation with others and different worlds. The people whose stories occupy the preceding pages provide details that reveal how modern travel is a quest where people connect the public and private spheres of life with the past, the present, and future, seeking to link themselves to a larger meaning of society as well as the cosmos. Despite the structures of a modern tourist industry, the world of travel is one where experience has not yet been determined. It is a place where people can encounter difference in terrain and in the other people they meet and thereby discover possibilities for remaking the self.

Upon leaving home, we view a horizon filled with promise, wonder, and mystery, and we cast ourselves into its future. The future is a landscape of discovery and becoming where "remains forever the play of possibility from which all things proceed. It is the land of hope's wild dreams" (Crites 1986, p. 167). There waits the "other," urging and prevailing upon us to make a response that redeems the details of how we belong to the world. The stories told of days on the road or on the trail express to others, as well as to ourselves, who we believe we are because of what we have done or seen. Yet, these stories provide few stable answers to the riddle of self. Instead, they reveal how journeys continually reformulate the questions of existence, always avoiding final solutions but probing continually at experience for the profound ways that it provides the self with a sense of location on the shifting terrain of contemporary life.

Note

1. These accounts are part of a larger research project that studied tourists at the Grand Canyon (Neumann 1991). The accounts were produced from a variety of sources. Some took the form of letters that were sent from tourists as a result of my request published in *Out West* magazine. I solicited other letters by writing to hikers whose names appeared on visitor registers at the Phantom Ranch Canteen at the bottom of the Grand Canyon. Some of these letters were followed with questionnaires that asked for descriptions of travel accounts. Finally, I interviewed people living in the Salt Lake City area about their travels to the Grand Canyon and the surrounding region.

References

Boorstin, D. J. 1961. *The Image: A Guide to Pseudo-Events in America.* New York: Harper & Row.

Braudy, L. 1982. "Popular Culture and Personal Time." *The Yale Review* 4:481-98.

Clifford, J. 1988. *The Predicament of Culture: Twentieth-Century Ethnography, Literature and Art.* Cambridge, MA: Harvard University Press.

Crites, S. 1986. "Storytime: Recollecting the Past and Projecting the Future." Pp. 157-73 in *Narrative Psychology: The Storied Nature of Human Conduct,* edited by T. R. Sarbin. New York: Praeger.

Csikszentmihalyi, M. 1982. *Beyond Boredom and Anxiety.* San Francisco: Jossey-Bass.

Emerson, R. W. [1836] 1971. "Nature." Pp. 7-45 in *The Collected Works of Ralph Waldo Emerson,* edited by A. R. Ferguson. Cambridge, MA: Harvard University Press.

Lefebvre, H. 1979. "Work and Leisure in Daily Life." Pp. 135-41 in *Communication and Class Struggle: Capitalism, Imperialism,* edited by A. Mattelart and S. Siegelaub. New York: International General.

MacCannell, D. 1976. *The Tourist: A New Theory of the Leisure Class.* New York: Schocken.

Mitchell, R. G. 1983. *Mountain Experience: The Psychology and Sociology of Adventure.* Chicago: University of Chicago.

Myerhoff, B. 1982. "Life History Among the Elderly: Performance, Visibility, and Re-membering." Pp. 99-117 in *A Crack in the Mirror: Reflexive Perspectives in Anthropology,* edited by J. Ruby. Philadelphia: University of Pennsylvania.

Neumann, M. 1991. "Tourism and Culture: The Meanings of Leisure Travel in the Grand Canyon." Ph.D. dissertation, University of Utah.

Neumann, M. and D. Eason. 1990. "Casino World: Bringing It All Back Home." *Cultural Studies* 1:45-60.

Patterson, D. 1988. *Literature and Spirit: Essays on Bakhtin and His Contemporaries.* Lexington: University Press of Kentucky.

Percy, W. 1989. *The Message in the Bottle: How Queer Man Is, How Queer Language Is, and What One Has To Do with the Other.* New York: Farrar, Straus & Giroux.

Riley, R. B. 1979. "Reflections on the Landscapes of Memory." *Landscape* 2:11-18.

Schiebe, K. 1986. "Self-Narratives and Adventure." Pp. 129-51 in *Narrative Psychology: The Storied Nature of Human Conduct,* edited by T. R. Sarbin. New York: Praeger.

Stout, J. P. 1983. *The Journey Narrative in American Literature: Patterns and Departures.* Westport, CT: Greenwood.

Zweig, P. 1974. *The Adventurer: The Fate of Adventure in the Western World.* Princeton, NJ: Princeton University Press.

PART IV

Transformations of the Self

10

Extraordinary Events and Mundane Ailments

The Contextual Dialectics of the Embodied Self

VIRGINIA L. OLESEN

If, as existential sociology claims, the lived body is integral to the continual transformation of self in situated contexts where self reflects upon self (Fontana 1987, p. 11), examination of context may well facilitate our understanding of that transformation. Using an analysis of lived experiences, and stressing that the body as well as the social life is lived, in this chapter, I explore two contexts, one *extraordinary* in which an event occurred "outside" the body, the other *mundane* in which the experience originates "inside" the physical body.[1]

These are two of four contexts that could be analyzed for extraordinariness/mundanity and "outside"/"inside." The other two—an extraordinary event occurring within the body and a mundane event outside the body—are

AUTHOR'S NOTE: The material quoted from *The San Francisco Chronicle* throughout the chapter was reprinted by permission. Quotations from *The New York Times*, copyright © 1990 by the New York Times Company, are reprinted by permission. Quotations from C. Foster, "Californians Adjust to Life on the Fault," are reprinted by permission from *The Christian Science Monitor*, © 1990, The Christian Science Publishing Society; all rights reserved. Andrea Fontana and Juniper Wiley provided helpful comments on an earlier version of this chapter, which was presented at the 1990 Pacific Sociological Association meetings. Carolyn Ellis and Michael Flaherty gave valuable and much appreciated criticism on this version.

not dealt with here, though they merit analysis at another time. Rather, the chapter focuses on patterns in the self-body dialectic in the aforementioned contexts to lead to a critical, conceptual discussion of self and body. I argue that symbolic interactionists need to amplify conceptual perspectives to understand transformations of self in embodied contexts.

To discuss the context of extraordinariness, I use published and reported accounts of individuals' experiences and feelings during, immediately following, and one year after the October 1989 San Francisco earthquake, including my own and those of colleagues and acquaintances.[2] I will treat these diverse reports as reflexive narratives of lived experience, recognizing that published accounts often reflect editorial processes that shape the tellers' original stories.

For the analysis of mundanity, I draw on interviews on self-care practices that my colleagues and I did at the University of California, San Francisco, between 1980 and 1985. Our respondents' experiences with everyday ailments and how they defined and managed them led us to theoretical concerns with the body-self relationships.[3]

The Extraordinary: The 1989 San Francisco Earthquake

With few exceptions, most people in the San Francisco area lived the October 17, 1989, earthquake. They experienced those 15 seconds not through the abstraction of the Richter scale (7.1) but through the body and its senses.[4] Frail human flesh absorbed and stored the feeling of structures shaking, the earth roiling, and tires bumping. An engineer who was driving on the Bay Bridge felt his car jump up and down and then, "We were falling through the bridge and there was nothing to catch us . . . I saw water below us. I felt for sure we were going into the bay" (*The San Francisco Chronicle*, Wednesday, October 18, 1989, p. 4). Fortunately, the car hooked on a piece of the damaged structure, allowing him and his passenger to climb to safety.

Sounds also registered the experience in the body: glass breaking, buildings groaning, concrete grinding. A truck driver remembered, "You could hear explosions. You could hear it [the Cypress Freeway] ripping" (*The San Francisco Chronicle*, October 18, 1989, p. 4). He experienced silence, too, "At first [after the quake] it was just total silence."

Further embedding the occasion in the body and in memory were extraordinary sights, such as telephone poles swaying, department store windows shattering, houses crumbling, and people staggering and falling in what one person described as "the dance of the medieval fools." The truck driver described the Cypress Freeway, "It was rocking and rolling back and forth. When the top zigged, the bottom zagged." At Candlestick Park Stadium, where the World Series was to be played, a baseball fan at the top saw the curved lip of the stadium move up and down. This awesome sight invoked the body, "My heart stopped. I thought, 'Don't let it come down.' That's all I could think of" (*The San Francisco Chronicle*, October 18, 1989, p. 7).

For those injured in the most devastating destruction, these experiences were even more dramatically and tragically embodied. A year later, a seriously injured survivor of the collapsed Cypress Freeway remembered that, as he watched cars and trucks in front of him drop off, he thought, "I hope just one of those big concrete slabs comes down and does it quick" (*The San Francisco Chronicle*, October 13, 1990, p. A12).

Those 15 seconds ruptured the taken-for-grantedness of body attached to earth and transformed the experiential environment. Groundedness ceased being familiar. Beingness in space was no longer unthinking or assumed but became quite conscious and problematic. In this "new" environment, uncontrollable, powerful forces threatened the body. The privileged, sacred body became the vulnerable body.

Because body and self are intertwined, reflections on this embodied experience activated a vulnerable or mortal self. A woman who had been on the midcity subway reminisced, "I thought we were all goners. I had this ghastly picture of everything caving in on me" (*The San Francisco Chronicle*, October 18, 1989, p. 6). In some cases, the dramatic and unexpected experience was so intense that this vulnerable self overwhelmed other conceptions of self (Adler and Adler 1989).[5]

For some, the immediate physical experience was sufficient for this new self to emerge. Others, however, reported that only when they reflected on what they had narrowly missed did a vulnerable self emerge, a complex rehearsal of vivid, could-have-been lived experience. An engineer came off the Cypress Freeway after his second trip of the day on that section; a woman in the financial district witnessed pieces of buildings falling into the street where she had been standing. At my home, after glass stopped crashing and the house stopped rolling, I realized that minutes before the quake I had been sitting where a heavy bookcase fell. I felt a chilling, even sickening wave of fear tinged with relief.

It is not surprising that strong emotion, fear often mixed with anguish at separation from or anticipated loss of loved ones, suffused the emerging vulnerable self.[6] "I was terrified," a research consultant who had been caught on the Bay Bridge exclaimed, "It was the most horrifying experience I ever had and it was horrible to be so far from my kids" (*The San Francisco*

Chronicle, October 18, 1989, p. 4). Some found their experiences so draining that they felt no emotion. A woman missed plunging from the sundered Bay Bridge but witnessed another auto fall into the gap, its driver the bridge's only fatality. Her feelings went beyond emotion, "I was numb from the time I saw the car go in until two weeks later. My brain would not acknowledge it" (*The San Francisco Chronicle*, October 12, 1990, p. 5).

Whereas Rehorick's (1986) insightful analysis of phenomenological aspects of a New Brunswick quake found that people quickly lapsed back into assuming benign groundedness, this did *not* occur quickly for many Northern Californians. Many, myself included, remained highly sensitive to locale. A colleague who went downtown a week after the quake reported that she and almost everyone kept glancing upward, as if to see what might descend unexpectedly. As in New Brunswick, "objects rarely attended to became indicators for suspected feelings of motion" (Rehorick 1986, p. 386). Weeks after the quake, when oxygen tanks rumbled by a classroom in which I was teaching, an event that would have been unnoticed before the quake, my students and I would go white with fear and apprehension, discussion would stop, deep breaths would be taken, and, as color returned to ashen, worried faces, talk would falteringly and slowly resume.

Months later, people were still avoiding elevators, rooms with certain kinds of doors and windows, even parts of their own homes that seemed potentially threatening should another tremor occur (*The San Francisco Chronicle*, May 25, 1990, p. 3).

Some apprehensive feelings understandably focused on places where major damage occurred: When the Bay Bridge finally reopened, a colleague reported that she crossed with some trepidation, saying to herself, "Please, don't let it happen now." Similar feelings were noted months after a 5.5 quake occurred in spring 1990 in the Los Angeles area, "Many residents seem to evaluate every locale for its escape factor. During rush hour, people seem to hesitate before stopping under a bridge" (Foster 1990, p. 7).

Even a year later, many still lived the physical environment as problematic. A Berkeley psychologist described hearing leaves rustling on a plant in her office. "If the wind is blowing and out of the corner of my eye I see it, I have to stop" (*The New York Times*, October 14, 1990, p. 20).

Why did the problematic linger for Northern Californians who, in the language of this analysis, continued to experience a vulnerable self? This had not occurred in New Brunswick, even though numerous lesser tremors were recorded for several months afterward. Both physical and symbolic reasons come to mind. Aftershocks, some as large as 5.5, continued for months. One of these occurred on April 18, 1990, the anniversary of the 1906 quake—and at the same time, in the early morning. These literally kept the body off balance. A paramedic worried, "The little ones, you don't take them for granted any more. You sit bolt upright in bed, holding your breath and wondering, 'Is this it?' " (*The New York Times,* October 14, 1990, p. 20). The aftershock experience also sustained the vulnerable self: "The aftershocks brought it all back," a public relations coordinator reported. "It pissed me off. I felt really angry at the earth for doing this" (*The San Francisco Chronicle*, May 25, 1990, p. B3). Another woman noted, "We keep being reminded of our vulnerability" (*The San Francisco Chronicle*, May 25, 1990, p. B3).

Along with the sheer physical experiences, symbolic materials also contributed to a lingering, shared vulnerability. Typifications of the event were influential: Experts quickly categorized it as the most severe quake in California since 1906. Predictions that forecast the timing and size of the "Next One" or the "Big One" continued into summer 1990. Then revised estimates showed an increased probability of another major quake, thus anticipating future vulnerability. Local newspapers, for the first time in history, began to carry weekly quake maps depicting seismic activity in Northern California. Cognition could then confirm what body and self had experienced.

The unremitting flow of mass media images and depictions, particularly on television, visualized, concretized, and symbolized the experiences even for those who did not watch, because the video coverage, as well as the quake, became a topic for conversation. The event was rendered collective, for individuals could compare themselves and their experiences with others'. This process also evoked gratitude for some that they had not suffered severely and guilt for others for the same reason. Both these reflections facilitated continuation of a vulnerable self.

Various themes influenced interpretations of self and earthquake risk. Continued emphasis on symbols associated with San Francisco transformed them to depictions of the experienced disaster. Notable among these was the broken San Francisco-Oakland bridge. A family and child counselor lamented, "I never in my wildest imagination thought the Bay Bridge would break. It became this symbol that life wasn't safe" (*The San Francisco Chronicle*, May 25, 1990, p. B-5).[7] The fashionable Marina district, well known to tourists for its bay-side Mediterranean ambiance, was endlessly shown as streets of shattered apartment houses, ruptured gas lines, and a dangerous fire that evoked memories of the devastating blaze after the 1906 quake.

Along with aftershocks and the symbolic deluge from mass media, extensive telling and retelling of personal experiences tended to keep taken-for-granted groundedness problematic and a sense of vulnerability fresh. The dramatic quality of many such narratives depended precisely on emphasizing the experience of problematic groundedness contrasted with the taken-for-granted physical world. These stories heightened individual reflexivity and shaped interpretation of the collective experience.

At the same time, however, the storytelling became part of a process in which self and body were reintegrated with the taken-for-granted world. Evidence from Los Angeles suggests that the problematic begins to be part of what is taken for granted. After the March 1990, 5.5 quake that occurred in Upland near Los Angeles, a newspaper columnist wrote, "People don't seem to be living in inordinate fear, but many are making small adjustments that show that 'the big One' has muscled its way into the collective consciousness and is planning a long stay" (Foster 1990, p. 7).

As the problematic became absorbed into the taken-for-granted, the vulnerable self merged into biography. Body and self were mutually implicated in that biography of vulnerability. An East Bay newspaper publisher put it personally: "I am never unmindful that in one split second this terrible thing can happen. Every lovely moment can suddenly be visited by that specter" (*The New York Times,* October 14, 1990, p. 1).

To summarize briefly, the quake severely disrupted body's taken-for-granted groundedness. This created an immediate problematic context and one for reflection, thus easing the emergence of a vulnerable self and confirming that "the lived body is at once physical and psychical" (Gallagher 1986, p. 166). Mass media of communication provided potent symbols that entered the self's further reflections on vulnerability, often with deep emotion. Interactions with others as stories were repeated eventually facilitated absorption of the problematic into the taken-for-granted and the emergence of a biography of vulnerability.

The Mundane Ailment

Unlike the experience of the earthquake that starts outside the body and disrupts "the natural attitude," mundane ailments originate in the body as sensations variously labeled as an ache, pain, discomfort, rash (Olesen et al. 1990) and are often relabeled as headaches, backaches, sore throats, and colds. These are everyday lived experiences for most of us in Westernized societies.[8] The very ordinariness of these ailments is such that, in British health care, they are termed "trivia." They usually do not disrupt the taken for granted but they do represent a departure in physical beingness on which self as knower reflects.

Unlike the dramatically embodied experience of the earthquake that people readily articulated, mundane ailments are so embedded in the taken-for-granted that people had difficulty discussing them in detail. We had to interview very skillfully to help our respondents reflect on these everyday occurrences. Yet, once commenced, such reflections contained rich insights into their views of the embodied self in the context of these ailments. Some respondents readily articulated the intimate connection between self and body. A 39-year-old financial consultant commented, "It's me. My body's me. We're both one. I'm in there. I know what's going on. Yeah. I think your body tells you just about everything. All you got to do is listen to it." A 26-year-old physical therapist echoed this, "I trust that it runs amazingly well for me and gets me through a lot of things. It's, it's, it's *me,* in a sense."

Perhaps the most poignant comments that pointed to body-self integration came from a young woman who as a child had been battered and sexually abused,

> I really almost did not see my body. . . . I used to have a sign up in my room which said, "You don't have a body, you are your body," which someone said a long time ago to remind me to be more integrated. . . . I always felt so totally fragmented that I did not ever pay attention to my body until it began to fall apart or got real sick or broke down. . . . I'm trying to pay attention to it for the first time in my life.

When we asked our respondents to detail how they experienced mundane ailments, and attributed meaning to and managed them, their wide-ranging comments described how these so-called trivial experiences of embodied-ness nevertheless occasioned self-reflexiveness.[9] One man declared about a rash on his hand, "This rash—it just wasn't me!"

Their accounts suggested the emergence of an altered "physical self." Though much like other social selves—self as student, friend, parent, lover—this self differs in that it is intimately integrated, indeed, is embedded in and emergent from reflections on embodiment. It is a complex self involving multiple meanings, such as body for self, body for others, and other parts of one's own self.

Some individuals reported that a view of the physical self, not always pleasant, came into focus with the experience of the trivial ailment. One woman recalled, "My skin just kind of started breaking. It was real itchy. . . . I felt I was like a snake or something shedding new skin you know." Another declared, "I don't feel it [acne] threatens my health. . . . On the other hand, I would say that it is a sort of negative aspect of my self-image. I would like not to have it." These recollections suggest that perceived or assumed visibility, as an attribute of mundane complaints, influences the self's assessment of the embodied experiences, probably in anticipation of interaction with others and in recollection of social norms of acceptability, or what has been called "the body for others" as against "the phenomenal body" (Denzin 1984, p. 111).[10]

The physical self is also tinged with vulnerability. Not all everyday ailments are only mildly irritating or worrisome; some were assessed as potentially serious for reasons having to do with reflection on self, for instance, as being a certain age. A young woman talked about a chest pain, "I wanted to check it out because I was scared. I'm too young for that [heart attack] and I'm not doing anything that warrants that kind of feeling so I checked it out." For another woman, a persistent back pain had affected her view of herself and occasioned a transformation of the physical self. Laughing, she first said, "It's made me, made me feel older."

Though emotion is readily understood in the embodied drama of the earthquake, it may seem surprising to see it in such everyday experiences. The woman just quoted described how her self had been altered in light of her painful back,

It's made me aware of being more careful and just, it's just changed my life-style to an extent that things that I'd never thought about being a problem before like a long car ride are now problematic, so that's changed my feelings about myself.

At this point, she broke down and cried.

Why should such "trivial" lived experiences occasion emotion? Part of the answer lies in the continually altering physical self. Depending on the meaning attributed by the experiencing self to the ailment, fear, disgust, or even pleasure can permeate the self. The meaning of the ailment and the subsequent sense of vulnerability, our accounts show, depend on previous experiences, duration, severity, age, and social context. A hairdresser reported that, after seven months, she had begun to think a cyst on her thumb was cancerous and she would no longer be able to work,

I was becoming quite terrified. . . . I was just praying that I would be able to do someone's hair again. You know, that's how I realized that, you know, my livelihood was more than just that. It was my whole way of living.

In this example, vulnerability experienced via the body and threatened physical self seeps into other aspects of existence and other selves, invoking fear for a current and future social self, in this instance, self as worker.

These reflections did not necessarily occur in interactions with others. Indeed, often there was no interaction with others. Transformation of self was accomplished via the self reflecting on body, objectifying body and symptoms, and reintegrating those into a new physical self, a kind of dialectic (Gadow 1982).

Very much as those who experienced the earthquake developed a biography of vulnerability, over a lifetime of mundane ailments and continual transformation of the physical self, for our respondents, there emerged a physical biography. This is composed of sensed vulnerabilities, potentialities, and emotions generated from a lifetime of experiences with trivial and nontrivial ailments. This is a source of definitions, symbols, meanings, and memories of past and anticipated physical selves. One man reflected on his physical biography,

> In the past two years I have had a whole series of things happen with my body. . . . I am in the process of reassessing what health means to me. . . . I don't consider myself a healthy person right now. There are things that I am dealing with, and I will be healthier, but right now, no.

To summarize, the self continually assesses embodied experiences with sniffles, headaches, rashes, and other physical symptoms, sometimes with great emotion. The view of self as one experiencing these mundane ailments, here conceptualized as the physical self, is over time incorporated into a physical biography of vulnerability and potentiality.

Discussion

Critical to both contexts I have discussed is the body's relationship to environment. An extraordinary event such as the earthquake, seemingly "outside" the body, is in fact integral to body and to self as feeling and perceiving body because "phenomenally or experientially, the environment is an indefinite extension of the lived body" (Gallagher 1986, p. 163). With regard to understanding the context of the mundane event "inside" the body, Mead's (1934, p. 172) writings are instructive, "Through self consciousness the individual organism enters in some sense into its own environmental field; its own body becomes a part of the set of environmental stimuli to which it responds or reacts." Body, as an ongoing resource and foundation of self, provides for the self ways in which self experiences self. "The experiencing of oneself," as Kotarba (1977, p. 261) has written, "is also an audience for self."

Thus body is at once part of the environment and constitutes a lived environment for self. Events within the seemingly external environment (e.g., slipping on ice, looking from a mountaintop, hearing fire sirens) implicate body and self. Additionally, the pains and pleasures of the physical body are the self's environment.

Characteristics of situated lived contexts offer a way to sharpen our understanding of these dialectics. The sudden, threatening experience of the earthquake upset the familiar environment and, as we heard through the voices of survivors, transformed self in the reflexive process. "It is because the experience of the familiar always involves a feeling of me-ness that the unfamiliar is so unsettling" (McCarthy 1984, p. 117). Mundane ailments, part of the ongoing body-self environment, for the most part familiar and nonthreatening, are assessed and integrated into a new physical self, sometimes with emotion and sometimes with a sense of vulnerability. Here we must look not only to reflection but to meanings attached to the familiar, meanings that may fall away as other selves are involved.

Symbolic interaction has both potential and limitations for analysis of these contexts of embodied experience. Mead's conceptualization of the physical, "the conversation of gestures," and his comments on memory facilitate these understandings; his emphasis on the self as cognitive makes analysis of emotion more difficult.

Mead's analysis of the physical, which is frequently overlooked, yet that Schutz (1962, p. 223) found fundamental to his own thinking, is highly relevant to analysis of "outside" the body events. Here I extend Mead's discussion of touch, which in one interpreter's view "has most reliably the character of reality" (McCarthy 1984, p. 117). Because we continually "touch" the earth with our bodies or extensions of our bodies (bicycles, cars, and so on), that touch produces pressure, which, like picking up an apple or leaning against a table, fills our world with physical objects and our sense of ourselves vis-à-vis those objects.

An earthquake, like falling down stairs or being hit by a car, thus alters "reality" with regard to taken-for-granted groundedness or touching the earth. Equally important, and following Mead's conceptualization of the body as center for self, these events in body environment rearrange the very coordinates of which body is the center and change one's relationship to physical objects as being below, above, or to the side of oneself, particularly if the reflecting self has assigned meanings of danger or threat to those spatial locations.

How is the embodied experience of the quake or the mundane ailment integrated into the transformation of self? One critic has written that, because Mead starts from an analysis of society and interprets the self as emergent from society, he "is unable to make intelligible the immediate relationship of the individual to his [*sic*] own body" (Nathanson 1973, p. 59). Yet, Mead does provide interpretation of ways in which bodily experiences become part of self, once self-consciousness is achieved. A partial answer is found in his delineation of the "conversation of gestures," the taking of the attitude of the other, and thinking about self or acting toward self as others have or would act (Mead 1934, p. 171). Because self continually senses body, a highly private set of reflections immediately ensue in the context both of the quake and of the mundane ailment. As self reflects on the experience undergone by body, self—at first without interaction with others—also alters. The internal dialogue shapes the new changing self, sensed as vulnerable because of potential loss, loss of self itself, or loss of social potential. When stories are told and retold to others and symbols are provided with which to interpret events, dramatic or mundane, the continual transformation of self continues. This phase is readily understood in classic interactionist terms, but these narratives may not occur at the outset of the transformation, if indeed at all.

Yet, this interpretation can only be partial. First, the body is not for the experiencing person an abstract set of scientific terms. It is a social body, a lived body; its parts, and experiences of it, are socially constructed with meanings derived from those experiences and related social definitions. To experience the body, as continually occurs, is to experience both feeling and meaning. Second, self as knower not only engages in a "conversation of gestures" but reviews a history of body's own experiences, some quite private, some interactive, many, in the case of dramatic events in the environment, quite emotional.

To what degree does the vulnerable self remain latent or marginal? What are the characteristics of contexts of lived experience in which this self reemerges? These are critical theoretical questions for understanding embodied experience as lived experience and the relationship to the transformations of self. Comments of a survivor of the Buffalo Creek Flood two years later hint that self is readily activated when individuals experience physical conditions similar to those of the original context. The biography of vulnerability surges to the fore,

Why it don't even have to rain. I listen to the news, and if there's a storm warning out, I don't go to bed that night. . . . Every time it rains, every time it storms, I just can't take it. (Erickson 1976, p. 17)

Mead (1934, p. 170) pinpoints the importance of biography in his comments on memory: "If we had no memory which identifies experiences with the self, then they would certainly disappear so far as their relationship to the self is concerned, and yet they might continue as sensuous or sensible experiences without being taken up into a self."

Thus self, reflecting on the event or ailment that has emerged in the body, draws upon biography, a social product of past as well as anticipated interactions and experiences, to interpret the bodily state. This reflection leads to a new structure, a renewed vulnerable self or a new physical self. Recognizing this "self-soma process" (Saltonstall 1990, p. 15), the analysis necessary to understand the embodied self in both contexts must be phenomenological and existential as well as interactionist.

In the interpretation of embodied experience of the earthquake and the mundane complaint, interactionism supplemented with phenomenological analysis moves us toward understanding the transformation of a vulnerable or physical self. This interpretive scheme is particularly necessary if we ask why people in those lived bodily contexts experience differing emotions, very strong emotions, in both the drama of the quake and the mundanity of the everyday ailment. Mead's comment that "the essence of self . . . is essentially cognitive" (Mead 1934, p. 173) does not facilitate understanding the fear, disgust, and grief experienced and expressed by individuals reflecting on these types of embodied experiences.

Some parts of Mead's writing are helpful, however. Self is a part of the field or an object for self, hence it is endowed with feeling, emotion, just as the self of another in social interaction is invested by the interactant with emotion and feeling (Denzin 1984, pp. 68, 132). Anger at continuing aftershocks, or sorrow over a continually painful back, reflects self's emotional assessment of, and investment in, self. Those feelings of self for self, Mead would argue, derive from real and imagined emotions of others and are laid down in biography (Denzin 1984, p. 58). A feeling of disgust at one's skin peeling off like that of a snake originates from socially defined standards of dirt or uncleanness and is perhaps interpretable within the "conversation of gestures."

Yet, one has the uneasy feeling that the attribution of meaning is only a partial explanation. As Ellis (1991) has noted about emotions more generally, and others (Baldwin 1988; Ferguson 1980; Kotarba 1984; Saltonstall 1990) have argued about the embodied self particularly, the overly rational perspective within symbolic interaction does not readily interpret emotion, embodiment, and self. Fresh approaches are required (Ellis 1991), particularly if we are to interpret more fully the experiences of the lived body and the implications for the continually transforming self.

Such fresh approaches might well include comparative analyses such as this one in which divergent contexts of bodily lived experiences are examined for their differences and similarities and for what conceptual and theoretical shortcomings they illuminate. For example, we could add to this comparison scrutiny of mundane events "outside" the body, such as falling or being accidentally bumped, with an extraordinary event "within" the body, such as a heart attack, a stroke, appendicitis, or a severe nose bleed.

Another potentially productive line of inquiry would be to explore men's, women's, and children's vulnerability in embodied experience. (See Note 5 for some of the experiences that could be analyzed.) We could explore how vulnerability emerges, how it feels in terms of emotions, what it means, how it becomes a part of biography, and how reflexive processes lead to a vulnerable self. This is a particularly intriguing set of issues because vulnerability is both experientially lived via the body and socially constructed.

As such, the phenomenological analysis reaches into the cultural: In modern America, besotted with high technology, technology wards off and manages body vulnerability (open heart surgery) but also induces it (genetic screening, conception, and birth), while streams of symbols delineate bodily vulnerability ("inside" such as cancerous agents in food, toxic wastes, and "outside" such as unsafe neighborhoods). In these embodied contexts, selves are transformed.

Summary and Conclusion

To understand the lived experience within contexts such as an earthquake or a mundane ailment requires that, insofar as is possible via an objectifying language, our analysis recognize that body and self are intertwined. In both these contexts analyzed here, self and body were seen to be intimately and reciprocally integrated. In both contexts, a biography of vulnerability and potentiality emerged, as the lived experiences accumulated, were reflected upon, were symbolized and narrated to others, and the self continually transformed and retransformed. Various emotions—such as fear, disgust, and grief—colored these reflections and transformations. It is important that neither the emotions nor the transformations were the outcomes, initially, of interaction with others but were an introspective assessment. To understand best these dynamics of the embodied self, we need to attend to cognition and emotion, using both phenomenal and interactive approaches.

Notes

1. This chapter thus differs from recent work on the body that implicates text, metaphor, social control, or power as adjunct to contemporary capitalism (Foucault 1978, 1979; Turner 1984; Martin 1987; Scheper-Hughes and Lock 1987; Freund 1988; Glassner 1988; Jaggar and Bordo 1989; Frank 1990; Featherstone et al. 1991).

2. Regrettably, at the time this was written, the firsthand accounts that the city's archivist had collected were not yet available to scholars, nor were materials on three other recent, severe quakes in Armenia, Iran, and Peru. Such comparative accounts would deepen our understanding of this embodied experience.

3. Full details about the sample and the study findings may be found in Olesen et al. (1990). Briefly, the research involved three related studies in which 60 men and women between the ages of 25 and 75 were asked to reflect in considerable detail on their experiences with mundane ailments and on their health in general. The study was sponsored by the Nursing Resources Division of the U.S. Public Health Service, the UCSF School of Nursing Research Committee, and the MaxiCare Foundation.

4. Some quake-wise San Franciscans immediately objectified the experience with guesses as to the Richter level. One colleague told me, "I said to myself, 'that had to be a 7.' "

5. That a vulnerable self should emerge following such dramatic rupturing of the body-environment connection, often with attendant perceived risk, is an instance in a more general class of contexts where there is a sense of vulnerability or a vulnerable self emerges. Persons who have experienced auto accidents, fires, muggings, rapes, or other assaults have reported this sense of self.

6. Emotion entered the temporal experience of many who experienced the quake and reported "that the 15 seconds seemed like forever" because, in Flaherty's (in this volume) terms, those few seconds were experientially saturated, or "bloated". Others, however, experienced the shaking as "quite short." I thought after the initial shake, "That didn't last very long."

7. Downtown Santa Cruz and Watsonville, both near the epicenter, experienced major destruction but are not as potent symbolically, and received much less media attention, though the suffering in those areas equalled that in the immediate Bay Area.

8. Our analysis made no claim to depict wider views of embodied experiences and self, because, following Whittaker (1990), we recognize that self may be conceptualized quite differently in other cultures, indeed if conceptualized at all.

9. Some research literature in the sociological social psychology of health and illness deals with the dynamics of self in highly dramatic illnesses, such as cancer, stroke, or related interventions, such as mastectomy, but overlooks the interrelationship of self and body in less dramatic contexts (Olesen et al. 1990). For an analysis of the embodied experience of serious illness, see Kesselring (1990).

10. Highly visible or socially unacceptable mundane ailments, such as rashes or flatus accompanying diarrhea, seem to invoke, even fleetingly, the kinds of management techniques employed by the stigmatized who are persons permanently disfigured or disabled. Poignant accounts of our respondents, who had undergone bowel surgery and who must wear appliances for body waste that are sometimes untrustworthy, suggest that strategies to manage potentially stigmatizing or embarrassing mundane ailments do emerge. Study of these would extend understanding of body-self and social interaction and the cultural codes of the time.

References

Adler, P. and P. Adler. 1989. "The Engulfed Self." Paper presented at the 1989 Gregory Stone-Society for the Study of Symbolic Interaction Symposium, Arizona State University.

Baldwin, J. 1988. "Habit, Emotion and Self-Conscious Action." *Sociological Perspectives* 31:35-58.

Denzin, N. K. 1984. *On Understanding Emotion.* San Francisco: Jossey-Bass.

Ellis, C. 1991. "Sociological Introspection and Emotional Experience." *Symbolic Interaction* 14:23-50.

Erickson, K. 1976. *Everything in Its Path: Destruction of Community in the Buffalo Creek Flood.* New York: Simon & Schuster.

Featherstone, M., M. Hepworth, and B. S. Turner. 1991. *The Body: Social Process and Cultural Theory.* Newbury Park, CA: Sage.

Ferguson, K. E. 1980. *Self, Society and Womankind.* Westport, CT: Greenwood.

Fontana, A. 1987. "Introduction: Existential Sociology and the Self." Pp. 3-17 in *The Existential Self in Society,* edited by J. A. Kotarba and A. Fontana. Chicago: University of Chicago Press.

Foster, C. 1990. "Californians Adjust to Life on the Fault." *The Christian Science Monitor,* March 28.

Foucault, M. 1978. *The History of Sexuality.* Vol. 1. New York: Pantheon.

———1979. *Discipline and Punish.* New York: Vintage.

Frank, A. W. 1990. "Bringing Bodies Back In: A Decade Review." *Theory, Culture & Society* 7:131-42.

Freund, P. S. 1988. "Bringing Society into the Body: Understanding Socialized Human Nature." *Theory and Society* 17:839-64.

Gadow, S. 1982. "Body and Self: A Dialectic." Pp. 86-100 in *The Humanity of the Ill,* edited by Victor Kestenbaum. Knoxville: University of Tennessee Press.

Gallagher, S. 1986. "Lived Body and the Environment." *Research in Phenomenology* 16:130-69.

Glassner, B. 1988. *Bodies.* New York: Putnam.

Jaggar, A. M. and S. R. Bordo, eds. 1989. *Gender/Body/Knowledge: Feminist Reconstructions of Being and Knowing.* New Brunswick, NJ: Rutgers University Press.

Kesselring, A. 1990. "The Experienced Body, When Taken-for-Grantedness Falters: A Phenomenological Study of Living with Breast Cancer." Ph.D. dissertation, University of California, School of Nursing, Department of Physiological Nursing, San Francisco.

Kotarba, J. 1977. "The Chronic Pain Experience." Pp. 257-72 in *Existential Sociology,* edited by J. D. Douglas and J. M. Johnson. Cambridge: Cambridge University Press.

———1984. "A Synthesis: The Existential Self in Society." Pp. 13-25 in *The Existential Self in Society,* edited by J. Kotarba and A. Fontana. Chicago: University of Chicago Press.

McCarthy, E. D. 1984. "Toward a Sociology of the Physical World: George Herbert Mead on Physical Objects." Pp. 105-21 in *Studies in Symbolic Interaction.* Vol. 10, edited by N. K. Denzin. Greenwich, CT: JAI.

Martin, E. 1987. *The Woman in the Body.* Boston: Beacon.

Mead, G. H. 1934. *Mind, Self and Society.* Chicago: University of Chicago Press.

Nathanson, M. 1973. *The Social Dynamics of George Herbert Mead.* The Hague, the Netherlands: Martinus Nijhoff.

Olesen, V., L. Schatzman, N. Droes, D. Hatton, and N. Chico. 1990. "The Mundane Ailment and the Physical Self: Analysis of the Social Psychology of Health and Illness." *Social Science and Medicine* 30:449-55.

Rehorick, D. A. 1986. "Shaking the Foundations of the Lifeworld: A Phenomenological Account of an Earthquake Experience." *Human Studies* 3:379-91.

Saltonstall, R. 1990. "Being Healthy: A Social Psychological Exploration of Self, Body and Gender." Ph.D. dissertation, University of California, San Francisco, School of Nursing, Department of Social and Behavioral Sciences.

Scheper-Hughes, N. and M. Lock. 1987. "The Mindful Body: Prolegomenon to Future Work in Medical Anthropology." *Medical Anthropology Quarterly* (New Series) 1:6-41.

Schutz, Alfred. 1962. "On Multiple Realities." Pp. 257-59 in *Collected Papers.* Vol. 1, *The Problem of Social Reality,* edited by M. Nathanson. The Hague, the Netherlands: Martinus Nijhoff.

Turner, Bryan W. 1984. *The Body and Society.* Oxford: Basil Blackwell.

Whittaker, E. 1990. "The Self." Unpublished lecture delivered at the Department of Social and Behavioral Sciences, University of California at San Francisco, May.

11

The Self, Its Voices, and
Their Discord

JOHN H. GAGNON

The Self

George Herbert Mead once wrote that the most important invention of the nineteenth century was the idea of the self.[1] I take it from his other writings that he did not mean by this that persons in prior ages or in other places did not know that they were individuals or that they did not know that they behaved differently in different social situations. Periods of social crisis in Western European history have produced outbreaks of heightened levels of individualism that modern observers have treated as qualitatively approaching or presaging the conventionalized experience of selfhood in the modern Western world (Morris 1972; Murray 1951; Tawney [1926] 1947). In addition, the recognition that persons perform different roles in varying social situations has a long historical record, though it is less often appreciated that the social meaning and practice of "role-taking" or "role-playing" differ from one historical era to another (Arditi 1989).

Mead's point was that, during the course of the nineteenth century, there had emerged a new species of mental life, a historically novel and therefore differently articulated mental apparatus. In the early decades of the twentieth

AUTHOR'S NOTE: This is a revised version of a paper presented as "Conversations in the Self" at the 1990 Gregory Stone Symposium: The Sociology of Subjectivity, St. Petersburg Beach, Florida, January 27, 1990. My thanks to Carolyn Ellis, Michael Flaherty, Bennett Berger, and Sharon Witherspoon for their helpful comments.

221

century, Mead labeled this new apparatus the "social self." Mead did not discuss, however, the material conditions for the emergence of this new species of mental life, its transformations across the 150 years from 1780 to 1930, or the changes mental life might continue to undergo after he made his own formulations. My goal in this chapter is to suggest the ways in which modern mental life—that is, how we *practice* mental life now (including those faculties or capacities that are now the subject matters of psychology)—has been culturally and historically constituted. I am not going to argue that mental life is the mirror of culture and social structure but, instead, suggest the ways in which mental practices have a historically changing relationship with social and cultural practices, even though it takes its origins from them. I want to argue that the emergent social and cultural conditions of nineteenth- and twentieth-century life required new forms of mental practice and that the requirements of late-twentieth-century life will provide the conditions for further changes in mental life in the future.

To begin at the beginning: At the end of the Enlightenment, the vast majority of people, including most of the urban intelligentsia, experienced their individuality as being constituted by a limited and seemingly coherent bundle of socially given roles that changed only slowly during the course of their lives. At this time, the worth of individuals was evaluated primarily by the competence of their public performance of these given roles. By the end of the eighteenth century and the beginning of the nineteenth century, however, a few individuals had begun to experience their relation to social life in ways that would be premonitory of the new forms of mental life that would emerge across the next century. An increasing number of people began to experience the relationships that they had with others, what we would now call "the roles that they were required to play," as detached from or alien to who they "truly" were or who they wanted to be. Thus a private protoself was being detached from public roles, a protoself that would change, though not isomorphically, as the roles that were played changed. This new mental formation, perhaps a private role that judged public roles, would "decide" what was inside and what was outside, what was self and what was other.

Mead's work comes a little more than halfway in this now 200-year-long process, and the mental structures that he proposed, the "I," the "me," and the "generalized other," are products of the intellectual climate and social situation of the United States in the late nineteenth and early twentieth centuries. The "I" is that which judges, accepts, and goes beyond the "me," which is the creature of the generalized other, the looking glass dimension of the self. This construction is a peculiarly "American" culmination of nineteenth-century ways of talking about mental life.

To think in this way about the origin and transformations of the self since the earliest stages of the nineteenth century requires a certain amount of conceptual legerdemain. While some of the words that we commonly use to describe interpersonal and intrapsychic practice (e.g., *role, role-playing, self*) were part of the language of persons who lived 200 years ago, they did not direct attention to the same features of the environment (here including the "structure" of the mind) and did not call for similar sets of actions (including verbal conduct). Thus people who participated in the earliest stages of the reconceptualization of these concepts did not know they were inventing new forms of mental life or that they were, in consequence, contributing to a new relationship between the individual and the social order. In the same way that the inventors of the economic relationships that would become capitalism were not themselves "capitalists" and the religious dissenters in Western Europe in the late fifteenth century were not contemporary "Protestants," those persons in the late eighteenth and early nineteenth centuries who experienced a sense of alienation from their surrounding culture and social relations were not modern readers of *Psychology Today* or members of the Society for the Study of Symbolic Interaction. To use contemporary terms in these historical circumstances without implicit parentheses falsifies what historical personages experienced and obscures the processes by which the terms took on modern meaning.

This historical process that generated the idea of self involved dialectical changes in both mental and material life. The crisis in cultural life of the late eighteenth century, variously identified with the collapse of the Enlightenment ideology, the failure of the French Revolution, the consolidation of early capitalism, and the establishment of a new dominant class, the bourgeoisie, led to diffuse existential experiences of alienation among cultural elites (Peckham 1986). These experiences required explanation and, through what we now call *feedback,* these explanations shaped experiences. During the remainder of the nineteenth century and into the twentieth, the definition of the self, its internal organization, its origins in the individual life history, its transformations throughout the life cycle, and its relation to cultural production have been influenced by changes in the material conditions of everyday life and changes in intellectual styles of explanation.

The earliest incarnations of this sense of alienation should not be interpreted in the modern sense as a simple desire for additional or different roles, or merely as a conflict between roles, but as the emergence of a new component in mental life that was a precursor to the experience of the self playing roles. In these early moments of a transformation of consciousness, there was a preliminary and tentative transfer of weight from the collective and public sources of connecting meaning and action to sources that are individual and private. In this process of social detachment (which is a double process, the detachment of self from roles and the detachment of roles from the other), a preliminary version of the self (the "something" that decided) had to be developed: a version that required ways of privately talking about the "self" as well as public actions that confirmed the presence of this "self" both to the individual making a claim to having a self and to the audiences for such verbal and nonverbal claims.

The locus of final authority in giving meaning to action had begun its two-century-long shift from the public to the private, from the demands of the "other" to the decisions of the self. As we get closer to the current time, this self begins to be experienced as separate from performances, separate from the new categories of "roles" that resided between the self and other persons, collectivities, and constructs. This self would ultimately become surrounded by a shell of roles that mediated between the private interior and the demands of social life. Such roles were not only judged by whether they were competently performed but by whether or not the roles themselves were appropriate to the self (their appropriateness had always been judged by the "other"). Even if individuals were not entirely free to "decide" their fate, their fate was experienced as being at least partially in their control when internal wishes met external demands on the contested terrain of roles.

It is important not to assume that this transformation came all at once either for individuals or for the cultures in which they lived. The self, like every human construction, is a sociocultural invention. Its transformations can be described as events in history. It was acquired at different points in the life course of individuals; it changed during the course of those lives, and it was itself changed as it was diffused into new social groups at different points in time. To have a self in the latter half of the twentieth century in the United States when it is an entitlement provided at birth is far different than the acquisition of the preliminary versions of a self in midlife by a woman in the nineteenth century after reading *Madame Bovary* or by a baptized native in a recently colonized society in Asia or Africa in the late nineteenth century.[2] The self was diffused both within the West and throughout the world and was transformed in this process of diffusion as surely as were sugar, literacy, European languages, Christianity, the automobile, and Coca-Cola.

The earliest manifestation of protoselves can be found in the works of those we now identify as members of the Romantic movement. The initial move involved the claim that their conduct that violated social expectations (including social expectations about appropriate artistic productions) was justified by the presence of a unique and private source of meaning. The source of this meaning could be identified as a "genius," a "vision," the "imagination," a unique biography, or a special collection of experiences that was greater than the sum of meanings and actions justified by social obliga-tions. This private source of meaning frequently existed as a form of resistance to the demands of what appeared to others to be legitimate social obligations. From the point of view of the resistor, the very legitimacy of the obligations made them part of the oppressive "other" (Becker 1976).

The existence and properties of the protoself could be explored or tested in a variety of ways, the majority of which involved a journey away (journeys were often not *toward*) from the demands of collective constraint. Such journeys could take place either in fantasy or in fact—one could journey into the collective past through writing novels or history, explore one's past through self-analysis, go abroad to strange countrysides and cultures, or disorient one's consciousness through alcohol or drugs. The key feature of the Romantic program of cultural detachment began with journey away from the demands of one's own culture.[3] During these travels, there would be a crisis of estrangement, and in the triumph over this crisis would be found a confirmation of the existence of a protoself that was independent, indeed transcendent over, the demands (here read *roles*) of social life.

This process of estrangement and transcendence may have produced for the first time in Western history a large number of individuals who began to experience "collective social life," not merely other individuals or other social groups, as oppressive. This experience, and the criticism of social life that emerges from it, is substantially more extreme than the views of even the most radical social utopians of the nineteenth century. The latter made the argument that it is not that individuals fail the social order but that the social order fails individuals, and therefore it is our task to construct a new social order that in its turn will reconstruct the individual (the dialectic again). The criticism of social life offered by members of the late Romantic move-ment was that what is oppressive is the experience of sociability and the need to act in a society, no matter how materially perfect. The antihero Axel Heyst in Joseph Conrad's novel *Victory* ([1915] 1957) is one of the first of many figures in modernist literature destroyed by the demands of virtuous social participation in an uncontrollable and sometimes malicious social world. This vision grows more bleak in more recent novels where the protagonist is crushed merely by participating in social life. In Joseph Heller's *Something Happened* (1974), the hero is without virtue and the social world is without malice; it has become like nature, indifferent.[4] It is now possible to respond to society the way de Sade in Peter Weiss's play *Marat-Sade* ([1964] 1977, p. 24) responds to nature:

> I hate nature
> this passionless spectator
> this unbreakable ice-berg face
> that can bear everything
> that goads us to greater and greater acts.

It is no longer that social life is not fulfilling; it *cannot* be fulfilling. Neither society nor the individual can be so transformed so that the former may fulfill the latter—unless we annihilate the individual (Zamiatin [1920] 1959).

What was central to nearly all of these nineteenth-century journeys away from social expectations, and their correlative twentieth-century escape attempts (Cohen and Taylor [1976] 1978), is that the majority of these travelers returned to their native territory and recorded their special and private experiences in publicly available media: in poetry, novels and memoirs, in painting and photography, in instrumental and operatic music, and in architecture (Peckham 1962). Like the persons who discover one of those wonderful out-of-the-way places, they had to come back and tell everyone about it; and soon the wonderful out-of-the-way place became just another stop on the tourist route. The cultural products that were the results of these journeys away were to serve as the ideological travel guides for all manner of more conventional persons who were members of the same as well as future generations. The Alps, the coasts of Africa, the South Seas, and the Indies, as well as Paris and Greenwich Village, are the names of some of the geographic places that were once adventure travel and are now the routine stuff of the package tour. The dissemination of the "idea of the self" along with the social practices associated with its personal affirmation produced a situation in which the avant garde was hotly pursued by members of "the other" (in twentieth-century terms, the "middle class" or "squares") seeking similar affirmations and experiences. Each journey that was created at great mental cost by the path-breaking members of the creative elite was to be taken by extraordinary numbers of quite conventional persons.

This belief in the possession of a private protoself that was to be the ultimate seat of authority for connecting meaning and action, which began as a minority and elite solution to a particular cultural crisis, was disseminated as a potential form of mental life to larger and larger audiences during the course of the nineteenth century. This dissemination, however, involved more than the production and consumption of cultural materials that were the evidence for new forms of mental organization and practices. Interacting with, and in some cases fomenting, these ideological developments were radical changes in the organization of everyday life and in the general accessibility of cultural resources. These provided for increased opportunities for social detachment and hence the reconstruction of mental life on a vast scale. I mention only four of these developments that provoked or affirmed a belief in various versions of the self among nonelites, beginning in the middle class and then spreading to everyperson.

(1) The rise of rail travel *provided, for the first time, mass access to easy rapid travel through space and hence the first quantum jump in the compression of time.* In addition, rail travel offered in its opening stages an entirely new experience of speed because travel was in open carriages. Even within closed coaches, the experience of movement was palpable, allowing the kinds of disorienting experiences recorded by Turner in his remarkable painting of 1844, *Rain, Steam and Speed—The Great Western Railway* (Butlin and Joll 1977).⁵ In the later era of closed and quieter cars with windows, people could sit and fantasize. Looking out at the moving landscapes of countryside and city without physical effort produced the lulling effects expressed in such music as *The Humoresque.* The railroad journey created a psychic open space as well as the rapid transition between home and work. This separation of connected activity sites offered the opportunity to play roles on quite different stages and to juxtapose the house, the neighborhood, and the community of residence with the office, the factory, and the space of the central city. Even short commutes on light rail, that is, streetcars and trolleys, offered a break from local surveillance and provided a quiet space for daydreaming. The railroad was a detaching experience both for the rider and for those who watched the trains go by. Reorganizing the structure of everyday life, the railway brought the machine into the garden and the individual into the machine (Schivelbusch [1978] 1979).

(2) The availability of reproducible images *of the individual, other persons, and other places occurred in the same time span as the railroad and with the same pattern of growth, first appearing in Europe and the United States and then spreading across the world* (see, for example, Booth 1984; Gernsheim 1965; Hales 1984; Hartmann 1978; McCauley 1985). For individuals who could not travel, the photograph brought home the fruits of those who could. Because photographs were then believed to be a representation of absolute truth, the difference between "there" and "here" was given a reality. One could imagine standing in front of those ancient monuments in Egypt, fighting in Mathew Brady's trenches, or attending the World's Fair in

Chicago. Someplace else was not so far away and beckoned with a reality not previously experienced. Indeed, contemporary first-time visitors know Paris in ways that only an accumulated set of secondhand experiences through still and moving images can provide (Greenblat and Gagnon 1983). The photograph provides the portrait and snapshot, the (potentially) continuous physical record of the face and body of the individual extended through time. Offering new limitations and opportunities for remembering, the photograph records who am I and who was I. The photograph thus presents both new scenes and stages on which to play and new occasions for the display of the uniqueness of the individual self.

(3) The experience of the shop window and fantasy consumption *represents the systematic provocation of private desire in the public forum.* In the contemporary world, the provocation of desire is usually the place of advertising, but the shop window and the department store, invented in the nineteenth century, go beyond the advertised image, particularly in the pretelevision era. Window-shopping in front of the temples of desire was an important feature of the lives of middle- and working-class women from the middle of the nineteenth century until now. The ability to display goods and to eat meals behind a simple pane of glass that separates the goods from those who want them and the food from the hungry suggests a transformation of the rules of desire. In the windows are what is to be desired, similar to the cinema of the 1930s and 1940s and television prime-time soap operas, and, as the displays are more elaborate, there are opportunities for those in want to fantasize their desires.

(4) The rise of literacy and the mass-produced book, magazine, and newspaper *offered an opportunity for individuals to experience other lives without leaving their own rooms.* The most powerful of role-playing media until the development of radio and cinema, the realistic novel reached its peak of development in the nineteenth century in all of the advanced nations of Europe as well as in the United States. Such novels, both of high and popular culture, provided the most intense opportunities for taking the role of the other. A late-nineteenth-century reader could be Clarissa, Robinson Crusoe, Becky Sharp, Ahab, Emma Bovary, Raskolnikov, or Tom Sawyer all in the space of a few weeks or months. Extending the limits of plausibility, the reader could be anyone and could follow the journeys of the authors to any clime, mental state, or biography.

Reading, particularly silent reading, could detach the reader from home, spouse, children, traveling companions—providing in most cases a temporary escape but, for some, opening the door to permanent change.

Its Voices

The last of these "material inventions" has the greatest substantive bearing upon the voices that are to be heard in the self and hence the internal conversations that are possible. The rise of literacy and the practice of reading, particularly the reading of novels, provides a rich opportunity for assimilating the contents of roles. This contrasts with the railroad, which provided occasions for social detachment, fantasy, and multiple stages for role performance and the new possibilities of remembering and traveling to distant scenes and climes offered by the photograph. It differs as well from the shop window that provoked the stylized desires of commerce. Indeed, novel reading was the most concentrated experience of what we now call role-taking possible in the nineteenth century. While other journeys may have been more disruptive of everyday routines, such as travel to foreign climes and cultures, taking perception-disorienting chemicals, or engaging in the violation of sexual taboos, the novel offered in a more compressed manner, particularly in terms of time expended, the greatest variety of "voices" and "conversations." In the words of the Russian literary theorist Bakhtin (1981, p. 261):

> The novel as a whole is a phenomenon multiform in style and variform in speech and voice. In it the investigator is confronted with several heterogeneous stylistic unities, often located on different linguistic levels and subject to different stylistic controls.

To paraphrase Bakhtin, the novel can contain "five types of compositional-stylistic unities": (a) the author's narrative, (b) stylized versions of everyday speech, (c) stylized versions of semiliterary everyday narratives (letters, diaries, personal journals), (d) literary speech assigned to other authors (philosophical statements, newspaper articles, memoranda, sermons), and (e) the speech of characters. Bakhtin (1981, p. 263) goes on to say:

> The novel can be defined as a diversity of speech types (sometimes even a diversity of languages) and a diversity of individual voices, artistically organized. The internal stratification of any single national language into social dialects, characteristic group behavior, professional jargons, generic languages, languages of generations and age groups, tendentious languages, languages of the authorities, of various circles and passing fashions, languages that serve the specific sociopolitical purposes of the day, even of the hour (each day has its own slogan, its own vocabulary, its own emphases)—this internal stratification present in every

language at any given moment of its historical existence is the indispensable prerequisite of the novel as a genre. The novel orchestrates all its themes, the totality of the world of objects and ideas expressed in it, by means of the social diversity of speech types (raznorcie) and by the differing individual voices that flourish under such conditions.

This is not merely a long way of saying that the novel is a baggy monster, though it shares some of that emphasis. The novel form, particularly in the nineteenth century, begins to contain an increasing diversity of voices presented in all possible styles and genres. Indeed, from Bakhtin's point of view, what distinguishes the novel from other literary forms is this diversity of voices. As the novel moves closer to the current time, an increasing variety of speakers are given voice, including speakers whose first right to be heard was often given legitimacy in the novel form (the peasant in Zola's *The Earth,* the pure revolutionary in Chernyshevsky's *A Vital Question or What Is to Be Done?*, the lesbian in Radclyff Hall's *The Well of Loneliness*). The form itself was (and is) not only incorporative of conventional voices but it offered access to new voices as well. The reading of novels provided an important context for readers to experiment with new elements in the self (new voices) as well as entirely new constructions of the self. Novels provoked a sense of possibility and hence alienation (I could be other than I am or what "I" could I be?) and were the occasion for the elimination of that alienation (This is what I am or this is the "I" that I could be).

It was reading silently, perhaps more than reading aloud, that provided the possibility of detaching oneself from the immediate demands of the environment. In the privacy of silent reading, people were offered the opportunity to hear new voices, often alien voices that would not be admitted if their words had to be spoken in the presence of others. In reading aloud, it is easy to choose Oliver Twist over Bill Sykes; when reading silently, the choice is not so obvious. Memorization and silent vocalization (moving one's lips while reading, so often characteristic of the "slow reader" of today) have an equally ambivalent quality. Memorization, the opportunity to make the words of the other one's own, is usually treated as a way of honoring the voices of the other, but it is in a deeper sense an opportunity to possess them. Even silent vocalization is the chance to say in one's own voice the words of others, words that become one's own. The novel thus offered the opportunity to journey, to take risks with the content of the self, at relatively low material cost. Silent reading is not only the opportunity to hear many voices, but it is, as Plato—speaking through the voices of Socrates and Phaedrus— understood, an opportunity for the reader to make a private meaning for the voices heard (Plato 1953). *Heteroglossia,* the existence of diverse and conflicting voices, is accompanied by *polysemy,* the proliferation of socially uncontrolled meanings for those voices. The world of private thought, so often denigrated as fantasy, is also a world of dangerous possibility.

As these opportunities for hearing many voices from the environment increased across the nineteenth and early twentieth centuries, so did the complexity and varieties of voices represented in conversations in the self. The relation between the density of voices in the everyday interpersonal and symbolic environments of individuals and the density of voices in the self appears to be relatively direct, at least in a crude quantitative sense. This is true both historically and in terms of the individual life course. Historically, there was a quantitative increase in the "voices" that most people heard in the public world and in their selves across the nineteenth century and, at least until the 1950s, most individuals gave internal voice to increasing numbers of speakers across at least the first two-thirds of their life course in modern urban-industrial media-based societies.

This view is based not only upon an understanding of the relation between language and the self held by the early symbolic interactionists and pragmatists in the United States but on the views of Bakhtin. To quote from a recent article by a Bakhtin scholar, Caryl Emerson (in Voloshinov 1986, p. 14), "Social intercourse, embodied in our outer speech, is gradually internalized to become 'inner speech,' and this becomes the semiotic material of consciousness." "The very act of introspection, Bakhtin claims, is modeled on external social discourse; all of our experiences exist, 'encoded in inner speech' " (Emerson in Voloshinov 1986, p. 118).[6] This process of "internalization" is composed of two methods. The first is "reciting by heart" or attempts to repeat the words of another exactly, to take them inside as the authoritative text. The second is "retelling it in one's own words," the opportunity to make speech one's own, what Bakhtin calls "internally persuasive" discourse. It is possible to notice an important connection between the pedagogy of Bakhtin (and Vygotsky) and John Dewey—learning to speak on one's own behalf, in one's own words, is similar to learning by doing, not learning by authority. It should be recognized that this choice on Dewey's part is itself an outcome of the rise of the idea of self as well as a faith in democracy (the political system of many voices) that characterized the social psychology of George Herbert Mead.

The self is composed of voices in conversation, voices that are given names and among whom there are rules for who speaks and in what order. These materials of the self—the voices, how they are named, and the regulations for orderly speech—are entirely social in origin.[7] While the materials of the self are entirely social, the conversations in the self are not conversations regulated in entirely the same fashion as are external conversations. The voices in the self are not isomorphic with voices in the world; except in the most rigid of mental lives, they do not speak in the same order, with the same weight, or with equivalent authority. The voices are also not in a one-to-one relation to social roles. That is, the number and variability in intrapsychic voices can be both larger and smaller than the concrete social roles available to enact. When one moves from internal speech to external speech, one moves, at least among sophisticated speakers, from being a playwright to being an actor, from meanings that depend on making oneself plausible to one's self to making one's enactment of the role plausible to concrete others (Simon and Gagnon 1988).

These conversations and how they are regulated are the self, though the self makes up only a portion of mental life. Mental life also contains nonverbal materials—images, nonverbal sounds, smells, tastes, physical abilities—but the interaction of these phenomena with the ability to speak and write, the usual forms of cognitive output, is poorly understood. In part, this relation is misunderstood because nonverbal experience is so frequently represented in verbal terms, that is, persons reproduce or recollect images by talking or writing about them rather than by representing the image itself. The same process occurs when reporting on our experiences with music or food and drink or sport; we rarely, when asked about a piece of music, play it; or when asked how something tastes, cook it; or when asked to describe a tennis stroke, take the racquet and reproduce it. There is a report, however, which I retell here as a counterexample, that, when Schumann was asked what a sonata he had just played meant, he simply played it again (Steiner 1978). The nonverbal components of mental life tend to be obscured by the fact that our recollections of all other modalities are reproduced as spoken or text narratives. As a consequence, we often assume that persons only have access to their mental life through verbal textual means.

The ability to talk to oneself and the complexity of such conversations are a matter of both history and biography—such skills are acquired and this acquisition is probably a matter of some difficulty. George Steiner's (1978, pp. 345, 366) remarkable and seminal essay, "The Distribution of Discourse," points out that

> linguists have given almost no thought to the formal characteristics, statistical mass, psychological economy or social specificities of internal speech. How often, under what lexical, grammatical and semantic categories and constraints, at what rate of flow, in what language (where the polyglot is concerned) do we speak to ourselves?

The unvoiced or internal components of speech span a wide arc: all the way from the subliminal flotsam of word or sentence-fragments . . . to the highly defined, focused and realized articulacy of the silent recitation of a learned text or of the taut analytic moves in a disciplined act of meditation. Quantitatively, there is every reason to believe that we speak inside and to ourselves more than we speak outward and to anyone else. Qualitatively, these manifest modes of self-address . . . test and verify our "being there."

In this essay, Steiner approaches descriptively Vygotsky's requested "historical theory of inner speech," pointing to changing distributions and social sources of genres of writing that are forms of "talking to oneself" or at least "talking to the page," the diary, the journal, letter writing. He points out that there has been a changing locus of various domains of speech on the dimension from private to public—what can be said to oneself and what can be said to others.

It is only in this conclusion that I would differ with Steiner's (1978, p. 368) argument,

that the shift in the balance of discourse since the seventeenth century has been outward. That there would seem to have been a concomitant impoverishment in the articulate means of the inward self. . . . Expending so much more of our "speech-selves," we have less in reserve.

I argue that, during this period, there has been a qualitative change in the structure of our speech selves and that there has been a massive quantitative increase in the extent, complexity, and variety of internal and external speech at least until the generations that grew up in the posttext world of television.[8]

And Their Discord

As the number of potential internalizable voices increased in number during the first half of the nineteenth century, novel difficulties in the "management of mental life" began to emerge. As the number of external voices increases, though not automatically or immediately or in all cases, so do the number of voices in the self—voices that speak for new wishes and desires. Indeed, the mixing of external voices in the mind is a source of novel voices, unheard in prior public conversations. Even the mishearing of other voices produces innovation in mental life. As the number of external voices grows, so does the number of external audiences, and the new audiences call for the rehearsal of new idioms.

This increase in the number of internal voices has created both problems and opportunities for actors at the levels of the intrapsychic and the interpersonal, and in relations between the domains of the private and the public. Making this matter more complex, it is likely that, from a historical perspective, what was problematic for many in the nineteenth century may have been transformed into possibilities for some during the late twentieth century. The increase in internal voices makes difficult the private decisions about which voice is allowed to speak as well as the order of precedence given to various voices. The internal problem is that the increase in voices weakens not only the singularity of the self but, in many cases, the hierarchy of voices. This is more likely to be experienced as a source of dismay in cultures that believe in individuals having strong and perduring characters that behave according to strict standards across time and context, those in which conduct is for all practical purposes context dependent and in which the relation between private states and public presentations is modest.

Most critical to the task of social interaction is who speaks last and thus has the voice carried into action. There is a fundamental tension between the multiplicity of internal voices and the necessity for the actor to speak in one voice in concrete performances with one audience or across a number of audiences (this is what is meant by being "ladylike" or "presidential" or "professorial"). This tension was probably more acute in the nineteenth century than in the twentieth on two grounds. First, the increased segmentation of roles found in contemporary life offers the possibility of speaking in different ways with diverse audiences. Second, the capacity of audiences to respond to performances that are ambivalent or presented in deliberately mixed modes has no doubt increased. Audiences in the nineteenth century had fewer ways of saying "get control of yourself" and fewer interpretative resources with which to account for "out-of-control" conduct. Duty and character were the distinguishing characteristics of the nineteenth-century singular self that spoke with one voice across many circumstances, even if alternative voices had been privately heard before speaking. This quiescence of dissenting voices is characteristic of most, though not all, competent social performances (not only nineteenth-century ones) because the act of speaking usually requires that other voices disappear from immediate consciousness. The demands of interaction often require a singularity of presentation that can only be maintained by a loss of ambivalence.[9] The more that is at stake and the greater the investment of time in the final choice, the greater the singularity of the statement and the wider the range of argument provided to sustain the dominance of that voice. It is in the early-twentieth-century products of high culture that dissenting voices appear for the first time in full cry, sometimes during, but always just after, the act of speaking. It is only later in the century that this condition would characterize increasing numbers of persons in the course of everyday life.

The everyday need to speak in a singular public voice while other voices are present leads to a number of adaptive problems. In some cases, persons find themselves limited by the singular voice of the role and begin to feel that the role is first "restricting" or oppressing and, more radically, that it is alien to them. In addition, people may find themselves dissatisfied with the repertoire of roles available to them and become critical of role-bound conduct in general. Others may have less trust or confidence in their internal voices and experience them as alien, either internally or in their public conduct, to who they are or wish to be. In a relatively simple formula, the problem of self-control can be experienced as a conflict at the boundaries of (self)/(roles)/(others). In more complex forms, the problem of self-control becomes more difficult, expressed as conflicts between voices that are entirely internal.

Freud's case histories of his patients at the end of the nineteenth century contain some of the earliest descriptions of persons who heard voices (interpreted by the analyst as desires or impulses) that they felt were alien to their "good self" that sought to be responsive to the voice of conscience and reality. From Freud's perspective, these voices spoke for desires or wishes that were rooted in the precivilized condition, primordial voices that were uneasily and incompletely repressed in the civilizing process. Prior to Freud's persuasion, his patients construed these voices as having more moral or religious origins, as evidence of sin or immorality. Beginning with the evidence of these alien voices speaking in dreams or interrupting normal discourse, Freud constructs a new set of speakers in the patient's mind. Each of Freud's internal speakers is a composite of other voices, some with external, others with internal, origins, that make mental life into an internal struggle between composite speakers. The Ego speaks for reality and community, the Superego for morality and the parent, and the Id for pleasure and nature. The voices of reality and morality speak to the external world and to each other and jointly share the task of repressing the primal voice of the Id restlessly babbling in code in the unconscious.

The process of psychoanalytic therapy is a conservative inversion of the Romantic journey in which the self becomes detached from the demands of culture (Gagnon 1984). The stressful journey into the miseries of childhood that is jointly undertaken by the analyst and the patient is meant to bring the latter into conformity with reality, that is, the demands of conventional social roles. In the process of therapy, Freud sought to gain control over that domain over which reality appears to have least control, the world of dreams into which individuals journey at night. While the Surrealists paid homage to Freud for his "discovery" of the unconscious and the symbols of the dream, they never understood that his desire was to gain control of nighttime and dream time. The therapist decodes the dream, emptying it of danger, foreclosing perhaps the last attempts of the patient to escape the demands of daytime and reality. It is always high noon and a cloudless day in the utopia of psychoanalysis.

Freud responded to the problem of alien voices by constructing a hierarchy of speakers and giving precedence to certain speakers based on their adherence to collective goals. Civilization may have its discontents, but where would we be without it? Even the more democratic George Herbert Mead quells the number of voices by collapsing their diversity. The Generalized Other (more benign than Freud's civilization) faces the Me (that portion of the self derived from and responsive to the other) and the I (that necessary source of autonomous action that anticipates the problem of oversocialization). Mead's faith in the democratic virtues of the Generalized Other proposes a more happy climate for human development than more European neo-Hegelians are capable of envisaging. Their experience of government and society provides little hope that the voices of the other can be trusted to become the voice of the self.

The difficulty for the Freudian attempt to control the conversations in the self is that they were too little, too late. The Freudian dream book, no matter how often revised, is too simple a decoder to interpret *Ulysses,* much less *Finnegans Wake.* From the first decades of the nineteenth century, the voices began proliferating at an increasing rate; at the end of the twentieth, they are now manifold. To which voice should individuals listen? Should the final word be spoken in the world or in the self? Even at the earliest moments of this century, as the dictum "pull [the parts of] your self together" was replacing "control your [singular] self," the hierarchy and precedence of the voices in the self were in a shambles. The institutional manifestations of psychoanalysis in institutes, certificates, mental hospitals, schools of social work, advice columns, community mental health centers, training analyses, developmental psychology—the concrete results of psychoanalysts' "ambition for their ideals"—have resulted not in civilization (the only good reason for repression) but in adjustment to the social order. Moreover, the patient can be adjusted to whatever social order in vogue, including a social order that permits "doing one's own thing" as often as "doing the social order's thing."

This dehierarchicalization of the self has been recognized by a diversity of serious figures in recent years, but it is spoken of in quite different ways. Thus Thomas Schelling (1980, pp. 96, 97) reports that he learned from his experience as a member of the National Research Council's Committee on Habitual Behavior and Drug Abuse that:

> people behave as if sometimes they had two selves, one who wants clean lungs and long life and another who adores tobacco, or one who wants a lean body and another who wants dessert, or one who yearns to improve himself by reading the Public Interest and another who would rather watch an old movie on television. And the two are in continual contest for control.

> How should we conceptualize this rational consumer whom all of us know and who some of us are, who in self-disgust grinds his cigarettes down the disposal swearing that this time he means never again to risk orphaning his children with lung cancer, and is on the street three hours later looking for a store that's still open to buy cigarettes; who eats a high calorie lunch knowing that he will regret it and does regret it, eats a high calorie dinner knowing he will regret it and does regret it; who sits glued to the T.V. knowing that again tomorrow he'll wake up early in a cold sweat unprepared for that morning meeting on which so much of his career depends; who spoils the trip to Disneyland by losing his temper when his children do what he knew they were going to do when he resolved not to lose his temper when they did it?

> Maybe the ordinary man or woman . . . doesn't behave like a single-minded individual because he or she isn't one.

This binary division of the economic monad perhaps produces as many voices as an economist can hear (or perhaps bear), the two voices that animate such cautionary tales as the prudent and the prodigal, illth and wealth, or the grasshopper and the ant. Even though Schelling's "science of self management" only treats the self as two voices representing two preferences, he opens the door to an image of the self as populated by a public of voices ranging from one to N, requiring some kind of voting scheme to make a final decision. In this circumstance, the management of the self becomes somewhat of a public goods problem, again without a Pareto optimal solution.

Consider a more radical vision of the "parliament of the mind" proposed by the novelist Luke Rhinehart in his 1972 novel titled *The Dice Man* (p. 252). A patient who has been cured though dice therapy by the analyst-hero (also named Rhinehart) reports on his precure paralysis:

I feel I ought to write a great novel, write numerous letters, be friendly with more of the interesting people in my community, give more parties, dedicate more time to my intellectual pursuits, play with my children, make love to my wife, go hiking more often, go to the Congo, be a radical trying to revolutionize society, write fairy tales, buy a bigger boat, do more sailing, sunning and swimming, write a book on the American picaresque novel, educate my children at home, be a better teacher at the University, be a faithful friend, be more generous with my money, economize more, live a fuller life in the world outside me, live like Thoureau and not be taken in by material values, play more tennis, practice yoga, meditate, do those damn RCAF (Royal Canadian Air Force) exercises everyday, help my wife with the housework, make money in real estate, . . . and so on.

And do all these things seriously, playfully, dramatically, stoically, hopefully, serenely, morally, indifferently—do them like D. H. Lawrence, Paul Newman, Socrates, Charlie Brown, Superman and Pogo.

It would be easy to point out that these are the voices of white, male, middle-class academics, probably with tenure, who can afford such internal-ized debate. At the same time, this richness and variety of the voices in these interiors parallel the new and multiform voices heard in the literary and political documents generated by the antiwar, feminist, ethnic minority, and lesbian and gay male social movements of the 1960s and 1970s. Each of these movements generated a complex, and often internally conflicted, set of "new" and "diverse" voices celebrated in book title after book title and even more often in blurbs and reviews (see Davies, this volume).

Along with the flourishing of new multivoiced and contentious move-ments are new amalgams of social types with rehappened histories and new ideologies. Sometimes they have a limited tolerance for ambiguity—"the white negro," "the lesbian feminist separatist," "the clone," and "the black neoconservative." At the same time, these new simplifications offer only short-lived attempts to control and manage the "baggy monster" of the self.

It is this issue of escalation of diverse and contentious voices that Rhinehart's therapeutic program in *The Dice Man* addresses. Rhinehart (both as author and hero) understands that one may choose a limited set of actions (sometimes only one) from the many voices and that choosing one course of action suppresses (and oppresses) all other voices. Because it is not possible to make a rational choice between the voices (except post hoc), Rhinehart recommends that his patients decide which of the myriad voices to listen to by casting dice.[10] He does not propose a voting scheme, a cost-benefit analysis, a negotiated settlement, an authoritarian dogma, or a even a psy-chotherapy to suppress the inconvenient voices; they are to be suppressed by lot.[11] What this procedure recognizes is the role of chance in the life course of most individuals and the contingent and rationalized outcomes of what appear to be rational choices. Good acts may produce evil consequences; evil acts may produce good ones.[12]

This dehierarchicalization of the self has leveled all voices. Discord, conflict, even mobocracy in the self are the consequences. Each voice represents a wish that, if it is enacted in concrete circumstance, will constrain other wishes, but there is no a priori way to decide among the wishes. In the modern situation, following from the quote from Rhinehart, morality (however voiced) ceases to be an authoritative voice and becomes a wish coequal with all other wishes.[13]

Conclusion

In this construal, the self is the sum of an individual's changing internal conversations, the forecastings, the recollections and the wishes, the voices that make up our intrapsychic life. The extent, divisions, hierarchies, components, structures, permeability, openness and closedness, the opposition or submission to "others" take their origins in socially acquired modes of talking that become the ways in which we experience our selves. In this view, there is nothing beyond these modes of talking—no groundedness in structural oppositions, no non-language-based machine that can be located in nature or culture or the design of the brain, no menu of desires fixed by the "needs of the individual" or the "needs of the society" or evolution or God that can place the causes of human conduct outside or above or below or prior to the conventionalized language of experience in a particular time and place. Such emblems are simply pragmatic devices that provide reasons for choosing one course of action rather than another, which allow us to enforce our interests by appeals to higher authority and, in the last analysis, limit the infinite regress of talking or explaining.

The domain of the private has ineluctably grown as cultures have become more complex and the intrapsychic; that is, the domain of the self has become the crucial mediator in a world in which the collective connections between meaning and action, meaning and meaning, and action and action have grown less compelled and hence less compelling. As concealment and the necessity for playing with roles has increased, so has the problem of intrapsychic "negotiation." In this way, the boundary between self and other, between public and private, has grown more permeable throughout the life course. External voices find their way more easily into the self, requiring acceptance or rejection or encapsulation. As the self becomes composed of more and more bits of what were once called ego-alien symbols and experience and desires, one comes to address more and more audiences but in increasingly limited ways. The illnesses that have emerged from these conditions will become the conventionalized and culturally acceptable strategies for dealing with the social realities of the postmodern world.

Notes

1. It is my recollection that this remark appears in Mead (1936). It was brought to my notice by Morse Peckham.

2. The self as an entitlement is part of both the everyday practice of parents in the United States and the practice of those experts who are given the responsibility for research on and the promotion of certain forms of mental life. The child development expert in the form of social worker, psychologist, schoolteacher, psychiatrist, pediatrician, psychoanalyst all foster the idea of the unique and individual self that emerges in the process of growth and development. Parents who work within this cultural tradition instruct children in decision making, autonomy, self-direction, and self-control. It is no wonder that individuals come to believe that they possess a self and use its authority for life management.

3. This use of the word *program* is a takeoff on the usage by the philosopher of mathematics and science Imre Lakatos (1970). He argues that there are programs of scientific activity composed of core ideas that cannot be falsified that are surrounded by a set of auxiliary ideas that are amenable to testing and refutation by experiment. My sense is that many social movements are programs in this same sense; they have a core of slow-to-change "ideas" surrounded by a penumbra of ideas and social practices that are concrete social experiments. There is a high turnover in these satellite ideas and practices and much debate about whether they actually bear upon the central theses.

4. There is equivalent language used by Jack London in his tale "Love of Life" in which a man in his first moments of abandonment by his comrade in the Yukon cowers "in the midst of the milky water, as though the vastness were pressing in on him with overwhelming force, brutally crushing him with its complacent awfulness." London, in his socialism, however, never confronts the complacent awfulness of social life with the same power (London [1907] 1980). It also seems to be a feature of modern literature, beginning perhaps with Edgar Alan Poe, to focus on the frigid last circle of hell rather than the furnaces above.

5. This painting is one of many that Turner painted after 1835 that were profoundly disorienting for audiences in his own period. Despite these consciousness-altering effects, this particular painting received relatively good press, and a number of newspaper commentators expressed the view that the train in the picture really looked as if it were traveling at 50 miles per hour. Many of Turner's paintings of this period, however, appear to be more accessible to modern audiences who have viewed abstract expressionist works. The decision to paint in this fashion characterizes many of Turner's later paintings, and his commitment to emphasize light and movement at the expense of conventional representation is likely to have come from experiences other than those of rail travel.

Many of Turner's paintings in this period and in this style are seascapes (e.g., *Snow Storm—Steam Boat off a Harbour,* exhibited 1842, Tate Gallery [V. 1, Catalogue 398, V. 2, Plate 388, 1977] or *Rough Seas with Wreckage,* c. 1830-35, Tate Gallery [V. 1, Catalogue 455, V. 2, Plate 438]) and there are landscapes of the period that are similar in technique (such as *Snow Storm, Avalanche, and Inundation—A Scene in the Upper Part of the Val d'Auoste, Piedmont,* exhibited 1837, Art Institute of Chicago [V. 1, Catalogue 371, V. 2, Plate 349]). (All citations to Butlin and Joll 1977.)

6. The attribution of V. N. Voloshinov's work to Bakhtin expressed in this quote has been revised as the result of the examination of other work by Bakhtin that was contemporary with the writing of *Marxism and the Philosophy of Language.* (See Morson and Emerson 1989.)

7. This argument is contra the important work of Dennis Wrong (1961). I agree with Wrong that human beings are not merely the sum of the norms they have internalized, nor is their conduct the result of an innate desire to please. The difference resides in my disagreement with Wrong's appeal to the presocial or the instinctual as the source of "human freedom." This decision by Wrong to locate the sources of human freedom in the unconscious and the irrational is part of an unwillingness of many sociologists to accept the consequences of their belief in the social determination of all of social life. The locus of freedom in the irrational is grounded in a belief in the inevitability of conflict between culture and the individual that is part of the inheritance of romanticism and psychoanalysis. More recently, Blau and Duncan (1967) located freedom in the amount of variance that was not explained in a regression equation, mistaking the failure to explain variance as the measure of individual autonomy (see p. 174, where the size of the square root of $1-R^2$ is treated a measure of free will).

8. This sense of muteness and inarticulacy of groups under 40 in the United States may only be a result of the increased notice given to groups always unvoiced. It is possible to argue, however, that the immediate satisfaction of the self and its wishes that is possible in a media- and consumer-driven culture may mark the end of the two centuries' long friction between self and other. The older social journeys that provoked and supported the self in its resistance to the other seem to have limited potency among the over-journeyed (in all senses), overexperienced, and marginally educated. Literacy and articulacy are now swamped in media speech that is often no more than white noise. Florence is no longer what it used to be; drugs and sex are commodities available to everyperson; the self is the object of sale and consumption. We may be at the end stage of a certain form of mental life.

9. The demands of competent interaction often impede those who would attempt covert participant observation in novel social settings. The effort of successful role performances interferes with successful recording of what seems to be going on and reduces the field report to retrospective reproductions (Van Mannen 1988).

10. The casting of dice to determine the outcome of choices is presaged in Rabelais, but the image of casting dice to decide court cases is used to illustrate corruption rather than the indeterminacy of choice (Rabelais 1944).

11. This decision to submit internal choices to a lottery seems to rest, at least in part, on a recognition that the distribution of costs and benefits in society is itself the result of a lottery. The fact that much of life is simply "one damn thing after another" violates the need of most persons to see events as having causes that are in some accord with the moral beliefs of the society (i.e., individuals deserve what they get). Most sociological theories share this belief in causation, which rests on a deeper moral belief that the world must

make sense. The denial by sociologists of the role of "luck" in economic success, proposed, somewhat temporarily, by Jencks (1972, pp. 227-28) is another measure of the resistance of social scientists to the temporary and contingent character of social life.

12. See the informative discussion of these issues in *Richard III* by the Shakespearean scholar Arthur Rossiter in his 1961 essay *Angel with Horns.*

13. In W. I. Thomas's formulation of the four wishes, the number four is simply a device for clumping together a variety of diverse concrete and specific desires. Thus a specific wish for a new sexual partner or for travel to a new locale can be classified under a general heading (e.g., the wish for new experience). Once we have classified the substantive wish, we believe that we have understood it and, by offering a classificatory explanation for the wish, control it. This is one of the comforts of theorizing.

References

Arditi, Jorge. 1989. "Social Structure and Role Behavior." Ph.D. dissertation, State University of New York, Stony Brook, Department of Sociology.

Bakhtin, Mikhail M. 1981. *The Dialogic Imagination: Four Essays.* Austin: University of Texas Press.

———[1965] 1984. *Rabelais and His World.* Bloomington: Indiana University Press. (First publication in English, 1968, original publication in Russian, 1965, probably completed in 1940)

Becker, George. 1976. "The Mad Genius Controversy: A Study in the Sociology of Deviance." Ph.D. dissertation, State University of New York, Stony Brook, Department of Sociology.

Blau, Peter and Otis Dudley Duncan. 1967. *The American Occupational Structure.* New York: John Wiley.

Booth, Mark Haworth. 1984. *The Golden Age of British Photography, 1839-1900.* London: Victoria and Albert Museum (An Aperture Book).

Butlin, Martin and Evelyn Joll. 1977. *The Paintings of J.M.W. Turner* (Vol. 1, Text; Vol. 2, Plates). New Haven, CT: Yale University Press.

Chernyshevsky, Nikolai G. 1886. *A Vital Question or What Is to Be Done?* New York: Thomas Y. Crowell. (Original in Russian)

Cohen, Stan and Laurie Taylor. [1976] 1978. *Escape Attempts: The Theory and Practice of the Resistance to Everyday Life.* London: Penguin.

Conrad, Joseph. [1915] 1957. *Victory.* Garden City, NY: Doubleday, Anchor.

Gagnon, John H. 1984. "Success = Failure/Failure = Success: The Co-optation of the Romantic Program in the 19th Century." Pp. 97-108 in *Romanticism and Culture,* edited by H. W. Matalene. Columbia, SC: Camden House.

Gernsheim, Helmut and Alison. 1965. *A Concise History of Photography.* London: Thames and Hudson.

Greenblat, Cathy Stein and John H. Gagnon. 1983. "Temporary Strangers: A Sociological Perspective on Travel and Tourism." *Sociological Perspectives* 23(1):89-110. (formerly the *Pacific Sociological Review*)

Hales, Peter Bacon. 1984. *Silver Cities: The Photography of American Urbanization, 1839-1915.* Philadelphia: Temple University Press.

Hall, Radclyffe. 1928. *The Well of Loneliness.* New York: Covici Friede.

Hartmann, Sadakichi. 1978. *The Valiant Knights of Daguerre.* Berkeley: University of California Press.

Heller, Joseph. 1974. *Something Happened.* New York: Ballantine.

Jencks, Christopher. 1972. *Inequality: A Reassessment of the Effect of Family and Schooling in America.* New York: Basic Books.

Lakatos, Imre. 1970. "Falsification and the Methodology of Scientific Research Programs." Pp. 91-196 in *Criticism and the Growth of Knowledge,* edited by Imre Lakatos and Alan Musgrave. Cambridge: Cambridge University Press.

London, Jack. [1907] 1980. "Love of Life." In *The Call of the Wild, White Fang and other Stories,* edited by A. S. Sinclair. London: Penguin.

McCauley, Elizabeth Anne. 1985. *A.A.E. Disderi and the Carte de Visite Portrait Photograph.* New Haven, CT: Yale University Press.

Mead, George Herbert. 1936. *The Movements of Thought in the Nineteenth Century.* Chicago: University of Chicago Press.

Morris, Colin. 1972. *The Discovery of the Individual, 1050-1200.* New York: Harper Torchbooks.

Morson, Gary S. and Caryl Emerson, eds. 1989. *Rethinking Bakhtin: Extensions and Challenges.* Evanston, IL: Northwestern University Press.

Murray, Gilbert. 1951. *Five Stages of Greek Religion.* Garden City, NY: Doubleday, Anchor.

Peckham, Morse. 1962. *Beyond the Tragic Vision: The Quest for Identity in the Nineteenth Century.* New York: George Brazillier.

————1986. *The Birth of Romanticism: Cultural Crisis, 1790-1815.* Greenwood, FL: Penkewill.

Plato. 1953. *The Dialogues,* translated into English by Benjamin Jowett. Oxford: Clarendon.

Rabelais, François. 1944. *The Five Books of Gargantua and Pantagruel,* translated by Jacque LeClercq. New York: Modern Library.

Rhinehart, Luke. 1972. *The Dice Man.* London: Granada.

Rossiter, Arthur P. 1961. *Angel with Horns and Other Shakespeare Lectures.* London: Longman.

Schelling, Thomas. 1980. "The Intimate Contest for Self Control." *The Public Interest* 60(Summer).

Schivelbusch, Wolfgang. [1978] 1979. *The Railway Journey.* New York: Urizen. (Original in German)

Simon, William and John H. Gagnon. 1988. "Sexual Theory: A Sexual Scripts Approach." Pp. 363-83 in *Theories and Paradigms of Human Sexuality,* edited by James Geer and William O'Donoghue. New York: Plenum.

Steiner, George. 1978. "The Distribution of Discourse." In *On Difficulty and Other Essays.* Oxford: Oxford University Press.

Tawney, R. H. [1926] 1947. *Religion and the Rise of Capitalism.* New York: Mentor.

Van Mannen, John. 1988. *Tales from the Field: On Writing Ethnography.* Chicago: University of Chicago Press.

Voloshinov, V. N. 1986. *Marxism and the Philosophy of Language.* Cambridge, MA: Harvard University Press.

Weiss, Peter. [1964] 1977. *The Persecution and Assassination of Jean-Paul Marat as Performed by the Inmates of the Asylum at Charenton under the Direction of the Marquis De Sade.* New York: Athaneum. (Original in German)

Wrong, Dennis. 1961. "The Oversocialized Conception of Man." *American Sociological Review* 26:183-93.

Zamiatin, Evgeny. [1920] 1959. *WE.* New York: Dutton. (Original in Russian)

Zola, Émile. [1887] 1954. *The Earth.* London: Elek. (Original in French)

Author Index

Subject Index

About the Authors

Arthur P. Bochner is Professor of Communication and codirector of the Institute for Interpretive Human Studies at the University of South Florida. He has contributed more than 35 articles and book chapters to both international and national publications on interpersonal relationships and is coauthor of *Understanding Family Communication*. His current research interests are on border crossings—how individuals formulate and/or manage identities that bridge different social groups—and on the reflexivity of communication research—how research affects the lives of researchers. He received the College of Arts and Letters "Scholar of the Year Award" in 1988 and gave a keynote lecture to the International Conference on Personal Relationships at Oxford in 1990.

Bronwyn Davies received her Ph.D. from the University of New England. She is currently Senior Lecturer in the Department of Social, Cultural and Curriculum Studies at the University of New England. Her major works include *Life in the Classroom and Playground: The Accounts of Primary School Children, and Frogs, and Snails and Feminist Tales: Pre-School Children and Gender.*

Norman K. Denzin is Professor of Sociology, Communications and Humanities at the University of Illinois, Urbana-Champaign. He is the author of several books, including most recently *On Understanding Emotion* (1984), *The Alcoholic Self* (1987), *The Recovering Alcoholic* (1987), *Interpretive Interactionism* (1989), *Images of Postmodernism: Social Theory and Contemporary Cinema* (1991), *Symbolic Interactionism-as-Cultural Studies* (1991), and *Hollywood Shot by Shot: Alcoholism in American Cinema* (1991). *The Alcoholic Self* and *The Recovering Alcoholic* were nominated for the C. Wright Mills Award in 1988. *The Alcoholic Self* won the Cooley Award from the Society for the Study of Symbolic Interaction in 1988 and was nominated for the Sorokin Award by the American Sociological Association in 1989. He is the author of more than 70 articles in various academic journals. He has been the editor of *Studies in Symbolic Interaction: A Research Journal* since 1978.

Carolyn Ellis is Associate Professor of Sociology and codirector of the Institute for Interpretive Human Studies at the University of South Florida. She received her Ph.D. in Sociology from the State University of New York in Stony Brook. She has published work on isolated fishing communities, sociology of emotions, and methodological issues in studying lived experience. Her current work attempts to combine narrative writing with qualitative research methods to explore the social construction of meaning in relationships.

Gary Alan Fine is Professor of Sociology at the University of Georgia. He is the author of *With the Boys: Little League Baseball and Preadolescent Culture* (recipient of the Opie Prize from the American Folklore Society) and *Shared Fantasy: Role-Playing Games as Social Worlds*. His current research is on the sociology of aesthetics (as examined through a study of professional cooks) and the sociology of nature (as examined through a study of amateur mushroom collectors).

Michael G. Flaherty is Associate Professor of Sociology at Eckerd College. His work concerns the analysis of self, interaction, and the social construction of reality. He is currently conducting research on the subjective and situated processes that condition the perception of time. His writings have appeared in *Social Psychology Quarterly, The Sociological Quarterly*, and *Studies in Symbolic Interaction*.

John H. Gagnon is Professor of Sociology at the State University of New York at Stony Brook. He received his undergraduate and graduate degrees at the University of Chicago. During the 1960s, he was Senior Research Sociologist and Trustee of the Institute for Sex Research at Indiana University. He has been a visiting professor at Cambridge University, the University of Essex, Harvard University, and Princeton University. He has conducted research on all aspects of sexuality and is now involved in a number of research projects on sexual conduct and AIDS. The chapter in this volume is the opening work in a larger project concerning the material origins of the self in the nineteenth century.

Laurel Graham is a doctoral student in the sociology of science at the University of Illinois in Urbana-Champaign. Her dissertation research examines Dr. Lillian Moller Gilbreth's constitution of three female subjectivities: paid worker, homemaker, and scientist.

Mark Neumann is Assistant Professor in the Department of Communication at the University of South Florida in Tampa. He received his Ph.D. from the University of Utah. He has published articles on leisure travel, casino gambling, and documentary photography.

Virginia L. Olesen is Professor of Sociology and Co-Director (with Adele Clarke) of the Women, Health and Healing Program in the Department of Social and Behavioral Sciences, School of Nursing, University of California, San Francisco. She received her M.A. in communications (Chicago, 1956) and Ph.D. in sociology (Stanford, 1961). She has published work on adult and professional socialization, women's work and lives, health and illness, social psychology of the body, emotions in institutions, and issues in qualitative research. She is coauthor of *The Silent Dialogue: The Social Psychology of Professional Socialization* (1968, with Elvi Whittaker), coeditor of *Women, Health and Healing: Toward a New Perspective* (1985, with Ellen Lewin), and coeditor of *Cultural Aspects in Menstrual Cycle Research* (1986, with Nancy Fugate Woods).

Laurel Richardson is Professor of Sociology at The Ohio State University. She is the author of *Writing Strategies: Reaching Diverse Audiences, The Dynamics of Sex and Gender, The New Other Woman, Gender and University Teaching: A Negotiated Difference*, and many journal articles; editor of *Feminist Frontiers*; and a published poet. Her interests in the sociology of knowledge have brought her to analysis of narrative in scientific discourses. Her quest is to write sociology as an effective and affecting discourse.

Carol Rambo Ronai completed her M.A. at the University of South Florida in Tampa. Her thesis was titled "Turn-Ons for Money: Negotiation Strategies and Emotion Work of the Stripper." An article from that work, "Turn-Ons for Money: Interactional Strategies of the Table Dancer," was coauthored with her adviser, Carolyn Ellis, and appeared in *Journal of Contemporary Ethnography*. She is currently pursuing a Ph.D. in sociology at the University of Florida in Gainesville, assisting Jaber Gubrium on "The Life Narratives of Older Persons Project," and working on a paper dealing with the semiotics of aging and exotic dancers. Her areas of interest include the sociology of knowledge, social psychology, and qualitative methods.